Capitalism

Revolutions of Our Time

Capitalism

John Vaizey

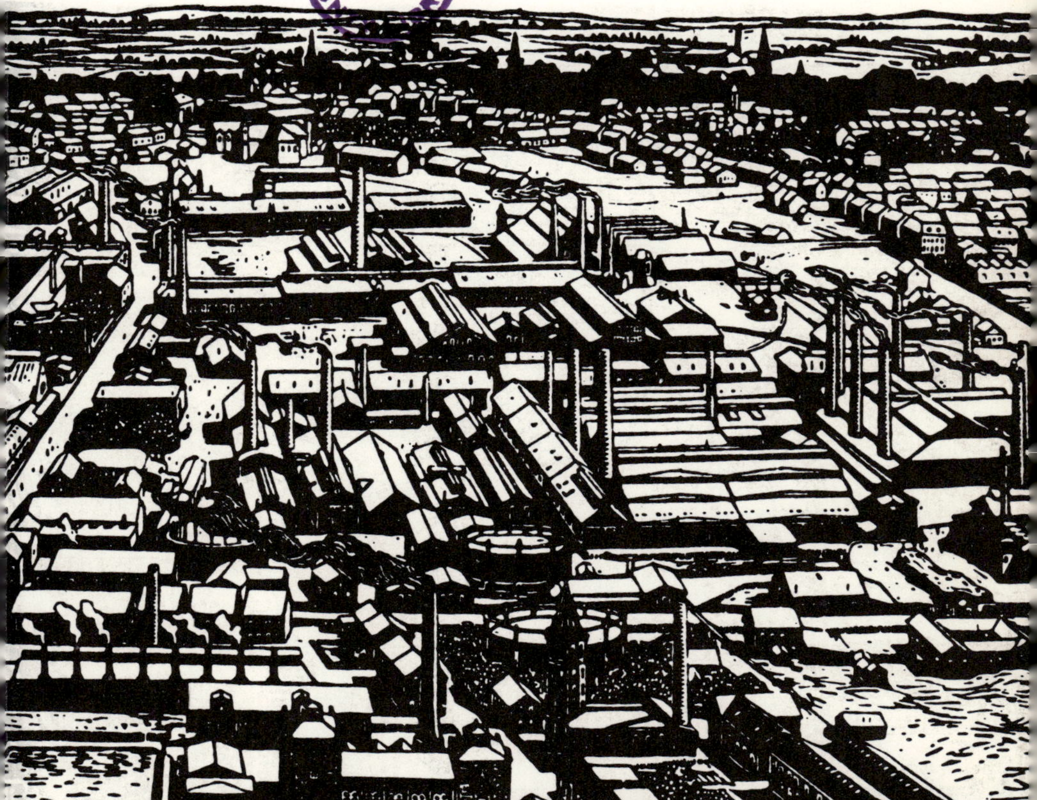

Weidenfeld and Nicolson 5 Winsley Street London W1

Printed in Germany by Mohndruck Reinh. Mohn OHG, Gütersloh

ISBN 0 297 00096 9

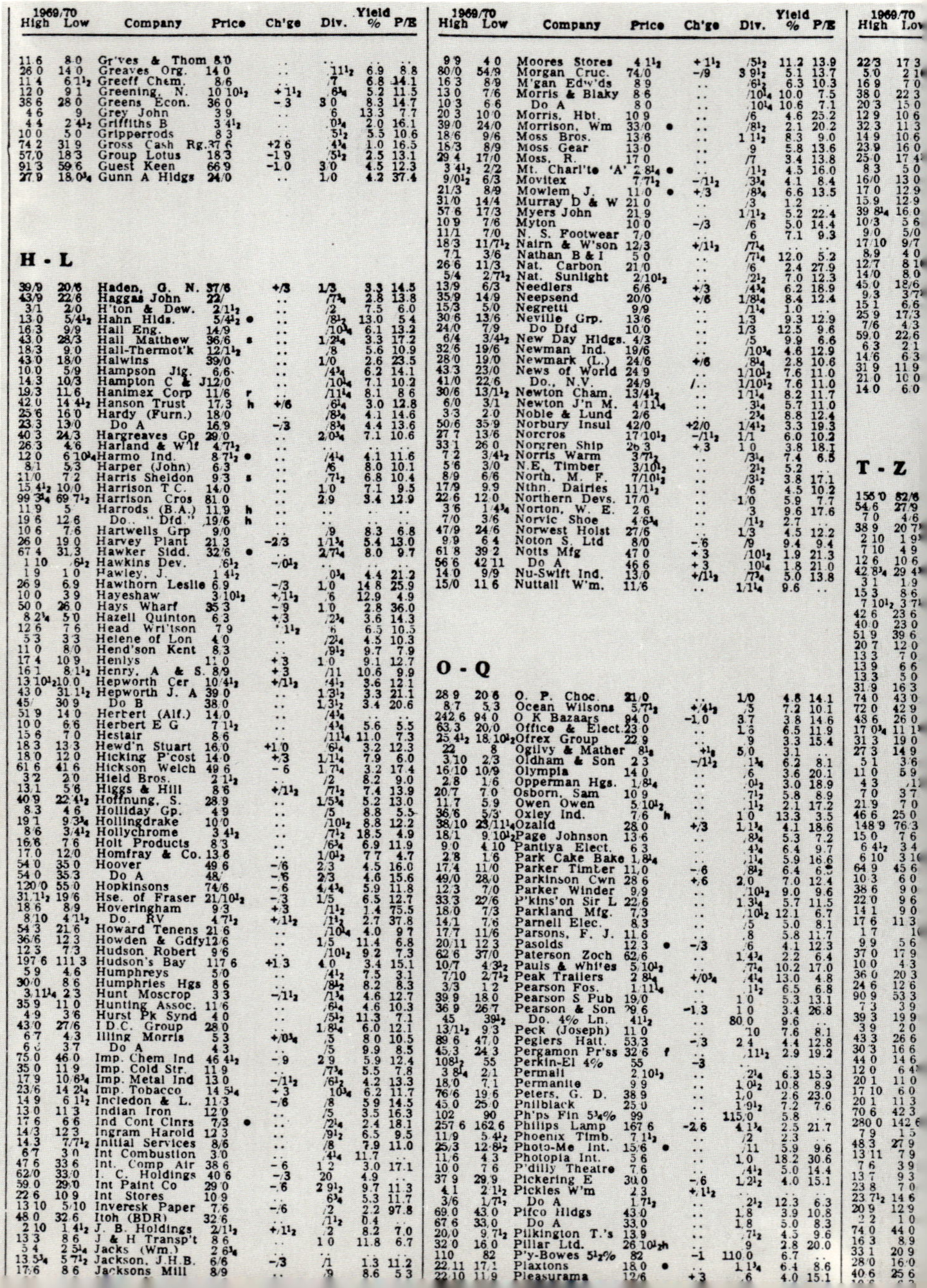

1969/70 High	Low	Company	Price	Ch'ge	Div.	Yield %	P/E
11 6	8 0	Gr'ves & Thom	8 0	..	..	..	..
26 0	14 0	Greaves Org.	14 0	..	11½	6.9	8.8
11 4	6 7½	Greeff Chem.	8/6	..	/7	6.8	14.1
12 0	9 1	Greening, N.	10 10½	+1½	.6¾	5.2	11.5
38 6	28 0	Greens Econ.	36 0	-3	3 0	8.3	14.7
4 6	9	Grey John	3 9	..	6	13.3	7.7
4 4	2 4½	Griffiths B	3 4½	..	.0¾	2.0	16.1
10 0	5 0	Gripperrods	8 3	..	5½	5.5	10.6
74 2	31 9	Gross Cash Rg.	37 6	+2 6	.4¾	1.0	16.5
57.0	18 3	Group Lotus	18 3	-1 9	.5½	2.5	13.1
91 3	59 6	Guest Keen	66 9	-1.0	3/0	4.5	12.3
27.9	18.0¾	Gunn A Hldgs	24/0	..	1/0	4.2	37.4

H - L

1969/70 High	Low	Company	Price	Ch'ge	Div.	Yield %	P/E
39/9	20/6	Haden, G. N.	37/6	+/3	1/3	3.3	14.5
43/9	22/6	Haggas John	22/	..	/7¾	2.8	13.8
3/1	2/0	H'ton & Dew.	2/1½	..	/2	7.5	6.0
13.0	5/4½	Hahn Hlds.	5/4½ •	..	/8½	13.0	5 4
16 3	9/9	Hall Eng.	14/9	..	/10¾	6.1	13.2
43 0	28/3	Hall Matthew	36/6 s	..	1/2¼	3.3	17.2
18/3	9.0	Hall-Thermot'k	12/1½	..	/8	5.6	10.9
43 0	18/0	Halwins	39/0	..	1/0	2.6	23.5
10.0	5/9	Hampson Jig.	6/6	..	/4¾	6.2	14.1
14 3	10/3	Hampton C & J	12/0	..	/10¾	7.1	10.2
19/3	11/6	Hanimex Corp	11/6 r	..	/11¼	8.1	8 6
42.0	14 4½	Hanson Trust	17,3 h	+/6	/6¼	3.0	12.8
25 6	16 0	Hardy (Furn.)	18/0	..	/8¾	4.1	14.6
23 3	13/0	Do A	16 9	-/3	/8¾	4.4	13.6
40 3	24/3	Hargreaves Gp	29/0	..	2/0¾	7.1	10.6
26 3	4 6	Harland & W'lf	4 7½	..	..	..	..
12 0	6 10¾	Harmo Ind.	8 7½ •	..	/4¼	4.1	11.6
8/1	5 3	Harper (John)	6 3	..	/6	8.0	10.1
11/0	7 2	Harris Sheldon	9 3 s	..	/7½	6.8	10.4
15 4½	10 0	Harrison T C.	14/0	..	1/0	7.1	9.5
99 3¾	69 7½	Harrison Cros	81 0	..	2 9	3.4	12.9
11 9	5	Harrods (B.A.)	11 9 h	..	..	..	..
19 6	12 6	Do.. " Dfd."	19/6 h	..	..	..	..
10 6	7 6	Hartwells Grp	9/0	..	/9	8.3	6.8
26 0	19 0	Harvey Plant	21 3	-2/3	1/1¼	5.4	13.0
67 4	31.3	Hawker Sidd.	32/6 •	..	2/7¼	8.0	9.7
1 10	.6½	Hawkins Dev.	.6½	-/0½	..	..	..
1 9	1 0	Hawley, J.	1 4½	..	.0¾	4.4	21.2
26 9	6 9	Hawthorn Leslie	6 9	-/3	1.0	14 8	25.9
10 0	3 9	Hayeshaw	3/10½	+/1½	/6	12.9	4.9
50 0	26 0	Hays Wharf	35 3	-9	1 0	2.8	36.0
8 2¼	5 0	Hazell Quinton	6 3	+/3	/2¾	3.6	14.3
12 6	7 6	Head Wri'tson	7 9	'1½	/6	6.5	10.5
5 3	3 3	Helene of Lon	4 0	..	/2¼	4.5	10.3
11 0	8/0	Hend'son Kent	8.3	..	/9½	9.7	7.9
17 4	10 9	Henlys	11 0	+3	1 0	9.1	12.7
16 1	8 1½	Henry, A & S.	8/9	+3	/11	10.6	9.9
13 10½	10.0	Hepworth Cer	10/4½	+/1½	/4½	3.6	12.1
43 0	31 1½	Hepworth J. A	39 0	..	1/3½	3.3	21.1
45/	30 9	Do B	38 0	..	1/3½	3.4	20.6
51 9	14 0	Herbert (Alf.)	14.0	..	/4¾	..	..
10 0	6 6	Herbert E G	7 1½	..	/4¾	5.6	5.5
15 6	7 0	Hestair	8 6	..	/11¼	11.0	7.3
18 3	13 3	Hewd'n Stuart	16 0	+1 0	/6¼	3.2	12.3
18 0	12 0	Hicking P'cost	14 0	+/3	1/1¼	7.9	6.0
61 6	41 6	Hickson Welch	49 6	-6	1 7¼	3.2	17.4
3 2	2 0	Hield Bros.	2 1½	..	/2	8.2	9.0
13.1	5 6	Higgs & Hill	8 6	+/1½	/7½	7.4	13.9
40 9	22 4½	Hoffnung, S.	28 9	..	1/5¾	5.2	13.0
8 3	4 6	Holliday Gp.	4 9	..	/5	8.8	5.5
19 1	9 3¾	Hollingdrake	10/0	..	/10½	8.8	12.2
8 6	3/4½	Hollychrome	3 4½	..	/7½	18.5	4.9
16/6	7 6	Holt Products	8 3	..	/6¾	6.9	11.9
17.0	12/0	Homfray & Co.	13 6	..	1/0½	7 7	4.7
54 0	35 0	Hoover	49 6	-/6	2 3	4.5	16.0
54 0	35.3	Do A	48/	-/6	2/3	4.6	15.6
120/0	55 0	Hopkinsons	74/6	-6	4/4¾	5.9	11.8
31/1½	19/6	Hse. of Fraser	21/10½	-/3	1/5	6.5	12.7
18 6	8.9	Hoveringham	9/3	+3	/1½	1.4	75.5
8/10	4 1½	Do. RV	4 7½	+/1½	/1½	2.7	37.8
54 3	21 6	Howard Tenens	21 6	..	/10¾	4.0	9 7
36/6	12 3	Howden & Gdfy	12 6	..	1/5	11.4	6.8
12.3	7 3	Hudson Robert	9 6	..	/10½	9 2	7 3
197 6	111 3	Hudson's Bay	117 6	+1 3	4 0	3.4	15.1
5 9	4 6	Humphreys	5/0	..	/4½	7.5	3.1
30/0	8 6	Humphries Hgs	8 6	..	/8¾	8.2	8.3
3.11¼	2 3	Hunt Moscrop	3 3	-/1½	/1¾	4.6	12.7
35 9	11 0	Hunting Assoc.	11 6	..	/6¼	4.6	10.3
4 9	3 6	Hurst Pk Synd	4 0	..	/5½	11.3	7.1
43/0	27/6	I.D.C. Group	28 0	..	1/8¼	6.0	12.1
6 7	4 3	Illing Morris	5 3	+/0¾	/5	8 0	10.5
6 6	3 7	Do A	4 3	..	/5	9.9	8.5
75.0	46 0	Imp. Chem Ind	46 4½	-9	2 9	5.9	12.4
35 0	11 9	Imp. Cold Str.	11 9	..	/7¾	5.5	7.8
17 9	10 6¾	Imp. Metal Ind	13 0	-/1½	/6½	4.2	13.3
23/6	14 2¼	Imp. Tobacco	14 5¼	+3	10¼	6.2	11.7
14 9	6 1½	Incledon & L.	11.3	-/6	/8	5.9	14.5
13 0	11 3	Indian Iron	12 0	..	/5	3.5	16.3
17 6	6 6	Ind Cont Clnrs	7/3 •	..	/2¼	2.4	18.1
14/3	12 3	Ingram Harold	12 3	..	/9½	6.5	9.5
14.3	7/7½	Initial Services	8/6	..	/8	7.9	11.0
6 7	3 0	Int Combustion	3/0	..	/4¼	11.7	..
47 6	33 6	Int. Comp Air	38 6	-6	1 2	3.0	17.1
62/0	33/0	I. C. Holdings	40 6	-/3	20	4.9	..
59.0	29.0	Int Paint Co	29 0	-/6	2 9½	9.7	11.3
22 6	10 9	Int Stores	10 9	..	6¾	5.3	11.7
13 10	5/10	Inveresk Paper	7.6	-/6	/2	2.2	97.8
48 0	32 6	Itoh (BDR)	32/6	..	/1½	0.4	..
2 10	1 4½	J. B. Holdings	2/1½	+/1½	/2	8.2	7.0
13 3	8 6	J & H Transp't	8 6	..	1 0	11.8	6.7
5 4	2 5¼	Jacks (Wm.)	2 6¾	..	..	..	..
13 5¾	5 7½	Jackson, J.H.B.	6/6	-/3	/1	1.3	11.2
17/6	8 6	Jacksons Mill	8/9	..	/9	8.6	5 3

1969/70 High	Low	Company	Price	Ch'ge	Div.	Yield %	P/E
9 9	4 0	Moores Stores	4 1½	+1½	/5½	11.2	13.9
80/0	54/9	Morgan Cruc.	74/0	-/9	3 9½	5.1	13.7
16 3	8/9	M'gan Edw'ds	8 9	..	/6½	6.3	10.3
13 0	7/6	Morris & Blaky	8 6	..	/10¼	10.0	7.5
10 3	6 6	Do A	8 0	..	/10¼	10.6	7.1
20 3	10 0	Morris, Hbt.	10 9	..	/6	4.6	25.2
39/0	24/0	Morrison, Wm	33/0 •	..	/8½	2.1	20.2
18/6	9/6	Moss Bros.	13/6	..	1 1½	8.3	9.0
18/3	8/9	Moss Gear	13 0	..	9	5.8	13.6
29 4	17/0	Moss, R.	17 0	..	/7	3.4	13.8
3 4½	2/2	Mt. Charl'te 'A'	2 8¼ •	..	/1½	4.5	16.0
9/0½	6/3	Movitex	7/7½	-/1½	.3¾	4.1	8.4
21/3	8/9	Mowlem, J.	11 0 •	+/3	/8¾	6.6	13.5
31/0	14/4	Murray b & W	21 0	..	/3	1.2	..
57 6	17/3	Myers John	21 9	..	1/1½	5.2	22.4
10 9	7/6	Myton	10 0	-/3	/6	5.0	14.4
11/1	7/0	N. S. Footwear	7/0	..	6	7.1	9.3
18 3	11/7½	Nairn & W'son	12/3	+/1½	/7¼	..	..
7/1	3/6	Nathan B & I	5 0	..	/7¼	12.0	5.2
26 6	11/3	Nat. Carbon	21/0	..	/6	2.4	27.9
5/4	2/7½	Nat. Sunlight	2/10½	..	/2½	7.0	12.3
13/9	6/3	Needlers	6/6	+/3	/4¾	6.2	18.9
35/9	14/9	Neepsend	20/0	+/6	1/8¼	8.4	12.4
15/3	5/0	Negretti	9/9	..	/1¼	1.0	..
30 6	13/6	Neville Grp.	13/6	..	1 3	9.3	12.9
24/0	7/9	Do Dfd	10/0	..	1/3	12.5	9.6
6/4	3/4½	New Day Hldgs.	4/3	..	/5	9.9	6.6
32/6	19/6	Newman Ind.	19/6	..	/10¼	4.6	12.9
28/0	19/0	Newmark (L.)	24/6	+/6	.8¼	2.8	10.6
43 3	23/0	News of World	24 9	..	1/10½	7.6	11.0
41/0	22/6	Do., N.V.	24/9	/..	1/10½	7.6	11.0
30/6	13/1½	Newton Cham.	13/4½	..	1/1¼	8.2	11.7
6/0	3/1	Newton J'n M.	4/11¼	..	.3¼	5.7	11.0
3 3	2.0	Noble & Lund	2/6	..	.2¾	8.8	12.4
50/6	35/9	Norbury Insul	42/0	+2/0	1/4½	3.3	19.3
27 7	13/6	Norcros	17/10½	-/1½	1/1	6.0	10.2
33/1	26 0	Norgren Ship	26 3	+3	1 0	3.8	18.1
7 2	3/4½	Norris Warm	3/7½	..	/3¼	7.4	6.5
5/6	3/0	N.E. Timber	3/10½	..	2½	5.2	..
8/9	6/6	North, M. F.	7/10½	..	/3½	3.8	17.1
17/9	9.9	Nthn. Dairies	11/1½	..	/6	4.5	10.2
22/6	12 0	Northern Devs.	17/0	..	1/0	5.9	7.7
3/6	1 4¾	Norton, W. E.	2 6	..	3	9.6	17.6
7/0	3/6	Norvic Shoe	4/6¾	..	/1½	2.7	..
47/9	24/6	Norwest Holst	27/6	..	1/3	4.5	12.2
9/9	6 4	Noton S. Ltd	8/0	-/6	/9	9.4	9.4
61 8	39 2	Notts Mfg	47 0	+3	/10½	1.9	21.3
56 6	42 11	Do A	46 6	+3	.10¼	1.8	21.0
14 0	9/9	Nu-Swift Ind.	13/0	+/1½	/7¾	5.0	13.8
15/0	11 6	Nuttall W'm.	11/6	..	1/1¼	9.6	..

O - Q

1969/70 High	Low	Company	Price	Ch'ge	Div.	Yield %	P/E
28 9	20 6	O. P. Choc.	21/0	..	1/0	4.8	14.1
8 7	5.3	Ocean Wilsons	5/7½	+/4½	/5	7.2	10.1
242.6	94 0	O K Bazaars	94 0	-1.0	3 7	3.8	14.6
63.3	20/0	Office & Elect.	23 0	..	1 6	6.5	11.9
25 4½	18.10½	Ofrex Group	22 9	..	9	3.3	15.4
22	8	Ogilvy & Mather	8½	+¼	5 0	3.1	..
3 10	2/3	Oldham & Son	2 3	-/1½	.1¼	6.2	8.1
16/10	10/9	Olympia	14 0	..	/6	3.6	20.1
2 8	1/6	Opperman Hgs.	1/8¼	..	.0½	3.0	18.9
20/7	7 0	Osborn, Sam	10 9	..	.7½	5.8	8.9
11.7	5.9	Owen Owen	5 10½	..	.1½	2.1	17.2
36/6	5/3	Oxley Ind.	7/6 h	..	1 0	13.3	3.5
38/10	23/11¼	Ozalid	28 0	+/3	1 1¼	4.1	18.6
18/1	9 10½	Page Johnson	13 6	..	.8¾	5.3	7.2
9.0	4 10	Pantiya Elect.	6 3	..	.4¾	6.4	9.7
2 8	1 6	Park Cake Bake	1 8¼	..	.1¼	5.9	16.6
17.4	11/0	Parker Timber	11 0	-6	/8½	6.4	6..
49/0	28/0	Parkinson Cwn	28 6	+6	2.0	7.0	12.4
12 3	7/0	Parker Winder	9/9	..	/10½	9.0	9.6
33 3	22/6	P'kins'on Sir L	22 6	..	1 3¾	5.7	11.5
18.0	7/3	Parkland Mfg.	7/3	..	/10½	12.1	6.7
14/1	7/6	Parnell Elec.	8 3	..	/5	5.0	8.1
17 7	11/6	Parsons, F. J.	11 6	..	.8	5.8	11.7
20/11	12 3	Pasolds	12 3 •	-/3	/6	4.1	12.3
62 6	37/0	Paterson Zoch	62/6	..	1 4¾	2.2	6.4
10/7	4/3½	Pauls & Whites	5/10½	..	.7¼	10.2	17.0
7/10	2/7½	Peak Trailers	2 8¼	+/0¾	.4¼	13.0	4.8
3/3	1 2	Pearson Fos.	1/11¼	..	/1½	6.5	6.8
39 9	18 0	Pearson S Pub	19/0	..	1 0	5.3	13.1
36 9	26 7	Pearson & Son	29 6	-1.3	1 0	3.4	26.8
45	39½	Do. 4% Ln.	41½	..	80.0	9.6	..
13/1½	9 3	Peck (Joseph)	11 0	..	10	7.6	8.1
89 6	47.0	Peglers Hatt.	53/3	-3	2 4	4.4	12.8
45.3	24 3	Pergamon Pr'ss	32 6 f	..	.11½	2.9	19.2
108½	55	Perkin-El 4%	55	-3	..	..	..
3 8¼	2/1	Permali	2 10½	..	.2¼	6.3	15 3
18/0	7 1	Permanite	9 9	..	1.0½	10.8	8.9
76 6	19 6	Peters, G. D.	38 9	..	1/0	2.6	23.0
45 0	25 0	Philblack	25 0	..	1 9½	7.2	7.6
102	90	Ph'ps Fin 5¾%	99	..	115.0	5.8	..
257 6	162 6	Philips Lamp	167 6	-2.6	4 1¼	2.5	21.7
11/9	5 4½	Phoenix Timb.	7 1½	..	/2	2.3	..
25/3	12 8½	Photo-Me Int.	15/6 •	..	/11	5.9	9.6
11.6	4 3	Photopia Int.	5 6	..	1.0	18.2	30.6
10 0	7 6	P'dilly Theatre	7 6	..	/4½	5.0	14.4
37 9	29.9	Pickering E	30.0	-6	1.2½	4.0	15.1
4 1	2 1½	Pickles W'm	2 3	+/1½	..	..	..
3/6	1/7½	Do A	1 7½	..	.2½	12.3	6.3
69.0	43.0	Pifco Hldgs	43 0	..	1.8	3.9	10.8
67 6	33.0	Do A	33.0	..	1.8	5.0	8.3
20/0	9 7½	Pilkington T.'s	13 9	..	.7½	4.5	9.6
32 0	16 0	Pillar Ltd.	26 10½ h	..	9	2.8	20.0
110	82	P'y-Bowes 5½%	82	-1	110.0	6.7	..
22.11	17.1	Plaxtons	18.0 •	..	1 1¼	6.4	8.6
22.10	11.9	Pleasurama	12/6	+3	.6	4.0	15.1

1969/70 High	Low
22/3	17 3
5.0	2 1
16 9	7 0
38 0	22 3
20 3	15 0
12 9	10 6
32 3	11 3
14 9	10 6
23.9	16 0
25 0	17 4
8 3	5 0
16/0	13 0
17 0	12 9
15.9	12 9
39 8¼	16 0
10/3	5 6
9.0	5/0
17/10	9/7
8.9	4 0
12/7	8 1
14/0	8 0
45 0	18/6
9 3	3/7
15 1	6 6
25 9	17/3
7/6	4 3
59.0	22/6
6 3	2 1
14/6	6 3
31 9	11 9
21 0	10 0
14 0	6.0

T - Z

1969/70 High	Low
155 0	82/6
54 6	27 9
7 0	4/6
38 9	20 7
2 10	1 9
7 10	4 9
12 6	10 6
42 8¼	29 4
3 1	1 9
15 3	8 6
7 10½	3 7
42 6	23 6
40 0	23 0
51 9	39 6
20 7	12 0
13 3	7 0
13 9	6 6
13 3	5 0
31 9	16 3
74 0	43 0
72 0	42 9
48 6	26 0
17 0¼	11 1
31 3	19 0
27 3	14 9
5 1	3 6
11 0	5 9
4 3	.1
7 0	3 7
21 9	7 0
46 6	25 0
148 9	76 3
15 0	7 6
6 4½	3 4
6 10	3 1
64 9	45 6
10 3	6 0
38 6	9 0
22 0	9 6
14 1	9 0
17 6	11 3
17	1
9 9	5 6
37 0	17 9
10 0	4 3
36 0	20 3
24 6	12 6
90 9	53 3
7 3	3 9
39 3	19 9
3 9	2 0
43 3	26 6
30 3	16 6
44 0	14 6
12 0	6 4
20 1	11 0
17 10	6 0
20 1	11 3
70 6	42 3
280 0	142 6
7 9	1 5
48 3	27 9
13 11	7 9
7 6	3 9
13 7	9 3
23 8	7 0
23 7½	14 6
20 9	12 9
2 2	1 0
74 0	44 0
16 3	8 9
33 1	20 9
28 0	16 0
40 6	25 6

Contents

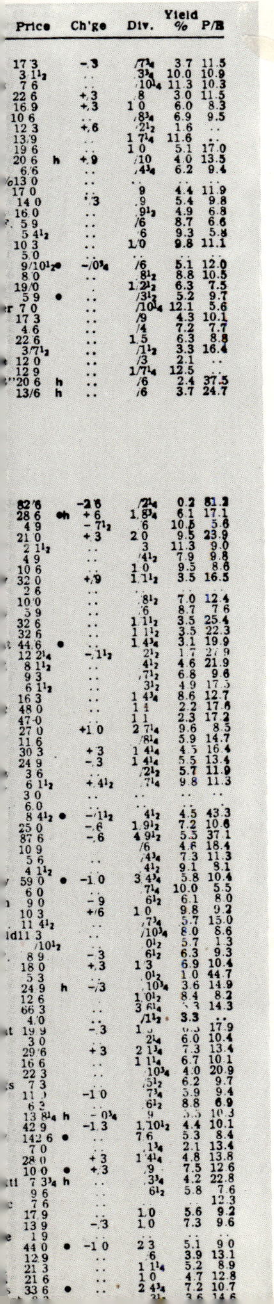

Origins

What is capitalism? 9
When did it begin? 13
The Ancient World 17
China 19
The Middle Ages 21
The rise of trade 26
The spread of mercantile empires 29
The accumulation of capital 33
The rise of a capitalist class 37
Technical innovations 44

Early capitalism

Adam Smith and Karl Marx 50
The steam engine and the energy revolution 54
Transport – canals and roads 61
Railways 66
The railway mania 72
Textiles and consumer goods 76
Agriculture 81
Technology, education and the transmission of knowledge 87
The immiseration of the proletariat 91
The conditions of industrial work 97
Profits and their spending 101
Money and banking 104
International trade 108
The state and the bourgeois 111
The state and the worker 115

High capitalism

New lands 118
The spread of trade 121
The migration of men and ideas 128
Bourgeois culture 132
La belle époque 135

The great boom 140
The rise of the consumer society 143
The great monopolists 147
The trades unions 150
The bourgeois state 154
The Edwardian compromise 156
The First World War 160
The disruption of world trade 164
The communist revolution 168

On the defensive

Unemployment 172
New industries 178
New techniques 182
The slump and the collapse of the gold standard 184
The rise of authoritarian politics 191
The New Deal 195
Keynes 198
The Second World War 201
Managerial capitalism 204
Is it still capitalism ? 212

Bibliography 218

Acknowledgements 219

Index 220

98 0	46 9	J'son Richards	46/9
21 3	8 9	Jute Indus	9 3
27 0	19 8	K Shoes	21 0
25 0	14 9	K.M P.H.	18 6
42 6	9 3	Kangol	9 6 •
31 0	10 0	Keay (T. C.)	12 6
2 4	1 3	Keith & H'son	1 10½
11 6	5 1	Keizer Venesta	8 3
13 9	3 3	Kenkast	3 3
5/10	3 9	Kennedy (A)	4 0
14 0	9/1½	Kennirg Mtr.	10 0 •
39 3	28 0	Ken Pal Hotel	28 0
39 3	25 9	Do A	26 6
21 0	10 9	Kent Castings	11 0 h
35 9	18 9	Kent (George)	25 3
16 6	9 0	Kier, J. L.	13 3
7 9	3 4½	Kirby's	4 4½
13 4	6 6	Kirkstall Fge.	9 1½
8 4½	3 9	Kitchen Taylor	6 6
42/9	25 0	Kleeman Ind.	36/3
65 0	4 0	Klinger Mfg.	4 4½
27 6	10 0	Ladbroke	21 0
17 9	7 9	Lafarge	8/0
26 6	15 9	Laing (John)	23 6
26 6	15 3	Do A	23 6
31 0	16 6	Lake & Elliott	17/0
7 4	4 3	Lambert H'wth	4 3
19 9	13 4½	Lamson Ind.	15 0
30 0	13 3	Lancs. Carpet	23 0
49 9	25 0	Lankro	36 6
49 0	24 9	Laporte Ind.	30 3
8 10½	6 3	Laund. Inv.	7 4½
44 9½	30 0	Latham J.	30 6
18 6	9 0	Lawtex	9 0
31 0	18 6	Lead & Alloy	27 0
21 11½	15 9	Lead Industries	18 6 •
16½	4½	Leasco Data	6
6 7	4 4½	Lee (Arthur)	5 6
26 3	15 6	Lee Cooper	15 9
45/0	30 0	Lep Group	32 0
95 7	13 0	Lesney	16 6
86 0	11 0	Do R.V.	11 0
23 0	6 0	Letraset	6 4½
56 6	39 0	Lewis & Peat	50 0
52 0	34 9	Do A	44 6
25 1½	15 3	Lex Services	2[illegible] 6
13 0	5 9	Leyland Paints	5 10½
20 7½	12 8½	Lilley F.J.C.	18 0
21 3	8 9	Limmer Hldgs	9 9
2 5	1 3	Lindop & Sons	1 3
26 3	10 0	Lindustries	10 9
29 9	12 0	Lines Bros.	12 6
13 10	6 9	Linread	8 6
19 1	8 9	Lister & Co.	8 9
55 0	40 0	Lloyd, F. H.	47 0
2 11¼	1 10	Locker, T.	2 0
2 9¾	1 4	Do A	1 10½
33 0	23 2¼	Lockwood Fds.	27 6
38 0	14 0	Ldn & M'land	22/0
25 5	9 5¼	Ldn & N'thern	15 6
19 9	8 7½	London Brick	9 0
21 3	13 0	Lon Prov Post	19 0 •
31 3	13 6	L R C Int	13 9
7 6	4 0	Lonsdale & Bar	4 0
43 9	17 6	Lovell Hldg.	20 0
32 9	24 6	Low & Bonar	26 6 •
13 9	7 6	Lowe & Bry'ne	7 6
13 0	7 3	Loyds Retail	8 3
80 6	43 6	Lucas Ind.	48 6
21 6	12 10	Lunt Comley	15 10½
93 6	61 6	Lyons (J) Ord.	68 6
91 9	68 0	Do A	68 0
6 6	4 7	Lytle (C. J.)	4 10½

M - N

27 1	16 9	M.K. Electric	18 0
8 6	5 0	M.L. Holdings	8/0
42 3	22 9	MTE Contactor	27 6
14 0	9 0	M. Y. Dart	9 9 •
22 0	12 3	Macready's Mtl	14 9
57 0	36 6	McCorquodale	36 6
18 0	9 6	Mackay (Hugh)	11 0
27 0	16 3	McKechnie Bros	24 0
26 6	16 0	Do A	23 9
17 9	6 6	Mcleod Russel	11 3
2 10	1 2	McManus Gp	1 3
20 0	12 3	Madame Tuss'ds	13 6
34 [illegible]	23 4½	Magnet Joinery	30 3
15 0	10 6	Magnolia Mfg.	11 6
16 0	9 0	Mallinson, G.	9 0
18 4	8 3	Mallinson Wm	9 9 •
13 0	[illegible] 9	Man Abell	8 0
93 0	11 0	Man Ag Music	34 3
26 6	15 3	Manbre & Gart	16 4½
19 3	11 4	Mann Egerton	13 6
12 0	8 0	Mann & Overtn	10 3
50 9	32 0	Maple & Co.	41 6
55 0	28 6	Marchwiel Hgs	43 0
20 0	14 0	Maro & Franc	14 3
10 6	5 0	Mark Lane Grp	9 4½
31 9	15 7	Marks Alfred	26 6
59 9	40 3	Marks & Spen.	56 3 •
26 6	10 9	Marley Ltd	10 9
25 9	3 9	Marling Inds.	3/9
9 4½	6 0	Marshall T Lox	6/0
9 3	6 0	Do 'A'	6 0
20 6	10 9	Marshall (H'fax)	11 6
38/0	14 3	Marshall (T) In.	26/0
7 0	5 1½	Martin Black	6 0
46/11	28 0¾	Martin-News	40 0
24 0	13 7½	Martin (Tom)	20 0
19 1	9 3	Martin Walter	9 3
40 6	26 9	Martonair	32 0
10 3	6 9	Mason (Frank)	6 9
8 0	4 3	Massey B & S	5 0
14 3	7 9	Massey Rbt B	9 6
18 3	15 0	Mass'n Sct Thr	15 0
22 6	14 7	Mather & Platt	18 1½
19 0	7 7½	Matthews Hdgs	7 7½
67 6	40 3	Maynards	41 6
19 0	8 3	Mears Bros.	8 3
25 0	13 1½	Mecca	15 10½
7 1	5 3	Medminster	5 3
10 2	5 9	Melbray Group	6 6
6 2	3 0	Mentmore Mfg	3 1½
18 9	13 0	Menzies (John)	13 9
14 0	4 3	Mercian Blds.	4 9
63 9	44 3	Metal Box	52 6
20 1½	14 0	Metal Closures	15 4½
5 6	2 9	Metal Prods.	4 3
6 0	3 9	Metalrax	4 10½
28 6	12 6	Metal Traders	20 6
46 9	15 9	Mettoy	16 3 •
11 10½	7 3	Meyer, M. L.	7 10½
17 9	12 [illegible]	Mid Elect Mfg.	15 6

9	11.0	
0	6.5	
.0	9.3	
4	12.0	
2	7.7	
.4	..	
.7	7.1	
8	6.4	
6	13.4	
.6	7.3	
.8	16.5	
.9	27.6	
.0	26.2	
.1	17.7	
.4	17.5	
.5	8.6	
.6	6.0	
.1	12.2	
.2	8.1	
.8	15.2	
.	..	
.9	8.8	
.1	10.1	
.3	27.0	
.3	27.0	
8	2.5	
.5	5.2	
.2	19.1	
.5	13.7	
.7	22.2	
.4	19.5	
.5	8.6	
.4	5.7	
.0	8.6	
.4	14.2	
.7	9.2	
.	..	
.8	10.8	
.9	7.0	
.7	14.8	
.4	20.1	
.0	13.4	
.2	10.9	
.3	16.4	
.7	14.3	
.8	14.4	
.0	9.5	
.0	11.0	
.1	14.8	
.0	3.0	
.8	7.7	
.7	8.6	
.4	11.6	
.0	14.9	
.4	15.7	
.9	8.4	
.4	7.9	
.9	14.8	
.5	8.2	
.8	10.3	
.9	11.8	
.4	7.9	
.5	13.5	
.4	7.9	
.0	6.1	
.6	13.4	
.7	6.8	
.5	12.5	
.7	11.8	
.7	13.5	
.1	17.0	
.2	16.9	
.2	11.2	
3.8	13.7	
8.3	8.2	
3.6	21.5	
3.3	17.5	
5.9	10.5	
6.6	13.8	
6.1	10.3	
4.1	21.4	
4.2	21.2	
8.9	11.9	
8.0	4.3	
4.1	16.7	
5.0	9.5	
3.5	10.0	
0.8	8.7	
7.7	8.0	
8.8	15.0	
5.8	7.8	
8.1	10.7	
6.5	12.7	
8.5	6.5	
7.2	14.8	
2.0	15.7	
3.6	13.0	
0.7	5.3	
2.8	20.1	
3.3	24.4	
8.1	19.4	
8.0	5.2	
0.0	8.7	
0.0	8.7	
6.5	9.7	
4.8	9.1	
0.0	7.5	
3.7	16.3	
2.7	18.6	
6.5	10.5	
2.5	17.6	
..	..	
..	..	
5.3	9.6	
6.4	10.8	
3.1	16.8	
5.9	10.6	
8.7	10.0	
7.6	8.8	
6.3	12.2	
8.6	9.5	
9.2	10.5	
6.7	10.2	
5.8	9.6	
5.3	18.8	
4.2	15.8	
4.1	12.6	
7.0	8.5	
8.5	8.0	
3.7	15.0	
6.6	11.0	
3.2	14.9	

25/0	10/4½	Pratt (F.)	14 0		-1/3	.10¾	6.4	18.2
17/6	6 3	Press (Wm.)	6 6		..	.2	2.6	9.0
36 9	24 3	Prestige Group	24 9		+/6	.10½	3.5	16.2
48 6	32 6	Price & Pierce	41 9		..	2.9½	6.7	8.7
36 3	12/3	Pricerite	12 3		..	.4¾	3.3	11.8
23 0	11 9	Pride & Clarke	11 9		..	/11½	8.1	..
47.9	35 3	Pritchard Cln	36 0		..	1 0	2.8	16.7
46 3	28 3	Prov Clothing	32 0		-/3	1 3	3.9	17 0
56 0	31 9	Purle Bros.	37 0		..	/4½	1.0	30.7
9 3	4 10	Pye Options	7 4½		..	..	..	..
5 0	3 9	Pyke W J	4 7½		..	/5	9.0	7.4
7/4	4 1½	Pyramid Group	4 7½		..	.6¼	11.2	27.2
7 6	6 0	Quality Clnrs.	7/0		..	/8¼	9.7	9.1
2/10	1/7½	Quick H & J	1 8¼		+.0¾	.1¾	8.9	8.2

R - S

4 10	2 0	R.F.D. Group	2 0		-/3	/2½	10.0	6.2
13 10½	7 10	R.K.T. Textiles	10 0		.	.9	7.5	8.3
23 9	13 6	Racal Elect.	14 1½		+.1½	.5	2.9	19.8
16 6	6 0	Radiant Met.	6 0		..	.3¾	5.2	10.1
3 4½	1 9	Raine Eng.	3 0		..	.2½	6.7	12.9
3 3	1 2	Ramar Textile	2 3	c	..	.1¼	4.4	15.5
129 0	77.0	Rank Org Ord.	91 0		+1 0	1 2	1.3	25.1
133/6	73 9	Do A	90 3		..	1 2	1.2	26.3
44 9	22 3	Ranks Hovis	22 10½		+.1½	1.9½	7.8	14.1
42 7	20 3	Do B	20 10½		+.1½	1.4¼	6.7	..
21 9	10 6	Ransome Hoff	10 6		..	10½	8.3	9.3
29 3	16 6	Ransomes S's	21 9		..	1 6	6.9	11.8
16 0	10 0	Ratcliffe F S	12 6		-.6	1 1½	9.0	8.3
30 6	11 6	Raybeck Ltd	11 6		..	[illegible]¼	3.5	9.3
11 0	5 7½	Rayne, H. M.	7 3		..	.7¼	8.3	9.3
8 10	5 3¾	Readicut Int	5 9		..	.3	4.2	11.0
26 9	15 10½	R. M. C.	16 3	h	..	.11	5.7	16.2
78 0	43 0	Reckitt & Col.	43 0		-.3	1 7¼	3.7	16.8
35/0	18 6	Redfearn Nat.	18 6		-3	.11½	5.1	10.8
23 7	13 0	Rediffusion	15 4½		-.3	.10	5.4	12.0
21 9	11/0	Redland	11 0		..	.7	5.2	12.7
12 4	7 7½	Redman H'nan	10 6		+.3	.5½	4.3	20.5
56 6	39/3	Reed (Austin)	53 6	●	..	2 9	5.0	12.6
56 6	39 10½	Reed Group	41/0		-1 0	2 6	6.1	11.4
18 9	13 9	Reed & Smith	15 6		..	1 2½	7.7	9.6
56 6	41 3	Reeves & Sons	49 6		..	3/0	6.1	14.1
11 3	6 0	Reeves, F. J.	6 6		..	7½	9.5	10.0
59 7½	38 0	Renold Ltd.	47 0		-1 0	2 3	4.8	17.8
16 9	12 0	Rentokil Ltd.	13 7½		+.1½	.4¼	2.6	24.0
28 3	17 6	Revertex	22 9		..	1 1¼	4.8	15.0
47/6	25/9	Rexmore	26 3		+.6	/10¼	3.2	10.5
76/0	33/6	Reyrolle Psns	34/3	●	..	3/0	8.8	6.8
22/3	12/0	Rhod. Cement	15 0		..	.10½	5.8	14.3
32 0	23 6	Ricardo Eng.	26 0		..	.10¾	3.5	11.1
29/9	18/9	Rich'rds & Wall	23/0		..	1.2½	5.2	20.4
8 4½	5 1	Richards Bros.	6 6		..	.6	7.7	11.8
43 0	34/0	Richardson A	35 3		..	1.7¼	4.5	15.3
9/0	4 6	Rich'dsons W	4/10½		..	/7¼	12.3	7.2
24 6	16 10	Rimmel	18 0		..	.7¼	3.3	18.0
4/10	1/6	Rippingilles	1/6		..	..	..	..
11/3	5/9	Rivlin I D & S	6 3		..	/7	9.4	7.3
2 1	1/4½	Rix (Oliver)	1/5		..	/1¼	7.1	13.9
11/6	6/9	Roberts Adlard	7/9		..	.8½	9.2	7.8
29/6	12 9	Robertson Fd.	12 9		..	/10¾	7.1	10.7
88 0	58/0	R'son Rentals	58/0		-1/0	2.0	3.4	21.6
25/6	11/6	Rockware Gp.	13/3		..	/9	5.7	15.1
49/1	15/3	Rolls-Royce	15 3		-1/6	2 2	14.1	6.5
13 9	4 3	Rootes Motors	5 0		+.6	..	..	..
10 7	3 6	Do A	4/3		..	..	..	..
19/1	11/3	Rose & Co.	11 3	●	..	1/1¾	10.2	6.4
20 0	10/6	Rotaflex	16/6		..	.4¾	2.4	18.6
35/6	17.0	Rotary Hoes	21 0		..	/7¼	2.9	16.2
30/0	11 0	Rotork Controls	11 3		+3	.8½	6.2	15.9
21/6	10 6	R'ledge & K'g	10 6		..	/9½	7.6	36.2
13 6	5/0	Rowe Bros.	6/6		..	/6	7.7	8.8
137 6	83/6	Rowntree Mc.	84 6		..	4/6	5.3	11.3
28 0	17 3	Rowton Hotels	18/0		..	.11¾	5.4	13.6
25 0	9 0	Royal Sovergn.	9 6	●	+/3	/6¼	5.4	10.1
55 0	33 3	Royal Worcs	33/3		..	.10¾	2.7	13.3
6/3	3/1	Rubber Regen	4 9		..	/4	7.0	11.2
25 9	10/0	Ruberoid	10 0		..	.9	7.5	12.3
26/10½	17.6	Rugby Cement	21 9		..	.7½	2.9	14.4
56.0	38 0	Do N.V.	45 0		-.7½	2/2	4.8	41.1
10 9	3 0	Russell Alex.	3/0		-/3	4½	12.7	12.9
5/4	3/1½	Rye (Claude)	5.1½	●	+.1½	/4	6.5	6.4
6/3	2/10½	Ryan (L.) Hgs.	2/10½		..	.3	8.9	10 6
13.3	4 9	Rycroft Hldgs	5 6	●	..	/6	9.1	7.1
18 9	3/10	Ryman Conran	14 9		..	/3	1.7	17 0
10 10½	4 3¾	Sabah Timber	8.9	c	-/6	6½	6.1	5.8
11 7	3 7½	S. & U. Stores	3/7½		..	7½	17.2	6.4
63¼	24	S.K.F. 'B'	24		..	17 8¾	3.7	6.2
18/0	9 6	Sale Tilney	16 0		..	1 0	6.3	10.1
24 3	16 6	Samuel H. Od.	21/6		..	8¼	3.2	16.5
25/0	16 0	Do A	18 9		..	8¼	3.7	14.4
32/9	24 6	Sandeman, G.	25 0		+6	1.5½	5.8	9.6
12/3	5 3	S'derson Mur.	6 0		..	..	..	..
45 0	27 6	Sanderson Kay	39 6		+.6	2 6	6.3	11.5
18/6	11 4	Sangers	15 6		..	4¾	2.6	11.3
27 9	17 0	Saunders Valve	19 6		..	/10½	4.5	15.3
60 5¼	34 6½	Savoy Hotel	51 3		..	1 7¾	3.2	17.0
32 6	20 6	Scaffldng. GB	23/0		-3	1/3	5.4	13.0
26 9	16 6	Scapa Grp.	17 0		..	/11	5.3	10.8
38 9	28 9	Scholes G. H.	29/0	●	..	1 7¼	5.6	13.1
32 3	16 4	Scotia Inv.	26 0		+/3	7¼	2.3	18.1
9/3	5 0	S.E.E.T.	5/1½		..	5½	9.0	7.6
13/1	6 4½	Scot Herit Tst	6 4½		..	4¼	5.6	9.8
23 0	5 6	Scottish TV A	6 0		..	..	..	67.3
16/8	8 8	Scott James	9 3		..	9¼	8.4	7.8
21 4	14 9	Scot Univ In	14 9		..	1-0	6.8	11.3
25 3	5 3	Scragg, E.	5 10½		-1½	5½	7.8	3.6
14 0	3 9	S & K Hldgs	4 4½		+/4½	9	17.1	6.4
44 6	19 0	Sealed Mtr	19 0		..	/9	3.9	13.5
45 9	20 6	Sears Hldgs	22 0	●	..	1 3	5.7	10.0
33/3	19 6	Do A	21 6	●	-.1½	1.3	5.8	9 8
10 8¼	6 2¼	Seddon Diesel	7 9		..	/3¾	4.1	12 7
3 1	1 10½	Selincourt	1 10½		..	/1¾	8.0	7.6
14 6	8 9	Sena Sugar	8 10½		..	/10¾	10 1	3 9
7 4½	4 1	Senior Econ.	6 3		..	/4¾	6.4	8 2
17 0	6 3	Serck	6 3		..	/3½	4.8	24.1
55 0	25 0	Settle Speak	39 0		..	3 3	8 3	6.1
6 3	3 9	Shannon "A"	4 6		..	2½	4 4	14 0
11 9	3 6	Shaw Carpet	5 6		..	..	..	..
12 10½	4 9	Shaw (Francis)	7 1½		+/3	6	7 0	4 7
85/0	72 10¼	Shaw, R. G.	82 6		..	3 8	4 4	14.9
17 6	11 9	Shpbridge Eng	11 9		..	/10¼	7 3	14 5
21 0	11 9	Sheffield Twist	12 9		..	.9	5 9	16 7
12 9	5 9	Shellabear Price	6 0		+.3	/7½	10 4	5 4
10 0	2 3	Sherman (Sam)	2 10½		..	..	..	5 3
3 0	1 9	Shiloh Spinners	2 0		..	/3	12 5	5 6
66.3	38 11½	Shipping Ind.	49 3		-9	.10¾	1 8	26 7
21 6	3 10½	Siipton Auto	4 3		..	/5¾	11.3	7 4
21 3	12 6	Siemssen Hunt	12 6		..	1 3½	10.4	7 7
111	97	Signode 7% Cn	97		..	140 0	7.2	
10 6	8 3	Sime Darby	10 0		..	6	5.0	14 5
12 6	5 6	Simms, W. J.	5 6		..	5½	8.2	5.1
42 0	29 0	Simon Eng.	33 0	●	..	1.6	4.5	13.3
16 6	11 0	Simpson, S.	11 6	●	..	/10½	7.6	12.5
16 0	10 0	Do A	10 3	●	..	/10½	8.5	11.1

27 3	15 0	Vosper	17/0		-/4½	/7	3.4	6.2
17 6	6 6	W.G.I.	7 0		..	9¼	11.1	9.3
5 3	2 7	Wade Potteries	3 9		..	.3¼	7.2	6.6
4 7	2/6	Wadham Str'er	2 6	●	..	3¼	10.8	12.1
42 0	22 6	Wadkin	22 6	●	..	1 1¼	4.9	13.3
43 6	27 9	Wagon Repairs	36 0		..	2 3	6.3	12.6
13 9	5 9	Walker C & W.	8 6		.	7¾	7.6	8.0
28 6	16 6	Walker Cros.	18 3		..	1 1¾	6.3	11 5
14 3	10 0	Walker J Gold	12 3		..	.7¾	5.3	15 8
13 7	7 9	Do N.V.	8 3		..	7¾	7.9	10 6
62 6	35 6	Walker & M'tin	37 0		..	2 6	6.8	10.8
3 7	2 3	Waller & Hart	2 10½	h	..	3	8.7	10.3
49 6	22 0	Walmsley Bury	22 6		-.6	2 3½	10.2	12.7
17/0	10 3	Ward & Gold	15 0		..	8¼	4 6	15 7
59 0	36 3	Ward, T. W.	38 6		..	2 9	7.1	8.3
8 4	2 7½	Wardle, B.	3 2½		-0½	2½	6 2	12.6
9 10	6 0	Warne Wright	7 0		.	7	8.3	6 1
5 3	3 6	Warner Hols.	4 0		..	3¾	7.8	6.5
42 0	23 6	Warren, J.	42 0		+2 0	2 6	6.0	15.4
30 3	21 3	Do A	27 6		+.6	2 6	9.1	10.1
27 9	5 6	Warwick Eng.	5 9		.	1	1.4	..
30 9	18 6	Watmough	20 0		-9	8	3.4	12.1
29 2	19 10	Watts Blake	22 0	s	+.2	/7¼	2.7	21.1
107 0	61 6	Wedgwood	61 6		..	1 1¾	1.9	17.2
29 6	18 0	Weir Group	18 3		+3	1/1¼	6.0	11.5
11 7	5 7½	Wellman Eng.	5 9		..	.4¼	6.1	12 9
11 0	4 9	Westbrick Pds	4 9		..	.7¼	12.6	5 0
7 0	3 9	W. Cum. Silk	4 3		..	/4¾	9.4	9.3
22 3	10 3	W Riding Wool	10 3		-/3	/11¼	9.1	11.6
44 6	20 9	W'house Brake	34 6		..	1 8½	4.9	9.9
21 10	6 0	West'and Air	6 3		..	.6¾	9 1	8.5
24 0	7 6	Weston, S.	7 6		-.1½	.5¼	5.9	8.8
12/1½	5 11¾	Weston Evans	10 9		..	7¾	6.0	9.6
16 9	10 0	Weyburn Eng.	11 0		..	1.0½	9.5	9.2
39 0	19 6	Wharf Hldgs	24 0	c	..	..	..	62.9
2 5	11¼	Whatlings	11¼		..	.1½	13.3	5.0
25 10½	14 3	W'sheaf Inv	19 7½		+.1½	/7¾	3.3	20.8
18 3	7 9	Wheelock Mard	14 10½		..	/6½	3.7	10.5
23 3	6 9	Whessoe	6 9		..	.9	11.1	4.8
10 3	5 0	White (John)	5 1½		+1½	6	9.8	6 5
19 9	12 6	Whitecroft	12 6		..	1 6	12.0	7 4
5 9	4 1½	Whitehouse G.	4 1½		..	.4¼	8.5	7 7
15 0	8 0	Whittingham W	10 3		..	/7¾	6.3	6.7
5 9	3 0	Whiteley BSW	3 4½		..	.2¼	5.5	10 9
5 3	3 0	Wiggins, C. S.	3 9		..	3¾	8.5	11.8
72 0	45 6	Wiggins Teape	45 6		-.6	2 4¾	5.3	11 9
10 6	4 6	Wilkins & Mit.	7 9		..	.6½	7.1	6 7
22 7½	7 0	Wilkinson Swd.	7 0		..	7¼	8.6	11.7
22 4½	5 0	Do A	5 1½			7¼	11.7	8.6
21/6	15 3	Wms. Humbert	15 3		-.6	.7	3.8	12 0
13 1	8 4½	Wms. Hudson	11 0		.	7¾	5.9	14.3
18/3	10 1½	Wilmot B'den	10 3		+1½	.7¼	5.9	10 6
13/0	5 0	Wilson Bros.	7 1½		+4½	.4¾	5.4	13 2
15 6	4/0	Wilson Lovatt	7 0		+6	/5½	6 6	4 8
3 1	1 1½	Wilson Mandle	1 3¾		+0¾	..	..	..
91 3	54 0	Wimpey, G.	60 6		+6	10¾	1.5	22 5
6 0	2 9	Windsor Sport	4 6		..	.	.	1 8
11 9	3 9	Wingard	3 9		..	2½	5.3	17 3
8/10	3 9	Winn Ind.	5 4½		..	6¾	10.4	7.4
28 1½	17 6	Winsor Newton	17 6		..	1 6	8.6	10.5
14 6	6 1½	Witter (Thos.)	6 1½		..	7½	10.2	13.2
27 1	17 3	W'sley Hughes	17 6		..	.9½	4.6	9 7
54 0	35 0	W'holm Bronze	35 0		..	1 3	3.6	12 6
2 8	1 6¾	Wombwell Fdy	1 7½		..	.2¼	11.0	8.1
41 9	19 3	Wood Bastow	19 3		..	10¾	4.7	12.4
34 0	19 6	Wood S W Grp	24 9		+9	1 0	4.0	14.5
8 3	3 9	Wood, W.	6 0	●	..	.5	7.0	11 0
18 4	9 0	Woodall D'ham	11 6	●	..	.10½	7.6	19.9
24 3	15 0	Wood Hall Tst.	17 7½		..	9½	4.5	12 3
26 6	17 6	Woodhead, J.	21 0		..	1 3	6.0	12 8
4 6	3 4½	W'dh'se Rixson	4 3		.	.3¾	7.4	8.6
17 10	7 9	Woolcombers	7 9		-3	.4¾	5.2	20 4
23 7	14 2¼	Woolworth	14 4½		-0¾	1 0	7.0	14 4
17 0	6 7½	Worth (Bond)	6 7½		..	1 1	16.3	13 1
10 9	3 1½	Wrighton F	8 9		..	.2¾	2.7	12.2
25 6	7 0	Wrights Bisc.	7 3		..	.9½	11.0	26.1
2 9	1 0¾	Yatton Furn.	1 1½		+0¼	1	8.0	8.9
24 6	12 6	Yarrow & Co.	12 6		-9	1 0	8.0	6.8
9 3	4 6	Yorks Fine W.	4 6	●	-3	.6¾	12.4	5 3
24 9	11 6	York Trailer	11 6		..	.7¼	5.2	13 5
16 6	6 3	Zenith Carb.	8 6		..	6	5.9	15 2
2 6	1 1	Zetters	1 10½		..	.1¼	5.3	20 5

FINANCIAL TRUSTS

7 6	4 6	Allied Finance	5 1½		..	..	..	..
15 1	6 9	Ang.-Cont. Inv	6 9		..	3	3 7	44 8
45 0	33 0	Argentine S. L.	33 6		..	1 8½	5 1	18 2
11 11	5 3	Assam Trading	7 0		..	..	..	..
28 10½	13 3	Astley Ind Tst	14 3		+3	1 0	7.0	17 9
11 8	6 4	Aust. Agric.	7 9		-1½	6	6 4	11 5
50 0	34 0	Aust. Estates	35 6		..	1 2½	3.4	12 0
40 6	24 3	Do A	30 0		..	1 2½	4.0	11 0
19 9	9 0	Aust. Past.	14 6		..	.4¾	2 8	13 1
11 9	3 10	Bank Bge. Sec	7 10½		..	3	3 0	20 2
18 6	13 9	B.E.T. Dfd	14 9		-.1½	.11	6 3	13 7
21 7½	5 9	Broadview	15 4½		-7½	3½	2 0	61.1
15 4½	8 6	Bryanston Fin	9 0	●	-9	7¼	6.7	7.3
101	43⅜	Canal-Randolph	43⅜		-⅞	9 2	1.1	.
22 9	10 6	Charterhse Grp	11 0		+.6	.9¼	7.0	12 8
15 10	11 3	Charterland	11 6		..	11½	8.3	8 3
114 5	71 0	Daily Mail Tst	71 0		..	4 9½	6 8	13 5
124 5	70 0	Do A	70 0		..	4 9½	6 9	13 3
62 3	43 6	Dalgety & N.Z.	46 6		+1½	2 7¼	5.6	13 8
54 0	21 3	Drakes	28 0		..	4¾	1 4	8.8
53 0	20 0	Do 10% Conv	27 0		..	1.0	3 7	..
116 3	111 3	Eng Assoc Am	116 3		..	4 1½	3.5	21 2
9 4	5 8	Est & Gen Inv	6 7½	●	..	.4¾	6.0	11 2
7 10	3 6	Exploration Co.	4 3		+6	2½	4 7	12.3
21 10	15 6	Fanti Cons	15 6		..	1.5¼ n	9 3	10 6
18 0	13 9	F.C. Finance	16 0		..	9½	5 0	18 2
49 6	32 0	First Nat Fin	35 6		+6	9	2 1	17 3
16 0	5 6	Fitzroy Inv.	5 9	●	..	6¼	9.1	6 9
38	8½	Gramco Man	$ 8½		-¼	.	.	.
13 9	7 9	Hume Hldgs A	8 6		..	.5	4 9	14 6
14 1	8 7½	Do B	8 0		.	.	.	..
46 4¾	25 0	I F I	25 0		-7½	9½	3.2	..
59 2¼	38 7	Inchcape	48 0		.	2 6	5.2	12.4
9¾	7⅜	I O S Ltd	7⅜		-⅛	.	.	..
66	6	I O S M	$ 8¼		+2¼			
19 3	3 3	Intl Secs	3 3			6	15 4	2 3
52 9	23 6	Jessel Secs	26 6		+1 0	1 6	5 7	12 0
47 6	13 4½	Do Dfd	16 6		+1 0			7 5
8 3	4 6	Kwahu Co.	4 10½		+1½	4¾	8 2	10 4
28 0	17 0	Law Deb Corp	17 [illegible]		+9	1 [illegible]¼	6 2	13 3
4 3¾	2 6	Malay R Loan	4 [illegible]½			2½	4 8	17 [illegible]
39 9	21 10	Mercantile Ord	25 [illegible]	●	+3	1 2	4 6	22 1
3 9	2 1	N M C Invest	2 6			3	10 0	11 6
11 7	7 6	Nat Mort Ag	8 0			7½	7 8	7 0
8 10	6 3	New World	7 0		+9	4¾	5 7	13 1
33 3	16 0	Raill Int	16 [illegible]½	h	-[illegible]	[illegible]½	4 3	2[illegible] 0
36 10	20 9	River & Merc	20 9			1 [illegible]	6 9	13 5
64 0	36 3	Slater Walker	41 6	h	+3	1 2½	2 9	[illegible]
36 3	5 10	Sterling Guar	[illegible] 3		..	[illegible]½	2 [illegible]	33 3
26 0	17 9	Trust & Agency	18 0		..	[illegible]¼	4 3	12 5
29 6	17 0	Utd Dom Tst	22 6			1 [illegible]¼	4 9	14 4
25 0	16 6	Wagon Fin	20 0		-3	1 [illegible]½	5 6	15 8
10 7	6 6	Western Credit	8 6		+1 0	6	5 9	

Origins

What is capitalism?

Capitalism is a word that has had many meanings, and is still in dispute. It arouses opprobrium and adulation; violent opposition and enormous support. It can be interpreted socially, economically, or politically; it can be described in engineering terms or in human terms. So what are the specific factors that this book will concentrate on?

Capitalism is mainly a feature of the North Atlantic. It probably started in Italy, spread into Holland, then England, and across the Atlantic to the North American littoral. After that it spread until its tentacles embraced parts of every continent. Capitalism, therefore, though based on the North Atlantic, was the first world-wide civilisation.

Its main feature has been steadily accelerating technical progress. As the early sections of this book will show, it would be a mistake — a grave mistake — to think that before capitalism the economies of the world were stationary, flat, and stagnant. Imperial Rome and Mandarin China reached peaks of technical achievement in some fields that were not reached again till the seventeenth and eighteenth centuries; the same is probably true of national income per head. Yet it is only since that time that continuously accelerating technical change has been a central feature of civilisation.

The causes of this continuous technical change are manifold. The application of science and technology to human problems is probably the key factor; it was the invention of modern science (based on the rediscovery of Greek learning) that supplied the dry kindle, for which technological innovation provided the flame. The beginnings of modern technology centre on changes in energy production and changes in transport; and the linking of these at first small but crucial changes to generally acceptable scientific principles invented a mode of changing human society that has proved irreversible.

opposite: A detail from 'The Banker and his Wife', by the Flemish artist Quentin Matsys (1460?–1530); the painting extols what were to be the Protestant virtues of frugality and thrift.

The continuous technical change — which is the central feature of capitalism — had to be embodied in physical capital and in the skilled labour force. The first condition, then, for the application of science and technology to human affairs was the accumulation of a surplus — capital that could be embodied in new machines and buildings. The accumulation of this surplus and its application to useful arts was therefore the economic condition that had to be established, before the scientific and technological changes could be firmly grounded. How to accumulate this surplus and apply it to the useful arts is the next question. The answer to that is the evolution of a number of separate groups or classes in society which could play important roles. The rich and powerful had always accumulated wealth; but so long as they used it on war, on ostentation, on religion, on themselves, it was not capable of application to useful arts. So somebody had to accumulate profits, or surpluses, by way of trade; somebody had to see openings, opportunities, occasions for profits to be made; somebody had to be prepared to employ large bodies of men and women; somebody had to be prepared to invest in factories, transport and production. These were not always the same people,

The two capitalist classes: the bourgeoisie and the proletariat. **left:** 'Réunion de Famille' by F. Bazille ; **right :** English factory workers during the First World War.

because the functions were diverse. But in a world of landowners, farmers, soldiers, aristocrats, priests and other feudal beings there appeared a new phenomenon — merchants, traders, bankers, manufacturers, employers and retailers, as a self-conscious group, were now borrowing money, investing it, getting profits and spending their profits on further investment. It was their concern with profit, and its reinvestment to yield still more profit, that differentiated them from other social groups. It is their ascension to a dominant social and cultural position which is the hallmark of capitalism.

The corollary of this is the rise of money, and the market system, to a dominant mode of relationships. Mankind moved from status to contract. It was money values, the anonymous arbiter of the price system, that tied all the different parts of the capitalist economic system together. It was not, as in Rome, allegiance to an emperor; or allegiance to a pope; or allegiance to a creed; or submission to a military tyrant: it was an acceptance of a link, via prices, to the profit and loss system of the market economy which indicated that a country, a region, a port or a city had gone over to capitalism.

A further feature of the capitalist system was the

Two views of labour under capitalism : **left:** Late nineteenth-century American ; **right** : French, 1907.

evolution of a group in the community — eventually to be numerically dominant — who were propertyless, not tied to the soil or to any specific place, who depended for their existence upon wages. The wages were paid to them by capitalists for work done ; and when there was no work, there was no pay. In earlier societies, whether slave societies, Asian societies, or feudal societies, the subsistence of the worker and his family was implicitly guaranteed by his status and was (to a greater or lesser degree) divorced from his work. Not so with capitalism. Work for wages and no other obligations was the order of the day. This propertyless, wage-earning, often unemployed group of people was christened by Marx 'the proletariat'. It was the proletariat which was to overthrow the bourgeois, or capitalist, state. It was the proletariat, it seemed, that in the North Atlantic world refused to overthrow the bourgeois state, and became itself a bit bourgeois.

What was the bourgeois state ? The early capitalists saw it as a referee, and no more. Its functions were to dwindle. Its swaddling clothes were to be thrown off so that the capitalists could be free to pursue profit. But eventually the state was rebuilt in a new form ; first, to wage war and to occupy colonial territories, and second, to cope with the immense social and technical problems of running the proper environment for a prosperous industrial society. Far from withering away, the state has become the most dramatic and important feature of capitalism. And it is the state, allied to nationalism, that has moved the world out of capitalism into the era of scientific-militarism.

When did it begin?

Capitalism has many faces and many aspects. Its start, therefore, can be assigned to many periods. It was in full bloom over most of the world between 1880 and 1914. Thereafter its geographical area began to contract. Its early blooming could be seen over most of Europe and the east of North America (as well as in a few offshoots like South Africa and the Australasian colonies) in 1820. It was coming into wide acceptance in Europe, and especially in Britain, by 1770. Most of this book, therefore, is concerned with the period post-1820. But much of the major manifestation of High Capitalism — capitalism in full bloom — could be seen in embryonic form from very early times.

Take, first, the advance of science. The rediscovery of Greek knowledge and the adaptation of Arab learning spread through western Europe after the fourteenth and fifteenth centuries. Galileo, Copernicus, Newton began a tradition of scientific enquiry that, with a few hesitations, became ever stronger, until its victory was assured at the time of Darwin and Huxley and the great nineteenth-century chemists and physicists. The triumph of the scientific spirit, which spread into history, biblical studies, the study of the classics, can be dated to the mid-nineteenth century; and its main foci were Britain and Germany.

The unleashing of continuous technological innovation is a little harder to date. The complexity of French clockwork, the ingeniousness of many Chinese devices (and they invented gunpowder), was matched to a degree by some of the achievements, especially in civil engineering, of the Greeks and Romans. By comparison, much of the engineering associated with the industrial revolution, such as the invention of the steam engine and its use to draw trains along the rails, was crude and unimaginative. But the industrial rev-

An English trade token (1792) celebrating the advances of mechanical engineering: Britannia's trident is replaced by a drill, her shield by a cog-wheel.

olution, and especially its embodiment in energy and transport, was linked closely to scientific principles, and through the development of both mechanical and civil engineering it became a continuously accelerating process applied to more and more walks of life. It would be wrong to think that change had not occurred before the invention of the steam engine. The sailing ship, for example, had evolved from a small, bulky and inefficient vessel, mainly propelled by oars, as used in Roman times, to fast schooners whose rate of travel was many times that of their predecessors. Each generation of ships embodied some improvements over what had gone before. But steam and steel meant a qualitative difference in the adaptation of techniques, and the process of change was rapid. As soon as an apparent plateau had been reached in technological design, as with the railway at the end of the nineteenth century, a new form of equipment came along — in this case the internal combustion engine. It would be right, it seems, to assign the period of the engineer's rise to dominance as the period in which the supremacy of the technologist, and his rooting in scientific principles, first became apparent. This can be dated fairly nearly to the spread of the steam railway in Britain, in the early 1830s, which is the period when most of Samuel Smiles's heroes in *Lives of the Great Engineers* were prominent.

The rise of capitalists was much earlier than the rise of capitalist technology. In all recorded time there have always been merchants and traders, and they were prominent in organising the trade routes (which reached India and China) of the Ancient World. The Arab traders were famous. The rise of Venice in the wake of the Crusades is well attested. By the thirteenth and fourteenth centuries the Italian city states and some northern cities were active centres of trade, with rich traders. By the seventeenth century whole countries — Holland and England — were ruled partly by merchants, whose family interests were linked to all the recognised sources of authority and power.

The application of farming surpluses to trade, and of manufacturing profits to agriculture, is a well-

Labour before capitalism – feudalism and slavery. **top**: Africans with their English master arriving in the West Indies to be sold as slaves. **centre**: A Russian 'muzhik' prostrating himself at a landowner's feet, 1789. **bottom**: Medieval serfs at work, watched by their feudal landlord.

attested phenomenon of eighteenth-century England. The brewers, who were among the first big industrialists, put some of their profits into farming, and big farmers put some of their profits into brewing. It is this sort of process — the utilisation of surpluses, through country banks, and the lending of the surpluses to industrialists — which is a central feature of capitalism. A well developed banking system existed in western Europe by the mid-eighteenth century. A tradition of engineering-minded entrepreneurs evolved, at first mainly in England but then elsewhere, who began to transform the economy. Wedgwood in pottery is an example of a name that became world-famous for the application of new techniques to a traditional occupation; and he became rich in the process, while his products were transported all over the capitalist world. It had been the same with Chinese pottery, but this had not been produced by Wedgwood's methods of bulk production, nor had it been financed and transported in the same way.

Marx and Engels have written vividly of the rise of the working class — the spread of the landless labourers. As methods of agriculture changed and as the birth rate rose, so the surplus of population congregated in the cities and worked for capitalists, for wages. By the mid-nineteenth century this was the most common way of earning a living in England, in northern France, and in parts of the United States. By the end of the nineteenth century it was the landed peasant who was untypical in western Europe and North America.

The emergence of the bourgeois state is associated with the overthrow of the feudal regulation of trade — Free Trade in England in 1846, the Cobden treaty with France in 1860, the abolition of slavery in America in 1863, the abolition of serfdom in Russia in 1861 — and the rise of a small bureaucracy wholly or partly responsible to a Parliament elected mainly by the business classes.

Engineering, the rise of capitalists, the emergence of the working class, and the transformation of the state all point to the early nineteenth century as the very period when capitalism, as it became known, finally emerged.

The Ancient World

It may be assumed that whatever mankind's particular genius may be, it was not less present in the time of the Ancient Greeks and Romans than it was in nineteenth-century western Europe. Yet the Ancient World, which had many of the preconditions for capitalism — that is for continuous technical progress, revealing itself in the steady accumulation of the means of production — did not achieve capitalism. Consider what Greece and Rome had. Science reached a peak that was certainly not recovered till the seventeenth century, and possibly even later. Roman roads were technically in advance of any means of transport till the canals of eighteenth-century England. Roman agriculture produced crops which in yield and quality were possibly not equalled till the eighteenth century. The aqueducts and roads, temples and houses were triumphs of civil engineering. The Roman Empire, especially, produced huge surpluses, which were available for investment. There was a large class of merchants and traders, which traded as far as China and India (the caravan route for silks was used by the Greeks in the fourth century BC). At the height of the empire civil peace prevailed over an area which reached thousands of miles — from Gibraltar to Asia Minor, from Scotland to Africa. The process of governing such a vast empire was developed to the highest degree of sophistication.

But it never developed into capitalism. Historians of classical times have long pondered the reasons. One is that the technology, though advanced, was not systematically linked to a body of scientific principles, so that a brilliant innovation was not necessarily part of a cumulative, reasoned process.

Another reason is that the ancients never operated a full money economy. Money, to them, it seems, was used in the way that small change is used. It was valued because it was made of gold, silver, or copper, not because it was a medium of exchange on which credit could be built. It was not the basis of credit; it was not accumulated in banks; surpluses were not systematically lent by one sector of the economy to another sector. So that, while there were merchants and traders they did not occupy the same social role that a modern capitalist fulfils. There was no class of men organising production on borrowed money and selling the produce at a profit, though apparently there were individuals, or small groups, who did so.

More important, the Ancient World was a slave economy. The spread of conquest brought in continuing supplies of slaves, and their labour was the basis of much production. When the supply of slaves dwindled, production languished. The significance of this is that the 'free' wage bargain, between a propertyless worker and an employer producing for profit (and using borrowed capital or credit to finance the process), was not capable of becoming a significant feature of Greek or Roman society so long as the slave owner could legally possess all the fruits of the slave's work. The productive possibility of the free wage bargain was not foreseen; nor could it be, until the crude exploitation represented by slavery was ended.

Above all, perhaps, the secularisation of the world that accompanied capitalism was never achieved by the Greeks and Romans. It was an era of militaristic triumphs and defeats, of gods and goddesses, of a society utterly unlike anything that has been consonant with capitalism. There is little point in arguing what is cause and what is effect; the fact of the matter is that in Greek and Roman life the community was dominant over the individual. The community's aims were not high production or individual profit, but the pursuit of military glory, social achievement, and religious satisfaction. These clever, achievement-motivated, remarkable societies (in many respects the most remarkable the world has ever seen) were not capitalist societies.

Might Rome have become one? Its embryonic monetary institutions were destroyed by a disastrous inflation, under Valerian in 256, which spread and could not be stopped. There were more large estates, and gradually the agricultural basis of the society diminished. The government extended its operations to cover many aspects of life; it was an autarchic and arbitrary society. Then the barbarian invasions began to erode the empire, until large parts of it collapsed. The slaves and the serfs merged into a class which bore the brunt of the economic and political crisis. A combination of attack from without and problems within brought economic activity to a lower level, from which capitalism ultimately emerged.

China

In the eighteenth century China may have had double the population of Europe, and it probably had a higher standard of living even than Holland, the richest country in the west. This fortunate economic position had lasted for many centuries; even at the time of the Roman Empire it seems probable that China was more populous and that its people were richer. The Chinese had relatively settled government, with a complex administrative system. Their scientific and technical achievements were ahead of those of the west. Their agriculture was more intensive. They had a skilled work force.

China was a world in itself, of many kingdoms, as early as the Egyptian and Babylonian civilisations. The country was a unity, but a unity as a civilisation (like medieval Christian Europe) rather than as a political entity like the Roman Empire. By the second century AD China had contacts with Persia, Rome and southern Asia, both by sea and by land.

The conquest of China by alien Buddhist nomads unified it politically, but the culture (which was Confucian, with ancestor worship at its centre) absorbed the conquerors, as the Indian culture absorbed conqueror after conqueror. Unlike Europe, China did not pass through a period of the 'dark ages'. The culture continued to grow richer, not thinner; the population continued to increase; and the bond of a common language grew tighter.

During the T'ang Empire (618–907) China extended its links with Byzantium, Japan, India and Persia. By this time it was clear that China had the most advanced civilisation in the world, and it was during this period that the Chinese came to regard all other civilisations as barbarous, akin to the barbarian nomads of the steppes, the foreigners with whom they were most familiar. The Chinese had a civil service recruited by competitive examination. They had widespread literacy and cultivation of the arts.

They had a relative abundance of food, provided from a carefully managed agriculture which relied on complex irrigation works, and they had advanced methods of manufacture of cloth and pottery and utensils.

Even when the Mongolians overthrew the T'ang dynasty and broke with its traditions, within a century the old order was reestablished. But the condition of the restoration was respect for the past, in every particular, and contempt for change and the outside world. By the fifteenth century, when America was rediscovered by the Europeans, China had a population of 200 million (probably three times that of Europe) and was living a settled, complex life, with a rich culture and moderate prosperity. Western visitors like Marco Polo were astonished at the wealth and vitality of Chinese cities and the complexity of their science and mechanical contrivances. The Ming civilisation, the civilisation which came into contact with Europe (chiefly the Portuguese), was not only an imitation of the T'ang traditions. In its porcelain, pottery, architecture and metalwork its developments were magnificent. But though these developments can be seen as representing a break with the past, generally it is true that the hierarchical nature of the society and its predominant tone of respect for the past (centred on the veneration of ancestors) were not conducive to a class of entrepreneurial innovators.

Gradually the Portuguese, the Dutch and the English established themselves on the coasts of China, in enclaves. It was from these enclaves that they brought back Chinese tea, porcelain and silks, and other rarities. But, because they traded from enclaves, their trading habits did not spread like an infection, as they did elsewhere.

European technical and commercial development, then, went on independently of China; and the isolation of China from the rest of the world meant that it fell relatively behind Europe, technologically. The Manchu conquest from the north, in the seventeenth century, was absorbed, like all other conquests. But it enfeebled the political and administrative structure of the empire, and as the threat from the north disappeared — since Manchuria and China were now one, and Manchuria, though the conqueror, adopted the ways of the conquered — China's military strength decayed. Consequently, when European imperialists arrived in strength, the Chinese were unable seriously to resist. The opium war of 1842 was based on a pretext: tired of trading with the Chinese mainly in silver, the East India Company insisted on exporting opium, and on the Imperial government's refusal to trade on this basis, gunboats were sent. There followed a series of rebellions, exacerbated by the pressure of population on land, which finally brought the Chinese Empire down.

Thus the great Chinese civilisation did not produce the scientific technology that was to transform the world, nor, having seen it, did it find that technology interesting or acceptable. The reasons were a combination of legitimate satisfaction with things as they were and a social structure with no room for entrepreneurs.

The Middle Ages

The Middle Ages stretch from the end of the Ancient World, in the fifth and sixth centuries, to the beginnings of capitalism, in the sixteenth and seventeenth centuries. The changes into capitalism began in western Europe in about 1500. It would be absurd, of course, to imagine that this period of a thousand years, followed by two to three centuries of preparation for full-blown capitalism, could be considered as a homogeneous unit; but certain central points stand out which are essential for a full understanding of capitalism as it emerged in western Europe.

First, the Roman Empire never wholly died, either in the east or in the west. The Byzantine civilisation continued many of the practices of the later Roman Empire, though it lost the aggressive expansionist militarism of the Romans, turning more to trade. Constantinople became the centre of trade for the Middle East, for distant Asia and for Europe. Next, the Latin successor societies to Rome in western Europe seem to have kept to a degree some of the urban life that had been characteristic of Rome; in France and Italy, some of the rural life probably survived substantially. The Arab invasions which swept across Asia, across North Africa, and into Europe, up to the Pyrenees and beyond, cut off western Europe from much of the

The Hanse towns

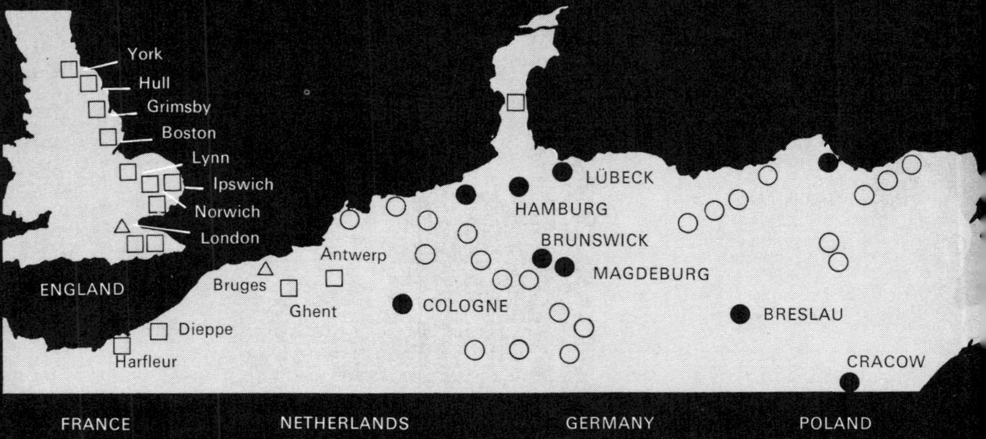

Trade Routes

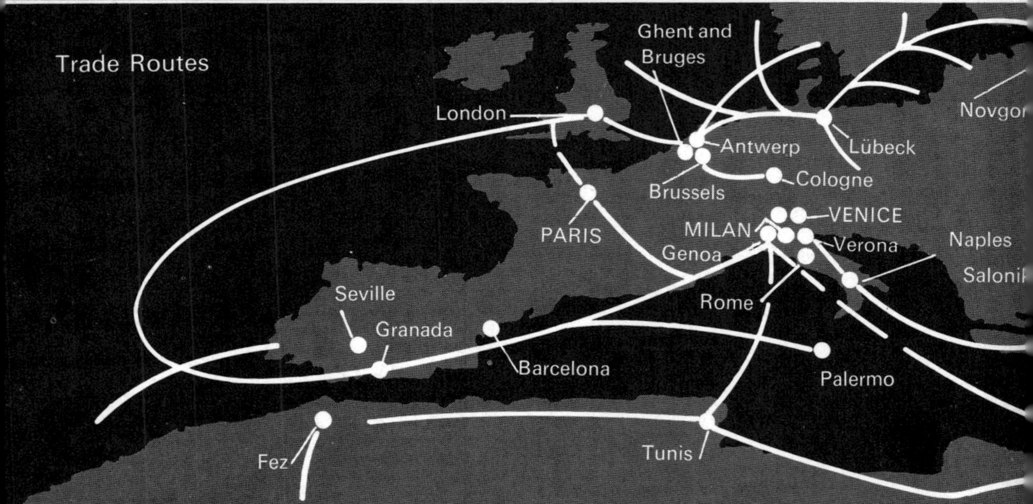

The Medici and Fuggers

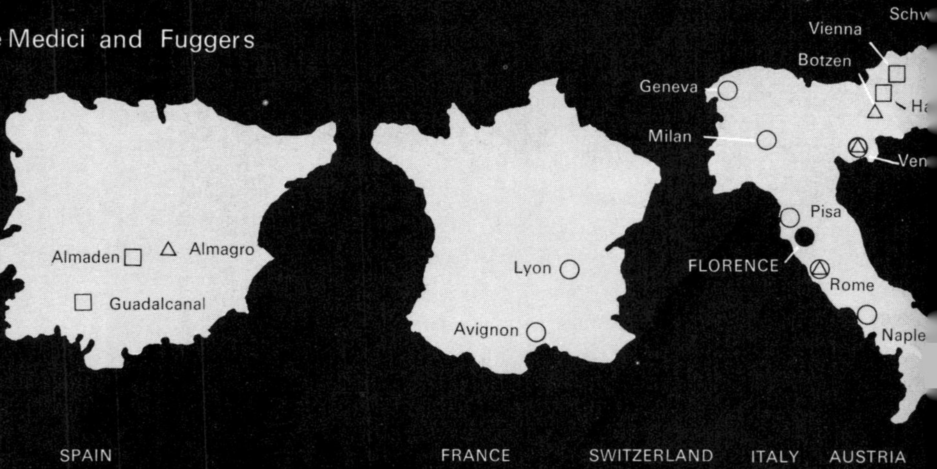

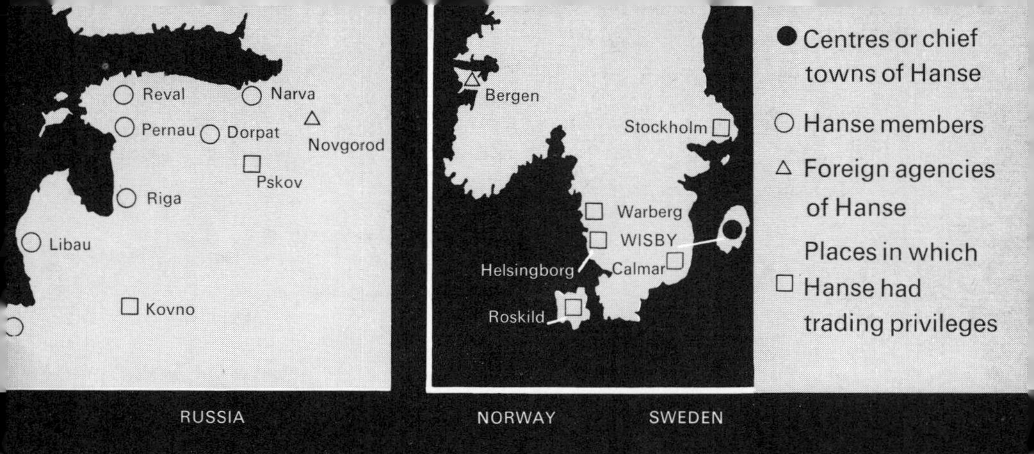
Centres or chief towns of Hanse
Hanse members
Foreign agencies of Hanse
Places in which Hanse had trading privileges
Reval
Narva
Pernau
Dorpat
Novgorod
Pskov
Riga
Libau
Kovno
Bergen
Stockholm
Warberg
WISBY
Helsingborg
Calmar
Roskild
RUSSIA
NORWAY
SWEDEN

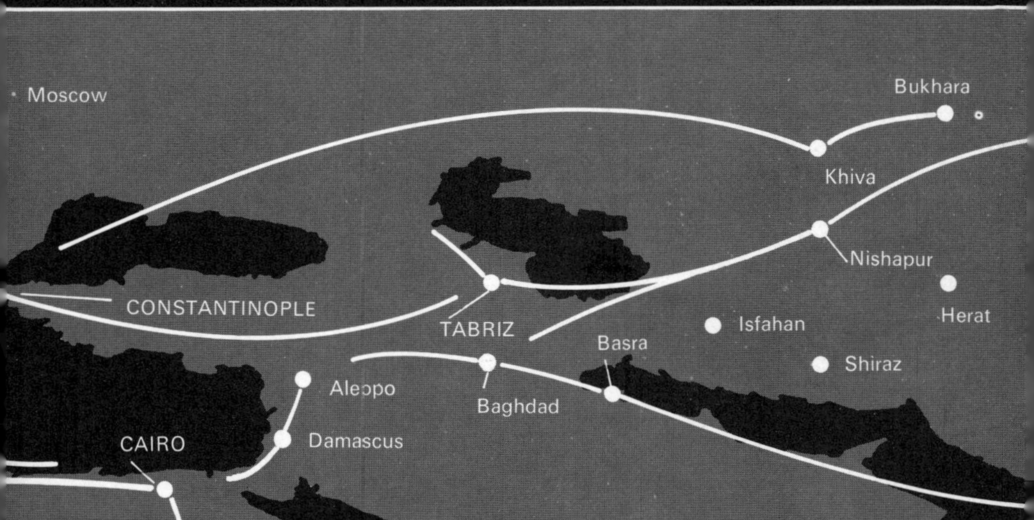
Moscow
Bukhara
Khiva
Nishapur
Herat
CONSTANTINOPLE
TABRIZ
Isfahan
Basra
Shiraz
Aleppo
Baghdad
Damascus
CAIRO

The Medici centre Florence
Medici branches
The Fugger centre Augsburg
Fugger branches
Fugger mines
Danzig
Amsterdam
Antwerp
Leipzig
Hochkirch
Bruges
Breslau
Cologne
Erfurt
Frankfurt
Cracow
Teschen
London
Nuremburg
Neusohl
Kremnitz
AUGSBURG
ENGLAND
GERMANY
CZECHOSLOVAKIA
POLAND

Arab merchants were responsible for much of European trade in the Middle Ages. A detail from a Catalan atlas of 1375, showing an Arab trading caravan on the Mongol silk route.

Byzantine trade, but the Arab traders in their turn developed a substantial land and sea trade across Islam. In Spain, where the Arab and Latin cultures mingled and to some extent merged, the Arabs and Jews became the centre of diffusion of Greek and Arabic scientific and philosophical works, so that Greek science and culture penetrated Islam and in turn penetrated the Latin cultures. The characteristic of later medieval society, therefore, was that it was unusually open (in comparison with other societies) to ideas from a variety of cultures.

Next, the development of sailing vessels, especially under the impact of Arab achievements and navigation, and small but significant improvements in many of the mechanical arts, gradually increased the productive potential of medieval society, which though less rich and powerful than Imperial Rome was less vulnerable to outside attack and inner collapse. During the period of the Crusades (roughly 1096 to 1204) the Venetians and their associates entered significantly into Mediterranean trade, both with Arabs and Christians. The Fourth Crusade, indeed, was marked by an attack on Constantinople, the capital of the Greek Orthodox Church, which gave Venice access to trading links that stretched across to China, where a Venetian merchant, Marco Polo, travelled in the late thirteenth century. Thus the Italian city states grew in wealth from trade with the whole Euro-Asian land mass, as well as with North Africa, and the level of intellectual, artistic, technical and scientific achievement rose significantly as the Greek, Arab and Latin cultures came into contact.

Northern Europe developed a similar sea-borne

trade, stretching from Ireland to Russia, with links round and across Europe to Italy. It was based on goods like wool, fish, timber, grain and cloth. Again merchants made fortunes, and cities like Bruges and Antwerp grew rich. A characteristic of medieval society, then, was the independence of trading cities; the fact that these cities — Genoa, Venice, Bruges, Pisa, and, a little later, London and Paris (in fact many of the great cities of modern Europe) — were rich, and powerful, and centres of intellectual life, was to become central to emerging capitalism. A network of trade existed all across Europe, with links round the world. There were vigorous intellectual centres at the key points of this trade network. At the heart of this intellectual activity were moneyed men, making profits by buying and selling, who dominated their cities.

They bought and sold partly on behalf of their fellow citizens and partly on behalf of the rural population. Late medieval life was predominantly rural (as was most of the world until the late nineteenth century), but it differed from classical times in that the central government was weak and the local lords were powerful. The feudal structure — oversimplified and formalised of course — consisted of a territory belonging to a feudal lord, a class of tenants, or yeomen, owing some feudal dues to the landlord, and a class of labourers, owing substantial dues, but in return expecting a living from the land. When a catastrophe like the Black Death took place, causing wages to rise, or when a substantial price inflation occurred, the feudal system began to break down. Some feudal lords began to use some of their surplus to enter trade, while some labourers were expelled from the land and began to form the beginnings of a class of landless labourers seeking employment in the towns. As prices rose and new knowledge began to affect production techniques, so agricultural relationships began to change. But in all this loosely organised medieval system tightly linked by trade, there was room for the towns to grow and prosper, and for the spirit of profit to dissolve feudal bonds.

It was in this fertile soil that the seeds of the new geographical and intellectual discoveries of the late fifteenth century were sown.

The rise of trade

Many medieval towns were based mainly on trade, and the trade network was to grow and become increasingly far flung. The rising incomes of the towns and their rural hinterlands demanded more and more silks, spices and other treasures, as well as basic commodities like wool and timber, salt and grain, wines and hides. The technology of the sailing boat and the art of navigation improved, so that expeditions were made along the shores of Africa, to India, and across the Atlantic to America. Vasco da Gama, Cabot, Christopher Columbus, Sir Francis Drake, are among the best known of scores of sea captains who pioneered new trade routes and discovered, or rediscovered, civilisations not known to the medieval world. Trade was extended to India and most of Asia on a big scale, and whole civilisations, like those of the Aztecs and Incas in South and Central America, were plundered. Wealth flowed into western Europe. Though initially some of the wealth went to maintain and develop the splendour of kings, princes, and bishops, as in Spain and Portugal, much of it enriched the merchants of the thriving cities of Italy and northern Europe.

At the same time, feudalism was breaking down. The rise of wages after the dreadful population losses of the Black Death and the Hundred Years War (about one-third of England's population died in two years, 1348 and 1349, during the Black Death) was but one of many causes of the decline of the manorial system. The growth of local trade made it profitable to produce agricultural commodities — especially grain — for local markets. Increasingly, feudal dues and services were commuted for money, and the landowner became a moneyed man as well as a lord. In some countries the feudal lords attacked each other, destroying their own power, as in England; elsewhere, as in France, they consolidated it with the monarchy. In those countries where the traders were allowed freely to operate, or where they were able to ally themselves with the political authority, the landowners began themselves to drift into trade. Allied to this shift in the importance of trade, which was promoted by an apparently noticeable rise in national incomes, was a shift of political and religious ideas.

The great trading routes rapidly spread across the

Atlantic, the Indian Ocean and the whole of Europe. The early capitalists — people like the Fuggers in Augsburg and the Medicis in Florence — were merchants turned bankers. As banking developed, together with significant advances in commercial practices such as double-entry book-keeping, it became possible to finance large-scale trade, enabling the products of large-scale industry to be exchanged. The earliest industrial revolution was probably in the manufacture of cloth, with the development of the watermill to enable mechanical fulling to take place (fulling is the process of removing grease from wool); cloth-making was the earliest large-scale manufacturing trade, in Flanders,

Jakob Fugger, founder of the Augsburg family who were bankers to the emperor Charles V.

A late fourteenth-century Genoese banker: in the lower picture he is using an account book.

A fifteenth-century Flemish manuscript showing a handloom used by Flemish weavers ; this type of loom remained in general use until the technical innovations of the mid-eighteenth century.

then in Florence, and finally in England, where it formed the basis of sixteenth-century expansion. Trade in agricultural products hastened the transformation of medieval farming, to enable the production of wool, of grain surpluses, and of timber to be stepped up.

By the late sixteenth century, then, northern Italy, parts of France and southern Germany, Flanders and England were linked by great trading centres (almost all ports) into a complex process of trade. This trade was rapidly increasing inside a number of countries, though in some countries it received political setbacks, in Germany's case from the Thirty Years War, and in Spain and Portugal from the development of theocratic absolutism.

Trade carried with it new attitudes to religion and politics. The nation state came into being, as did Protestantism, which by a process of pressures also called into being a reformed Catholicism. Luther, the original heretic, was as opposed to usury as the medieval papacy had been ; Calvin, however, was the archetypal Protestant whom later historians were to identify as the embodiment of the Puritan spirit of early capitalism. His emphasis on hard work, frugality, thrift and self-reliance was an essential ideology sanctioning the capitalist spirit of enterprise, profit seeking, and the utilisation of retained profits in other enterprises.

Early bankers made some of their income by lending to princes; though they were to continue to do this, the new and acceptable way was to lend it to finance enterprise.

By the end of the medieval period, then, with the fall of the Universal Church, the opening up of trade, the rise of New Learning and the scientific spirit, and the development of respect for a merchant-venturer class in a significant number of big cities in growing nation states, output was rising and a growing surplus was falling into the hands of families anxious to use it to develop productive enterprise, in order to engage in ever more profitable trade, both local and long-distance. The self-sufficient man was already old-fashioned; the age of specialisation had begun, and with specialisation large-scale production of single commodities could be undertaken. Given the existence of adequate capital, growing markets, and the possibility of a rational development of technology, the capitalist revolution was now possible. The seventeenth and eighteenth centuries therefore saw a great growth of trade, great increases in output, and a continuous expansion of western Europe's frontiers, both by means of trade and conquest. Population increased, as did the care of cultivated land. On the swelling tide of this prosperity, Europe's new limits were quickly to outdistance those of Imperial Rome; and its ideas — essentially the Enlightenment, the very spirit of capitalism — were to conquer most of the world in a way that Rome had never done.

The spread of mercantile empires

The ubiquity of capitalism in 1900 was at least partly explained by the fact that the dominance of western Europe was established by 1700. The spread of European empires was related to the spread of capitalism in a complex way. Capitalism eventually reached parts of every country in the world, and almost every country in the world was controlled by people of European stock. This may have been an inevitable consequence of triumphant capitalism — as trade developed, so the flag was bound to follow: but the evidence is to the contrary. Trade and the flag went jointly and, having conquered much of the world, capitalism rushed in to fill the vacuum. When it was a decadent or bastard capitalism, as in Spain and Portugal, then those areas of the world colonised by the Spanish and Portuguese had a decadent and incompetent colonial capitalism. When, as with North America, the conquest was by high capitalism, the consequence was an even more triumphant transplanted capitalism.

How then did Europe conquer the world? In the first place by trade and plunder. The Portuguese, Spanish, French, British and Dutch established trading posts from China to Peru, from the Cape to Newfoundland. These trading posts became centres where indigenous produce was collected, and where goods for Europe were bartered. The home ports became great entrepôt centres, where goods were exchanged from all over the earth. In some cases, however, the trading posts became centres of immigration, as happened all up the eastern littoral of North America, in parts of South America and on the Cape of Good Hope. In America, North and South, some of the native population was murdered, part was assimilated, and

The headquarters of the Dutch East India Company in Amsterdam, in a seventeenth-century engraving.

the rest was driven into the wilderness, the High Andes and the mountain chains of North America. In West Africa, the population was decimated by slavery. In India, China and Japan, however, no large permanent settlements were made.

Two marked features stand out. Latin America apart, the great conquests of world trade routes were made by Companies of Merchant Venturers, like the Dutch East India Company or the Hudson Bay Company. The profits of these quasi-military, quasi-empire, quasi-merchant bodies, gained by trade conducted against a background of superior physical force, went straight to merchants, not to governments. In Spain and Portugal, of course, the surpluses went to princes and kings. The merchants used their profits to earn more profits; the kings used their surpluses for the glory of themselves and of their God.

Secondly, the impact of trade was to dissolve existing civilisations. It has already been argued that trade had dissolved the medieval Christian civilisation of Europe, just as a pertinacious weed will force apart huge stones in a great castle or triumphal arch. Trade was even more effective in dissolving the high civilisations of the Muslims, the Hindus, China and Japan, to say nothing of lesser cultures like those of the Incas and the Aztecs. The pursuit of profit in South America was transmuted to the pursuit of loot, and the dissolution of the Aztec and Inca civilisations was accomplished by a hateful force, reminiscent of the violent atrocities of our own day against the Jews, the Kulaks and the Biafrans; but the energy which caused the initial contact was the pursuit of trading routes to the east. In India, by contrast, blessedly free from hidalgos and priests, the British, Dutch and French traded; then the British conquered. But they hardly ever looted, they never massacred and they never settled. Yet the native civilisation deteriorated and withered. It is this aspect of the conquest of the rest of the world which is most interesting, for what the Spaniards did in Peru was not much different from what the Anglo-Saxons had done to Roman Britain, or the Goths to Italy. The holding of India by a group of merchants, with very little force, is a remarkable feature of world history. India was not converted to capitalism, except in spots

The central office of the Dutch East India Company at Hugli in Bengal, 1665.

below: A Japanese view of the Dutch trading post at Nagasaki in the early eighteenth century ; note the Japanese servants in European dress.

like Calcutta and Bombay. It was embraced by it, and gently milked, first of its treasure — gold, and silks and spices — and then of its commodities, like rice and cotton. It was kept like a fattening cow in capitalism's farmyard; Latin America was ruthlessly despatched in the Spanish abattoir. Latin America nominally became Catholic; nobody seriously bothered to make India Protestant. A contented Hindu cow yielded a lot of milk.

China and Japan are two more variants of a pattern which became very general. Neither was conquered, yet the high Chinese civilisation virtually dissolved as its principal centres fell into the trade network. Japan, after resisting involvement for several centuries, underwent a hysterical conversion and became almost more capitalist than the capitalists. In neither case did the Europeans bother to conquer, or to convert the inhabitants to their official religion. All they wanted was for the Chinese and the Japanese to trade; and, by trading, the old ways were broken and new ways were adopted.

The Merchant Venturers initially sought, then, precious or rare goods — furs, spices, silks, jewels, gold and silver. By the end of the nineteenth century their trading empire had progressed from producing rare raw products, or ingenious handicrafts, to the bulk production of raw materials — wood, cotton, grains, meat, timber, coal, copper — which were manufactured in Europe or North America and sold back to the empire. Some parts of the world, indeed, were so warmly embraced that they themselves built their own Manchesters: Calcutta, Buenos Aires, Sydney, Johannesburg became outposts of industrial capitalism.

The accumulation of capital

Trade, especially trade with Asia, America and Africa, was the source of much capital. It accumulated in the hands of the merchants, who used it to finance more trade, as well as to finance the production of the goods which were taken out from Europe to be sold. The profits from the East Indies trade and from the slave trade were enormous; the merchants engaged became some of the wealthiest men in Europe. They married, especially in England, into almost the best families,

An eighteenth-century client at the Bank of England deposits a bag of coins, receiving in return a paper bill of credit.

and achieved great political influence. It was in this way that they helped to create the conditions in which mercantile capitalism could prosper still further. Permission to charge interest (which offended the laws against usury), internal peace and security, the protection of the fleets of merchant vessels — all these were matters of concern to the great merchants, and in northern Europe especially they had their way.

There were other sources of capital. As some of the merchants became bankers, so the practice of extending credit spread, and it became possible to borrow to finance trade and production. This practice, which was to be the basis of high capitalism, began in a small way in Italy and southern Germany (where it was handicapped by the usury laws) but it took a qualitative forward leap in England in the eighteenth century. By 1800 there was a network of country banks, based on London, which was a viable system, accustomed to extending short-term credit to businessmen. Above all, there was a network of city financial institutions which was used for financing foreign trade.

The 'price revolution' of the sixteenth and seventeenth centuries, which accompanied the flow of gold and silver from Latin America to Europe, was a potent force in enabling capitalists to accumulate surpluses. This price revolution, which may have been due to the quite unprecedented expansion of the money base through the importation of precious metals, had a series of direct and indirect economic and social consequences which were of supreme importance. It impoverished many landowners, whose real incomes fell, and encouraged them to sell their lands, thus bringing more and more of agriculture into the capitalist sector of the economy. The wage earners certainly lost part of their incomes as a result of the inflation. Thus the poor, having increased their earnings after the population scarcity in the fourteenth century, and achieved for some of their number an escape from feudalism, now found their real wage levels falling. The relative impoverishment of both landowners and workers helped to enrich the merchants and the capitalists who employed wage earners. The great rise in profits during the sixteenth and seventeenth centuries enriched a great

The first great stock-market scandal involved a trading company, shown in this contemporary Dutch cartoon of the South Sea Bubble (1720). The heading reads: 'The wind-buyers or wind catchers, who, for wind, lose money and goods and ruin their wives and children'.

many quite ordinary people and encouraged more and more people to attempt to become capitalists. As the ideological temper of society changed, too, more and more people came to regard it as worthy and worthwhile to become profit earners, to become merchants and manufacturers.

The sources of capital accumulation greatly expanded, coming from overseas trade, internal trade, and a rise in the profits level. So, too, did the opportunities for the profitable use of capital. It was used first in trade and in the transport associated with trade. There was a significant advance in the technology of shipping, an improvement in ports and the safeguarding of overland routes. Capital was also increasingly applied to agriculture, manufacturing and mining; in many branches of industry there were series of small changes which cumulatively became significant. Nef has documented this for English coal mining. It was notable in European agriculture, and, to take another example, the manufacture of cloth became progressively cheaper. Thus profits were rising because technology was causing costs to fall in many lines of business.

One less obvious fact, which is nonetheless important, is that in many parts of the world the 'wasteful' use of a surplus was far less than it had ever been before. Europe may have been divided by religion and factions, and may hardly ever have been wholly at peace; political history is full of wars. But during this period they were minor wars. Apart from the Thirty Years War, few devastated whole territories: even the French revolutionary wars, and Napoleon, who conquered huge amounts of territory, did little damage to property or people. And when institutions were destroyed, they were often (not always) replaced by institutions more favourable to capitalism than those they replaced. Napoleon, in many respects, made Europe ripe for capitalism by giving it a framework of law, and aggrandising the capitalist class. Also, after Islam finally lost its dynamic, Europe was free from serious attack from without; Islam's capture of Constantinople in 1453 turned out to be the last serious attack on Europe by non-capitalist forces. And the conquest of the rest of the world was achieved at little cost to Europe in blood or treasure. It is this sense of a world that was mainly secure, in which accumulation could safely proceed, which contrasts most significantly with the arbitrary tyrannies elsewhere, and the constant threats from without which had often made the tyrannies necessary for defence and security.

Flamboyant expenditure was less of a drain, too. Many of the cities were beautiful. Monarchs, princes, merchants and bishops still built ever more sumptuous palaces and castles; the baroque was one of the world's great architectural styles. But in the capitalist world more and more building was for use, and not for religion, a trend which culminated perhaps in the Empire State Building, built for offices in 1931, at a cost of $40 million, 'as a monument to man's lofty ideals', as the publicists said. It would be quite untrue to say that the rise of capitalism was accompanied by a dying down of aesthetic or spiritual achievement. But it would be true to say that less of the surplus was devoted to the equivalent of the pyramids or the medieval cathedrals. Even Versailles, or Schönbrunn, were relatively cheaper than the pyramids. And western Europe, as it entered early capitalism, was richer than almost any society that had ever been known. Its poor people were probably not much richer than their predecessors of several hundred years before, but the surplus which their labour helped to achieve was not spent on the glorification of their masters, or on the destruction of mankind, but mainly on the creation of useful objects. Capitalism may have been immoral, unattractive, destructive, but it was a furnace which forged ploughshares, not swords — and ploughshares of ever improving quality in ever increasing numbers.

The rise of a capitalist class

The early capitalists were merchants. Some of them, like the Medicis, came early to political power. In Venice they controlled the state. Others, like Sir Josiah Child in England, were powerful men of influence. In general, it is safe to say that by the seventeenth century many important international trading cities were governed by groups of merchants, who were increasingly exercising powers over the nation states in which they were found. The most vivid instance of this was the

The first capitalists were merchants: **(right)** Frontispiece to Jacques Savary's treatise 'Le Parfait Négociant' ('The Ideal Merchant'), 1675. As the merchant accumulated a surplus, he turned banker: **(below left)** Nathan Rothschild (1777–1836) epitomises the stock figure of the 'fat capitalist'. By the mid-nineteenth century the entrepreneur or industrialist had emerged as the capitalist par excellence: **(below right)** this Dutch cartoon of c. 1900 calls him 'the man of the century'.

power of the City of London in England, which not only dominated the country almost openly under Oliver Cromwell, but continued to be of supreme importance under his Restoration successors. Thus the merchant, operating perhaps in a Company of Merchant Venturers, living with his family in a city dominated by other merchants, was one representative of the rising capitalist class. In England he might marry his daughters into the gentry, and thus gradually the influence of his family and his money would spread into agriculture.

Other capitalists, hardly worthy of the name it might be thought, were local merchants, corn chandlers, leather sellers, dealing in local commodities locally. But gradually, in England, the Low Countries and North America, such small fry became a powerful and significant group, linked as they were to the yeomen farmers by bonds of marriage and credit. It is worthy of note how important the family was in capitalism. The essence of credit is trust: you have to have faith that your loan will be repaid. A tight-knit family was often the best guarantee of security. Thus capitalist families, great and small, were built up, linked with each other by marriage, and, usually, by common religious convictions.

To this growing class of big and small merchants and bankers the early capitalist industrialists and farmers must be added. The essence of a capitalist industrialist was that he was an organiser. The earliest industrialists were 'putters out'. A clothier, who has been claimed to be the origin of the industrial capitalist, was a man who owned the wool from the time it left the sheep's back till the time it went to a tailor. The specialisation of labour usually entailed at least a dozen stages between shearing the sheep and selling the cloth, each performed by a different group of people. The clothier organised the whole process. To do so he needed organising — 'entrepreneurial' — skill, capital, and good business contacts. It was, of course, by modern standards a technically extremely inefficient system. The rate of loss was very high. Efficiency eventually dictated that some of the stages at least should be performed under one roof. That roof was owned by the capitalist, and the machinery that came to be invented was installed and owned by him as well. The early industrial capitalists, therefore, evolved from merchants who acted as coordinators of an industrial (or agricultural or extractive) process into owners of fixed capital who employed workers by the hour or day or week, on their own premises. Some of the earliest capitalists in this sense were the coal owners (for the demands for energy soon grew as industrialism began), and the capitalist farmers. But the industrial revolution as commonly understood first manifested itself in the consumer goods trades, of which textiles, pottery and brewing were the most important. The capitalist owned not merely the materials used in production, but the tools and the buildings. The fixed capital (as opposed to the 'circulating capital' represented by the raw materials being processed and the wages advanced to the workers before the final goods were sold) embodied the technological progress known as the industrial revolution. The fixed equipment, which used energy derived ultimately from coal, was extremely expensive and the industrial capitalists often therefore became big capitalists. By the mid-nineteenth century the term 'capitalist' applied at least as much to manufacturers as it did to traders, to industrialists as much as to bankers.

These industrialists had to have high technical ability. So, too, a successful banker or farmer had to be up-to-date in his knowledge and skilful at his business, to survive in an increasingly specialised and competitive world. For a feature of capitalism, compared with the societies that preceded it, was the high degree of specialisation that took place. It was the market system that permitted and encouraged specialisation. As soon as there was a market, and people could charge what the market could bear, and could make new products rather than selling conventional products at a 'just' price fixed by a guild of producers, then the competitive skill of a producer became of dominant importance in determining his personal fortune. If he was to keep ahead of competitors, he had to try to modify and improve his products. Thus the early capitalists came to be highly technically qualified people.

The capitalist class, then, included merchants, small and big traders, bankers, manufacturers and farmers.

Through their family networks they came to include many of the members of the professions; but their central focus was 'business'. The capitalist class was differentiated on the one hand from the landowners and peasants by deriving its income from business rather than mere ownership – 'business' being defined precisely as buying and selling goods and services — and on the other hand it was differentiated from the working class by the possession of capital. Its members lived mainly in the towns, and their connections came to occupy prominent — even dominant — positions in society. And as the 'bourgeoisie', or those who controlled the towns, were the rising class, it tended to be their cultural values that became the dominant values of society as a whole. Thus the bourgeoisie came to control more of the state; it was their tastes that determined the market for art; and it was their thought that became the fashionable thought.

The capitalist class, then, was much wider than the group of businessmen who ran the capitalist economies. It was a group which formed the elect in many walks of life, from the church to the arts. Yet it would be wrong to think that the bourgeoisie was unopposed, or that it was itself homogeneous. As late as the 1860s even in England, Parliament was still numerically dominated by the landowners, though the landowners had for long been intermarried with the bourgeoisie. In Germany the princes and the hereditary aristocracy were the governing class until the 1860s. Indeed, in France, in many respects a pre-industrial capitalist country, the second empire and the third republic were remarkable for their bourgeois character, compared with other European countries. The trappings and often the realities of power rested with the landowners, especially in Russia, the Iberian peninsula and other parts of Europe. The workers and the peasants too provided occasional rumblings against capitalism which broke out into violence from time to time, as in 1848 and 1871 in France. The bourgeoisie itself was deeply divided: first by nationality, and then by religion and cultural allegiance. Despite the international character of capitalism, it was associated with the rise of nationalism and ideologies, which, ultimately, brought it several times almost to the ground.

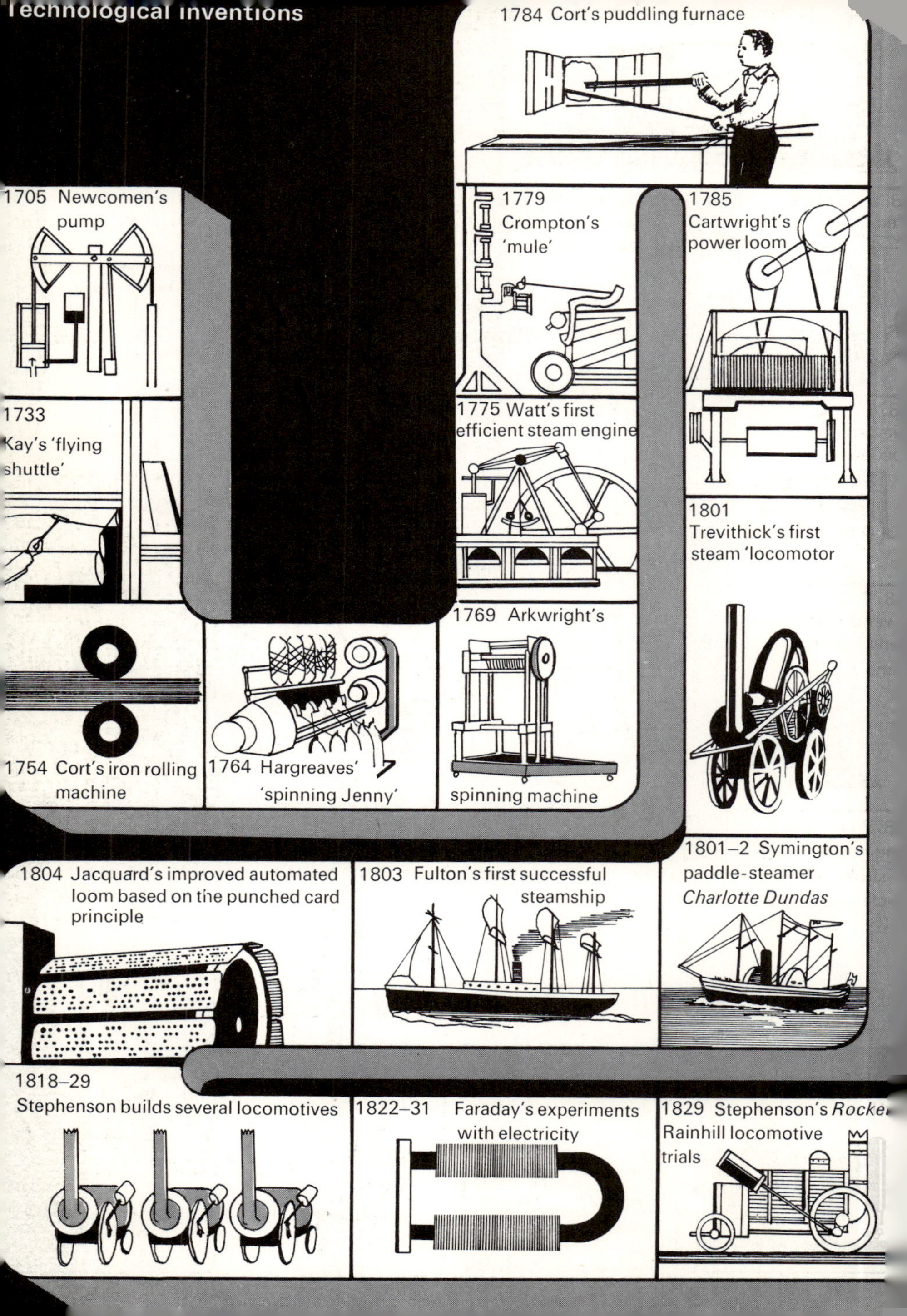
1705 Newcomen's pump
1733 Kay's 'flying shuttle'
1754 Cort's iron rolling machine
1764 Hargreaves' 'spinning Jenny'
1769 Arkwright's spinning machine
1775 Watt's first efficient steam engine
1779 Crompton's 'mule'
1784 Cort's puddling furnace
1785 Cartwright's power loom
1801 Trevithick's first steam 'locomotor
1801–2 Symington's paddle-steamer *Charlotte Dundas*
1803 Fulton's first successful steamship
1804 Jacquard's improved automated loom based on the punched card principle
1818–29 Stephenson builds several locomotives
1822–31 Faraday's experiments with electricity
1829 Stephenson's *Rocke* Rainhill locomotive trials

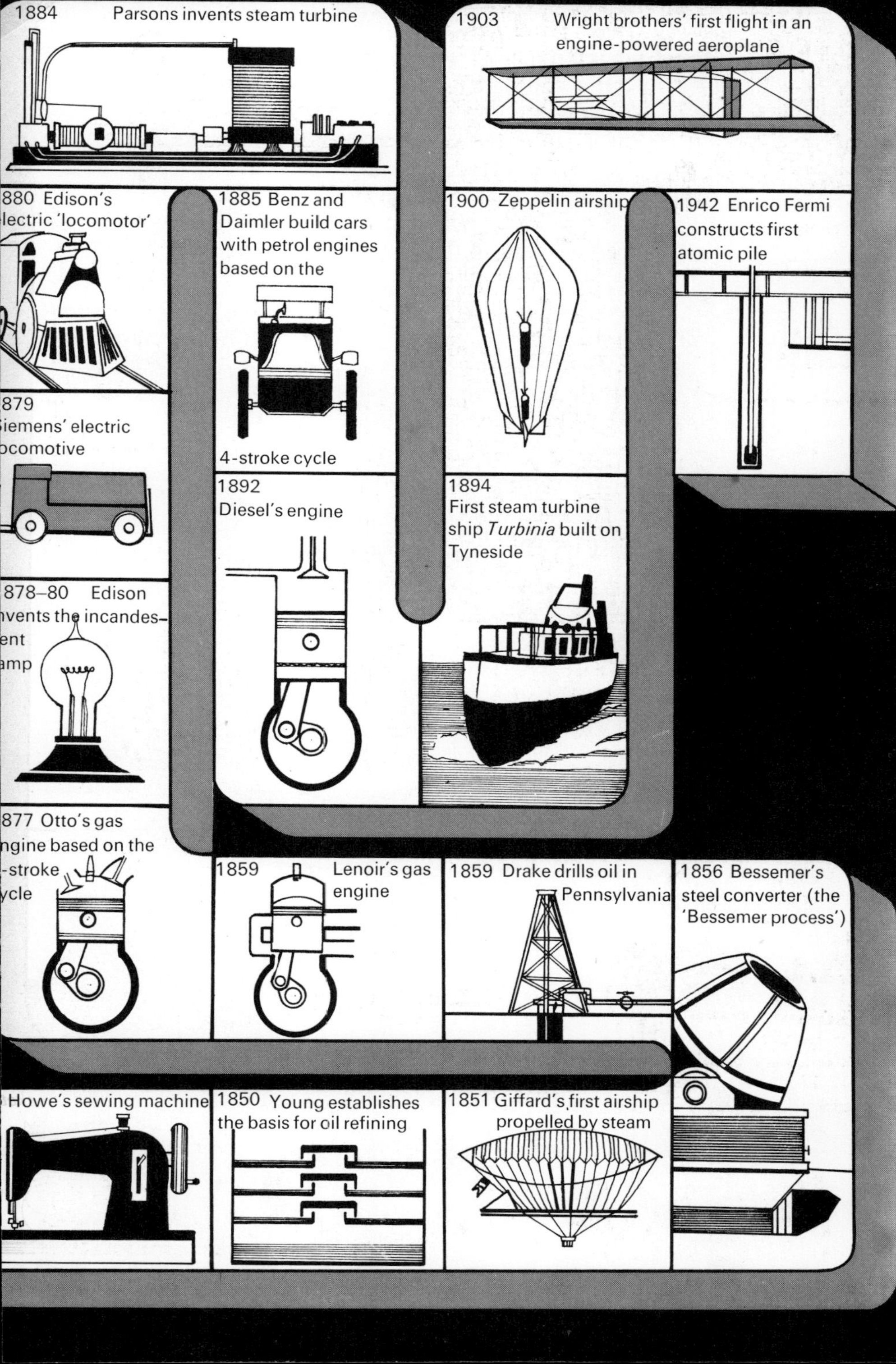
1884 Parsons invents steam turbine
1903 Wright brothers' first flight in an engine-powered aeroplane
880 Edison's
lectric 'locomotor'
1885 Benz and Daimler build cars with petrol engines based on the 4-stroke cycle
1900 Zeppelin airship
1942 Enrico Fermi constructs first atomic pile
879
iemens' electric
ocomotive
1892
Diesel's engine
1894
First steam turbine ship *Turbinia* built on Tyneside
878–80 Edison
nvents the incandes-
ent
amp
877 Otto's gas
ngine based on the
-stroke
ycle
1859 Lenoir's gas engine
1859 Drake drills oil in Pennsylvania
1856 Bessemer's steel converter (the 'Bessemer process')
Howe's sewing machine
1850 Young establishes the basis for oil refining
1851 Giffard's first airship propelled by steam

Technical innovations

Capitalism was synonymous with technical progress. For millennia, of course, technical change had taken place, but had done so fitfully and with frequent regressions, as civilisations rose and fell. Only such basic discoveries as fire and the wheel seem to have survived from civilisation to civilisation; more complex techniques had to be reinvented. From the fifteenth and sixteenth centuries, however, technical progress moved forward with increasing rapidity. The significant advances were in transport, energy, textiles and other consumer goods, metalwork and agriculture.

The evolution of the sailing ship has already been mentioned. It made possible rapid, frequent and reliable sea journeys, carrying bulky cargo and considerable numbers of passengers. Road transport improved quickly with the coming of the turnpikes in England. Thus when the steam engine was introduced to railways and ships, it came into a situation where a big transport system already existed, visiting all continents, and enabling substantial trade to be carried on.

Before the invention of the steam engine the only inanimate sources of energy available to man were water and wind. **below**: A watermill (c. 1600); **opposite:** a windmill (1762 from Diderot's 'Encyclopédie').

The second acceleration of technology was in energy. Windmills and watermills were not new, windmills having been used in Europe since the twelfth century, and watermills probably a little earlier, though both had a Chinese ancestry. By the seventeenth century both windmills and watermills

were ubiquitous. Coal had been used for centuries as a domestic fuel, before it became widely used in England as an industrial fuel in the seventeenth and eighteenth centuries. To mine coal for domestic use from deep seams, the first steam engines were developed by Savary and Newcomen to pump out water. Newcomen's engine, developed in 1712, was the first successful steam engine. Carlo Cipolla, the brilliant economic historian, points out that by the time of its invention, western Europe's per capita consumption of energy was already greater than Roman society had ever known; he attributes this higher rate of energy consumption to the absence of slavery (or muscle power). It is also attributable to the steadily rising demand for manufactures which created conditions where technical improvement steadily paid off the cost of innovation. It was against the background of rising energy consumption that James Watt's development of the steam engine occurred; and with that development the enormous forces of the industrial revolution were let loose. Watt's engines, and those designed by his successors, had become prevalent by 1800 in the textile industries and in brewing. By 1850 'the age of steam' was well under way. Thus the end of the eighteenth century saw a rising output of coal and a steady development of steam power. This revolution in energy consumption was the clue to the nature of the industrial revolution, and hence to the nature of industrial capitalism. For the consumption of energy now rose to unprecedented levels, and at a continuously accelerating pace. Capitalism can almost be defined as the range on the curve of per capita energy consumption where it rises above 15,000 calories per day (according to Cipolla), and derived to the extent of 85 per cent from plants, animals and men. (This 15,000 calories includes food.) By 1900 energy consumption was mainly derived from mineral fuel (except, again, for food).

Textiles and consumption goods were rapidly changing at the same time. Compare the roughly constructed medieval house, with little glass and rough carpentry, with an eighteenth-century brick villa, full of windows, careful carpentry and metalwork. The improvement in workmen's tools — saws, chisels, adzes — is as important as the improved quality and reliability of the bricks, glass, door furniture, sash-cords and water closets that went into the house. Almost any other commodity would show a change from rude individuality to sophisticated smoothness. The rise in technical proficiency is obvious. The methods of production became increasingly mechanised, with a steady improvement in the reliability and consistency of the products. The invention of more and more machinery to process wool and cotton textiles — to spin, to weave, to dye — required a substantial development of the engineering trade. It was this mechanisation, too, which raised the demand for energy. The energy was derived first from water-mills and then from steam engines. The immediate demand for more energy, then, was caused by the rapid growth in the volume of manufactures and by the mechanisation of the means of producing them. This is why the textile industry — especially the

right: A German doll's house, 1675; **opposite**: an English doll's house, eighteenth century. Building styles reflect the startling advance in technical proficiency during the eighteenth century.

cotton industry of Lancashire — may be regarded as the pioneer of the industrial revolution. It was the first to become mainly mechanised, the first to use steam engines widely, and the first to congregate substantial numbers of workers in factories. The story of the Lancashire cotton industry is the story of early capitalism. But cotton was not the only consumer goods industry to be revolutionised. It was significant because it was an apex of a trade triangle — cotton came from North America and the Caribbean,

it was sold overseas, and slaves were transported from Africa to America. Cotton, therefore, combined mechanisation, a labour force, capitalists, merchants, and use of the new reliable trade routes, in an entirely pathbreaking way. But similar tales can be told of other products — beer, wool, iron and brass goods, for instance. All demanded machinery, energy, capital, markets, labour and entrepreneurs.

Timber was of course used in making the machinery, but above all iron was needed. Therefore, the growth of the iron trade was significant. It used wood and coal as a source of energy and was essential for many small artefacts — nails, joists, hinges — for machinery, and (when railways came in) engines and rails. It was round the iron industry that major technological innovation based on science was centred. The use of coal to convert ore into pig iron was not possible before the middle of the eighteenth century; its use was an early application of chemistry to manufacturing. Iron manufacture was one of the earliest American industries, because of the abundance of timber in North America; but it was above all in England that the process most rapidly developed. As a result of Abraham Darby's discovery of the method of converting iron ore into iron by using coke, the use of coal was possible. Then Cort invented the puddling process, which gave a purer product in larger quantities, and he next invented the rolling mill which enabled large quantities of iron to be pressed and shaped. This raised the output of iron tremendously, because costs fell and the technical conditions for producing large quantities now existed. Huntsman then invented a process which enabled steel to be made with greater reliability. The engineering industry was now able to call on cheap iron and reliable (though not cheap) steel. The consequences of the manufacture of large quantities of cheap iron were tremendous; the coal and engineering industries were based upon the abundance of iron.

An English trade token of 1811, showing the ironworks at Bilston, Staffordshire.

Lastly, all this industrial activity took place with an emerging market and an ever growing labour force. Apart from the Irish Famine of 1845–50 and Stalin's Ukrainian famine of the early 1930s, Europe no longer knew mass hunger. For this and other reasons the population was growing rapidly. It was fed by an ever increasing agricultural production. More and more land was brought into production, in Europe and America, as forests and woodlands were cleared. New crops, especially rootcrops, were developed. Tropical products, like tea and sugar, became more common. Above all there was an improvement in agricultural methods. This came partly from an improvement in knowledge. The principles of selective breeding became pragmatically clearer. Animals grew bigger and were better tended. Crops improved. The land was scientifically enriched by manure and by rotation of crops, and by new techniques of ploughing, hoeing and sowing. To enable these new principles of farming to be applied, England pioneered the principle of enclosing fields with hedges or walls, to replace the medieval system of strip cultivation in large open fields; it seems that, outside England, such principles were first adopted in Holland. As the animals were improved by selective breeding, their feeding was also improved by the use of rootcrops and turnips, enabling them to be kept through the winter. Continuous meat production, instead of annual autumn killings, became possible. Thus all over Europe, and eventually all over the colonies, progressive landowners became capitalist farmers, applying a developing agricultural technology, by means of capital, to their land. The consequence was a growth of agricultural production on a scale that had never been seen before. It was on this abundant food that vast new populations were enabled to live; and they formed the labour force for industrial capitalism. In the process, some parts of agriculture itself became increasingly capitalist. But in some countries, notably France, where the peasants gained possession of the land after the revolution, they were resistant to change, as were many Russian landowners. In these countries the progress of agriculture into capitalism was barred by institutions which eventually were overthrown by a combination of low prices and revolutionary change. Despite its progress into capitalist forms of production agriculture remained, in almost all countries, a reservoir of hostility to capitalism.

Early capitalism

Adam Smith and Karl Marx

Adam Smith, a Scot, was born in 1723 and died in 1790. He was a well-known though not a distinguished professor of philosophy in Glasgow, but in 1776 he published *The Wealth of Nations*, which was to become the cornerstone of the philosophical interpretation of capitalism. Adam Smith was almost the first economist (itself a capitalist occupation) and the first serious analyst of the process of economic growth. His work became the basis of the capitalist programme.

Economic growth, he reasoned, depended on the division of labour, which improved the skill of the labourer and enabled different specialist occupations to be developed. As the market economy spread, so the possibilities of the division of labour increased. The key to specialisation, therefore, was the growth of the market. Technology developed as fast as the market allowed it. Wage-labour in capitalist occupations yielded a surplus (which labour engaged in service occupations — such as government — did not). It was the surplus, invested by the capitalists, which was the engine of capitalist progress, since it was this surplus which enabled them to feed the labourers in the interval between buying the new materials (or sowing the seeds) and selling the finished goods or crops. For Adam Smith, labour was the source of value, and it was differences in inputs of labour which explained differences in the prices of various commodities. Therefore, labour for Smith was the factor of production which yielded the means which enabled progress to occur. The surplus fell into the hands of the capitalists, who used it as capital both to employ (and feed) more labour and to construct plant and machinery. The landowners took their toll of the surplus but their use of it was worthless, mere idle consumption, as was the share of the surplus appropriated by the church and the government. A society, once provided with a framework of law and order, would achieve its greatest level of economic welfare if the product of labour were divided between subsistence wages for labour and the profits of capitalist enterprise.

Smith's argument yielded several important conclusions for policy. One was that anything that limited the spread of the market limited the exploitation of advancing technology (which he called the division of labour). He was a free trader, and looked forward to a world whose goods would be freely exchanged with as few restrictions as possible and where prices would find their true level. A second conclusion was that landowners were unproductive drains on the economy except where they acted as capitalist farmers. Thirdly, government should do as little as possible, except to keep the peace, because every penny not used by a capitalist in productive enterprises was a waste.

It should be said at this point that Smith was probably more right than he was wrong. Eighteenth-century governments were organisations for finding jobs for unemployed aristocrats, and a few landowners apart the huge incomes of the aristocracy were wasted on ostentatious consumption. The great mass of the growing population would have starved unless they had been given the opportunity of employment, and the only way they could be given employment was by the accumulation of a productive surplus which could be used to create fixed capital and finance the stocks of raw materials and semi-finished and finished goods that an advancing economy requires. What is happening in India now is what would have happened in nineteenth-century Europe if Adam Smith's arguments had not prevailed. His doctrine of free trade, and of the essentially productive nature of profit and unproductive nature of government activity, became the central points of the capitalist doctrine. It was with this manifesto that tariff barriers were lowered all over the world and that the free movement of capital and labour was not only allowed but encouraged. It was with this manifesto that governments were everywhere exposed to reform, with a reduction of their activities ensuing.

Smith's brilliant arguments were carried further

opposite: A drawing of Adam Smith, 'The Author of the Wealth of Nations', by John Kay, 1790.

by two English economists, T. R. Malthus and David Ricardo. Malthus (1766–1834), a Cambridge clergyman, was concerned with the rapidly rising population and extended Smith's reasoning to argue the proposition that the population tended to rise in geometric progression, while food supplies rose only in arithmetic progression. The supply of labour therefore tended constantly to exceed the means to feed it; and the pressure of the supply of labour tended constantly to push the wage level down to subsistence. Philanthropists who sought by private philanthropy or government action to redistribute income to the poor were self-defeating, because the population would automatically increase to eat up the surplus. The only hope lay in population control (by voluntary restraint) and in the accumulation of a productive surplus. There is little doubt that one of Malthus' main arguments was correct: the way to cope with the population increase was not philanthropy, but to extend production. However, he underestimated the possibility of raising production. In fact, his mathematics could almost be reversed, to suggest that food supply under capitalism would tend after a certain period constantly to exceed population. But the way that food supply was increased was through the productive investment of the surplus produced by the wage-labourers and invested by the capitalists.

Ricardo (1772–1823) was a stockbroker, drawn from the world of finance, and his contribution to classical economic theory was a fundamental one both because it was the highpoint of classical economics and because it formed the basis of the most ruthless refutation of capitalism, by Karl Marx. Ricardo adopted Adam Smith's position, but assigned a heavy role to the rate of profit. According to Ricardo, there was a tendency for the rate of profit to fall and so for the rate of economic expansion to slow down, since the rate of expansion was determined by the surplus available for investment in the means of production. The only factor offsetting this fall was technological progress; and technological progress depended, in turn, upon the capitalist class's spirit of enterprise. Ricardo was in effect saying that wages could not rise, that the rent of land (the income of the landlords) was unproductive, and that the engine of capitalist progress — profits — had a tendency to run down. Therefore, it was implied, profits must be carefully preserved. He was against the Poor Law, against the Corn Laws, and against any restriction in the free forces of the market.

Karl Marx (1818–83), the German philosopher, who came to England and wrote *Das Kapital* in the British Museum, accepted classical economics as a description of the way capitalism worked, but saw capitalism as a stage in the world's history. Each civilisation had an economic system, whose character accorded with the technical conditions of production. The social and political superstructure was erected on this economic basis, classes represented groups of different economic interests, and their relationships were objectively and immutably determined by the conditions of production. Each economic system contained its own contradictions, which expressed themselves in a class struggle, and the victorious class established a new economic system, which in turn produced its own classes. Thus the feudal system expressed the dominance of the landowning class when settled agriculture was being established. The bourgeoisie represented the revolutionary trading class in feudalism. Having overthrown feudalism, capitalism established the conditions where capital could be accumulated in industry. The bourgeoisie's historic role was to accumulate capital and to transform the conditions of production. To do so they employed the proletariat, who were propertyless and ever increasing in number. As output rose, owing to the accumulation of capital and technical progress, the profit rate fell (as Ricardo had adumbrated it) and consequently the steam would go out of capitalism. The capitalists would increasingly exploit the workers, whose increasing numbers would cause them to compete for work, keeping wages down to subsistence. But as the capitalists accumulated the means of production, they would find it increasingly difficult to sell their products. Search abroad as they would for increasingly cheap raw materials and labour (to keep costs down and profits up) and for new markets, the working class, contin-

Karl Marx addressing the London Instructive Society of German Workers in 1850.

ually impoverished by exploitation, would not be able to buy the products of its own labour. Marx, his friend and collaborator Engels, and his disciple Lenin, pictured a world of capitalist monopolies warring with each other for a way to avoid the implications of the falling rate of profit. The crisis of overproduction would eventually cause the working class to rise in revolution, overthrow the rule of the capitalists, and use the means of production which had been forged in the capitalist furnace to produce the economy of abundance, which would be socialism. Under socialism the bourgeois state, the very machinery of oppression, would rust away unused, and a new man freed at last from economic shackles could walk free — 'to each according to his needs, from each according to his ability'. Under communism the contradictions would be ended. Capitalism would have dug its own grave, but while doing so it would have left a legacy of productive capital which would provide its successors with the means to the good life.

The steam engine and the energy revolution

Capitalism, then, according to Smith, Ricardo and Marx, is the story of the creation of industrial hardware, of which the steam engine was the essential apparatus. James Watt developed Savery and Newcomen's steam engines by separating the condensing chamber from the chamber in which steam was generated; and by the use of a piston, forced forward by the pressure of the steam, he was able effectively to transform heat into usable energy. By applying the piston to a rotary motion he could take advantage of the procedures used in the watermills, at that time the main source of industrial energy. After many technical and financial struggles Watt teamed up with Matthew Boulton, and in the years between 1785 and 1800 (when their patent expired), their enterprise built two hundred and eighty-nine steam engines for cotton mills, breweries and other factories. Steam engines rapidly became technically more efficient as boiler-making developed as a craft, as pig iron quality improved, as new high-grade steels came into use, and as the size of engines (measured in horsepower) increased.

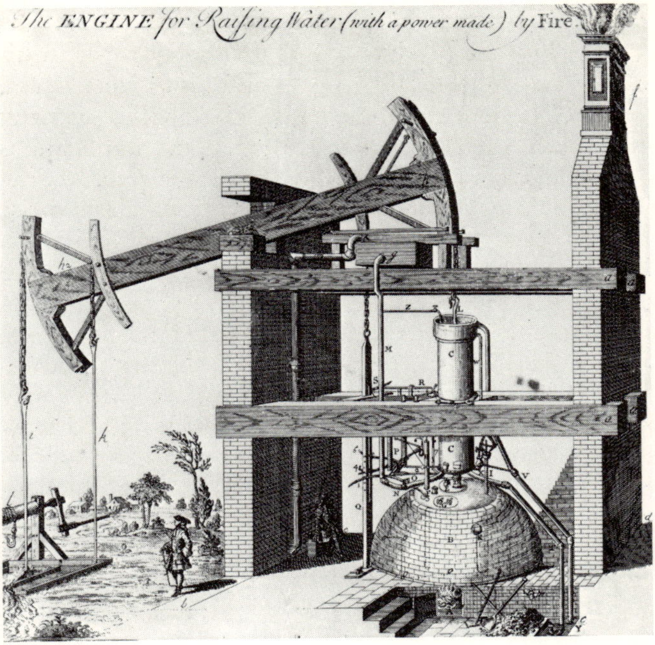

Newcomen's steam engine, in an engraving of 1717. James Watt modified this engine to make it commercially viable.

The English coal industry was the first large-scale extractive industry organised on a capitalist basis, and it provided the biggest single new source of energy to mankind probably since the windmill became generally used, and possibly since the horse was first used as a draught animal. The main centre was in Northumberland and Durham, where for the first time deep mining was developed. The men (and until 1842 some women) were lowered by cable; then they worked with a pick and shovel, and used gunpowder occasionally at the more recalcitrant spots. There were light tramways, pulled by human labour, to take the coal along the mined seams to the shaft. The working conditions were appalling and the dangers — from rockfalls but above all from explosions — immense. In the pits, employment ranged from very small numbers to hundreds of people. The mine owners were often big capitalists and sometimes wealthy landowners from whose soil the coal was extracted, men like Lord Fitzwilliam, Lord Crawford, Lord Durham, Lord Londonderry and the Bishop of Durham. They gained a reputation for

The rapid growth of the English coal industry in the nineteenth century was due to the steam engine: this print of Hetton Colliery (c. 1822) shows steam power working the pumps inside the mine and a Stephenson locomotive in the foreground.

ruthlessness which was wholly deserved. Yet the colliery workers were amongst the highest paid wage earners in the country, and were to become part of the aristocracy of labour, leading the field in forming trade unions and in political activity. Their villages were closed, tight-knit communities, where there was a common consciousness of hardship (especially when demand for coal fell and there was unemployment) and of comradeship in an exceptionally hard life. All over northern England — Lancashire, Staffordshire, Yorkshire, Cumberland — and in Scotland and south Wales, the coal industry grew rapidly — from about 10 million tons of coal output in 1800 to 44 million tons in 1850, an amount which was tripled again by 1880. As coal was virtually the sole source of industrial energy (and increasingly of domestic heating), especially with the invention of coal gas for commercial use (Regency London had gas lighting), coal output is an excellent index of the spread of industrialism — though as the efficiency of engines improved it progressively understates industrial expansion as the nineteenth century went on. By 1850 there was a substantial export of British coal, showing the rise of overseas industry, and the Belgian, French and American coalfields were coming into serious production.

British coal was exceptionally cheap at this time and it formed a basis for low cost energy. The demand for coal — good quality steam coal — came from the stationary engines increasingly applied in industry. The development of engineering skills enabled the steam engine to be used in different branches of trade. Maudslay developed the technique of manufacturing cylinders and valves, of screw-cutting lathes, of planing and milling machines. Steam hammers, accurate measuring machines, all increased the power and precision of steam-equipped tools, so that identical machines could be produced in large numbers, enabling large-scale production units to be equipped. Engineering became an industry which was strongly localised in London, Lancashire, Glasgow and some midland towns like Birmingham. Machines were developed to produce rails, struts for bridges, iron beams for factories; mechanised printing became possible; and iron ships.

Thus the steam engine not only harnessed coal power but by the development of the engineering industry enabled energy to be applied to a wide variety of occupations. The revolutionary development of the application of steam power to transport enabled the railway and the steamships to reduce transport costs, increased the availability and speed of communications, and enabled bulk cargoes to be easily carried. The expansion in coal consumption after 1830 is attributable in some large part to the rapid spread of the steam train; and then the development of the steamship and the steam tram increased the market for coal still more rapidly.

Despite the early industrialisation of the Belgian coalfield, as well as of the adjacent part of northern France, a few small areas in Germany and a few places in America, by 1850 the British coal and engineering industries dominated the world. Over two-thirds of the world's coal was mined in Britain; some went for export; and about half the world's energy produced by steam power was produced in Britain at that time. It is no wonder that the economic and social drama being played out in Britain was the model from which capitalism's nature was deduced, both by Ricardo and by Marx, and that the political and social doctrines evolved in Britain were widely adopted as the doctrines of capitalism.

England adopted, in the age of steam, the policies of laissez-faire. The Poor Law of 1834 left the poor

overleaf: The north of England became notorious for its grim industrial towns: Sheffield in the mid-nineteenth century.

to a bare and intolerable relief when they were destitute — otherwise they had to fend for themselves. Free trade was enacted and agricultural protection was eliminated. The state machine was reformed. The bourgeois spirit infiltrated venerable institution after venerable institution.

Notable among the consequences of this steam revolution was a relocation of economic, social and political power in the country. The steam revolution was mainly based on the coalfields (since it was cheaper to transport finished manufactures than to transport coal), and the bulk of industry therefore was located on the coalfields. (The older trades continued to be located in the big cities of the pre-steam era — notably in London.) It was to these coalfields and the industrial areas adjacent to them that populations flocked. Living conditions in the towns were so bad that the death rate exceeded the birth rate, but the population was continually sucked in from the adjacent countryside and from Ireland, so that huge concentrations of people grew up round Manchester, Liverpool, Birmingham and the smaller industrial towns of the north. It was within these industrial areas that new political and social movements had their base. Both the ardent free-trade doctrinaires and the early socialists were products of the industrial districts — John Bright and Richard Cobden, laissez-faire's chief political spokesmen, were Manchester Liberals, and Peel, the prime minister who first achieved a substantial degree of free trade, was a Lancashire cotton mill owner's son.

The introduction of steam, then, occurred first in Britain, giving Britain a world leadership which it exercised throughout the nineteenth century, until it was overtaken by Germany and the United States. Within Britain, and more especially within England, it relocated economic power, and consequently the social and political balance shifted. The composition of Britain's exports moved to manufactured goods (especially cotton and engineering goods) and coal; its imports became, increasingly, basic foodstuffs and raw materials. The unleashing of steam's energy was the prime cause of the spread of capitalism, by railway and ship, throughout the world.

Transport—canals and roads

If early capitalism is synonymous with the rapid increase in per capita energy consumption associated with steam power, it is also synonymous with the development of a speedy, secure and unsurpassed network of communications. It was the railway and the steamship which fully integrated the steam revolution with the spread of capitalism, but the early years of industrialism in England were pre-railway and pre-steamship. The steady improvement of sailing ships has already been mentioned: the American merchant navy reached its apotheosis in the 1830s and 1840s, with the development of the beautiful clippers and schooners which sped across the Atlantic and round Cape Horn. But the development of sailing ships was a continuum from the original Viking sailing ships that had gone to America a millennium before. The steamship in an iron hull was a radical advance which did not become at all widespread until the 1860s, though it was used on American rivers from the 1810s. Railways became the basic means of transport in Britain in the 1850s and somewhat later in Europe and North America. Until then capitalism spread by water, helped by radical improvements in the road system.

The internal means of transporting goods in most countries before 1800 were mainly by river and canal. The canalisation of rivers to make them navigable had been going on from the Middle Ages, but canals (which the Romans had constructed) were not generally dug until the seventeenth century, when Colbert built the Languedoc Canal. This, together with the improvement of the French road system by Henri IV, was primarily defensive in origin, whereas

Stourport Canal, in an eighteenth-century print.

Navigation Office, Stone.

Messrs Wedgwood & Co

The Company Consider themselves entitled to detain Goods for Freight in Arrear.

To Hugh Henshall & Co Dr

1806	For Freight		Weight T	C	Q	lb	Paid on L	S	D	Rate	Amounts L	S	D
Mar 15	To Bill delivered										221	16	10
22	9 Crates	L'Pool a Etruria					"	3	"		"	3	"
	Clay	Pike & Jones	14	17	"	"		4	11	12/-	9	3	2
29	3 Crates	Etruria a [illegible]		12	"					"	"	9	"
	8 Empty Casks	Stourport Etruria	"	"	"	"	3	4	6		3	12	6
	10 Empty Hhds	" Park	"	"	"	"	1	18	8		2	8	8
April 5	4 do Crates	L'Pool Do	"	"	"	"	"	3	8		"	3	8
	10 do Hhds	Stourport Do									"	10	
	Clay	L'Pool [illegible]	14	9	"	"	"	4	10	12/-	8	18	3
	2 Casks Lead	Preston [illegible]	1	11	1	2	"	15	8	7/5	1	7	3
	1 Crate	Etruria [illegible]	"	4	"	"						3	7
12	Chirtstone	Leek Etruria	6	10						3/9	1	4	5
	Clay	L'Pool Fayle	14	2	"	"		4	8	12/-	8	13	11
	1 Empty Crate	" "							4		"	"	4
19	1 Hhd, 1 Tierce	Etruria [illegible]									"	14	
	1 do 1 do	" [illegible]									"	14	"
	24 Empty Crates	L'Pool Etruria									"	8	"
	1 Puncheon Spirits	[illegible]		9	"	"				19/10	"	8	11
	1 Crate	Etruria [illegible]		4	"	"					"	3	7
	1 Hhd, 1 Tierce	" [illegible]		14	"	"					"	12	7
	1 Box	" [illegible]	"	"	2	29					"	1	"
May 3	Clay	L'Pool Etruria Fayle	8	7	"	"		2	9	12/-	5	3	"
	"	" Do	16	10	"	"		5	6	"	10	3	6
	"	" Do	15	10	"	"		5	2	"	9	11	2
	1 Crate 1 Box	Etruria [illegible]		4	2	10					"	4	7
	Clay	L'Pool a Etruria	16	2	"	"		5	4	12/-	9	18	7
	2 Crates	Etruria [illegible]										7	2
17	1 Hhd Ware	L'Pool Stoke	"	"	"	"	"	"	"		"	"	"
	128 Casks Clay	" Etruria	32	"	"	"		4	6	"	19	8	6
	33 do	" "	8	5	"	"		1	"	"	5	"	"
	90 do	" "	22	10						"	13	10	
	2 Bags Potatoes	Winsm [illegible]		3	2	20				6/5		1	3
											335	4	5

the English canal and road building of the eighteenth century was almost wholly commercial. England, surrounded by sea and with navigable rivers stretching far inland, was well placed to develop commerce in bulky goods, and did so; the next step was to connect some places to the rivers by canal, or to connect the rivers with each other. The Duke of Bridgewater had a canal constructed by a civil engineer (formerly a millwright) called James Brindley, to connect his collieries at Worsley to Manchester. This was then linked to a project of Josiah Wedgwood, and others, to join the potteries in Staffordshire by canal to the Mersey, the Trent and the Humber. This Grand Trunk Canal was the first major canal system; it enabled coal, salt (from Cheshire) and pottery to be transported easily and cheaply to Liverpool and Manchester and down through Hull to London. A further canal linked the system to the Severn, and so to Bristol. A link through Coventry and Oxford to the Thames, completed in 1790, meant that most of the major manufacturing towns of England were linked by the internal canal and navigable river system.

The canal mania, when canals were started all over Britain, came in 1790–4, but canals continued to be built until the 1830s. Ireland was crossed by two canals, from Dublin to the Shannon, and Scotland was bisected by the Caledonian Canal. Thus by 1830 the British enjoyed an internal transport system linking their excellent ports and rivers with each other and enabling goods like wool, timber, clay (for bricks), iron, manufactured goods and stone to be transported quickly and easily. The effects of this transport revolution (for it was no less) in speeding up the movement of goods, people and ideas were notable. 'Sea coal' became a common domestic fuel; bricks became cheap, enabling a wide development of housebuilding, and markets became ever wider. Not less important, the canals were owned by companies, which accelerated the process of the creation of financial institutions. The institution of transferable 'shares', which earned profits, was not entirely new (it had played its part in the founding of the great mercantile companies) but it was first widely

opposite: An invoice of Josiah Wedgwood for the transportation of goods by canal, 1806.

developed by the canal companies and was a notion that was developed to embrace the concept of a permanent company, owning considerable installations and operating them on a continuing basis as generations came and went. This was the form with which the railways were launched; the company was soon to replace the one-man family business and the partnership as the typical form of capitalist enterprise.

Europe also built canals, based on the great river system, which increased the level of commerce significantly, especially after the Belgian development of the 1820s, which used the Scheldt estuary as its means of transport. The American river system was used extensively as the interior was conquered. In 1807 the Hudson was the site of the first commercially satisfactory steamboat, the *Clermont*, on the Hudson River between Albany and New York, and the Mississippi and the Ohio began to be successfully used by steamboats in the 1820s. The first major canal system was the Erie Canal, which links the Hudson River and New York City to the Great Lakes at Lake Erie. This linked Ohio, the Great Lakes and New England, and so stimulated New York's development as a great port and as the centre of industrialisation in New England.

The energy revolution reduced the costs of energy. The canal system reduced the costs of transporting energy potential, always the biggest costs in energy production. The fall in costs per ton mile was probably to one-tenth, and even one-twentieth, of what it had been by road; and transport was technically possible for large bulky commodities, which it had not been before.

There was a significant improvement in road transport simultaneously with the building of canals; by the beginning of the seventeenth century the European road system was in a worse condition than it had been under the Romans. The horse was strengthened by selective breeding and better feeding. Wheels were improved, carriages were lightened, and springs were introduced into them. Above all, the roads themselves were made on new principles. In the Middle Ages pack horses proceeded in convoy along stone causeways, which ran along the roads. The roads were deep muddy tracks in wet weather, dusty paths in dry. The French constructed a national system of roads for military purposes, just as the road from London to Holyhead was a military highway. The French *routes royales* were built by the *corps des ponts et chaussées*, and were well constructed. But it was the British, through the turnpike trusts, who advanced technologically in road construction. The turnpike trusts, bodies of local worthies, kept the roads in repair by charging tolls for passage. John Metcalf, a northern road-builder (1717–1810), dug ditches by the roadside to drain them and put foundations underneath. Thomas Telford (1757–1834), who built iron bridges, strengthened the foundations; John McAdam built up the surface from stone chips, so that it was not broken by the iron rims of the wheels of the fast carriages, which had destroyed the surfaces of earlier roads.

It was on road administration that all attempts at road reform had previously broken down: either the road was ill or well constructed, but it was almost always ill-maintained. Most of the turnpike trusts saw to it that repairs were undertaken. Consequently road travel times were cut to about one-third of what they had been early in the eighteenth century. This speeded up communications, and the movement of people became faster and safer. The amount of travel was by modern standards very small; and only Britain, the Low Countries, France and the United States had a passable road system. Where there was industrialisation there were improved roads. Elsewhere, communication was exceptionally difficult.

A late eighteenth-century English trade token, testifying to the improvement in road transport, issued by the proprietor of the 'Swan with two necks', London.

Thus by 1830 canals and improved rivers had made industrial loads technically and economically possible to transport. Steamships were beginning to be used on rivers and for coastal traffic (from Britain to Ireland, from England to the continent, in the Mediterranean). Sailing boats were far quicker and bigger than they had been. The roads in industrial areas had cut travel time by two-thirds. The effect of this transport revolution may be seen in the greater volume of trade, both overseas and inland. But it was the steam engine that really revolutionised the world.

Railways

Railways were made of iron and were first laid to solve the problem of bearing the weight of carts full of coal drawn by horses from the mines to the nearest point for loading onto a barge. Northumberland, Durham and South Wales had several hundred miles of track before 1820, and there were also a few miles of track in northern France and in America, chiefly for coal. Steam engines were first used on roads, but their weight and power destroyed the road surface. After two other pioneers had made attempts, with some success, George Stephenson began on his famous railway steam engines; in October 1829 his *Rocket* won the competition, established by the new Liverpool to Manchester line, for the best engine, stationary or locomotive. Suddenly it was clear that the alternative to costly roads and slow canals had been found.

The railways were very expensive to build. A new technology had to be pioneered; land had to be bought; canal interests had to be bought out. By the end of the 1830s the outline of England's trunk system had been completed. Before 1860 Parliament in London had authorised the building of over a hundred lines; and over eight hundred Railway Acts were passed in the twenty-five years between 1825 and 1850. The first lines were solidly profitable — the volume of traffic, both of goods and of people, rose at geometric rates. By 1850 there were 6,625 miles of route in operation, linking nearly all the principal British towns. Railway shares had become a major form of investment, held by almost the whole middle class. There was a railway mania (discussed on p. 72), which caused speculative booms and slumps, virtually the first of a recognisably 'modern' kind.

The economic effects of the railways can scarcely be exaggerated. First, their cost of construction was high. In England, the first country in which they were built, thousands of 'navvies' were employed. Great civil engineering concerns, headed by Brunel, Peto, Brassey, Locke, and others, organised large gangs of highly paid workers and a flow of materials and equipment to the line, which spread across the country on embankments and in cuttings like a series of scars. This raised employment and disturbed existing social patterns.

A track built at Newcastle for the transportation of coal by horse and cart, 1764.

Next, the demand for iron and coal speeded up the development of iron works and coal mines, which also reduced their costs as the costs of transport fell. Whole new coalfields came into operation. The demand for engines and equipment, for carriages and wheels, for signals, for many iron and steel goods, provided a great new opportunity for the engineering industry. The electric telegraph was introduced in 1839 to keep stations in touch with each other, and this led to a further development of engineering. The great firms of Napier, Armstrong and Whitworth and Maudslay (to name but a few) developed heavy and light engineering techniques to a new degree of precision. The railway companies themselves set up locomotive repair and engineering departments.

The railways employed a great many people — clerks, drivers, porters, engineers — by 1851 reaching in Britain a total of sixty-five thousand. New towns, like Swindon, were created for and by the railways.

Above all, however, the railways speeded up transport and reduced its cost. The passenger time was reduced to one-third of that prevailing on the fast turnpike roads, and then to one-fifth. Transport time for goods was one-tenth of that by the canals, and the loads could now go to parts of the country not connected with the canal and river system. The consequences for industrialism were obvious. The movement of population became far easier, travelling now being within the reach of all but the very poorest of the working class. The price of industrial goods fell, and the price of bulk goods (raw materials and food) fell even more dramatically. The railway engine brought full-blown capitalism to Britain as well as to other countries.

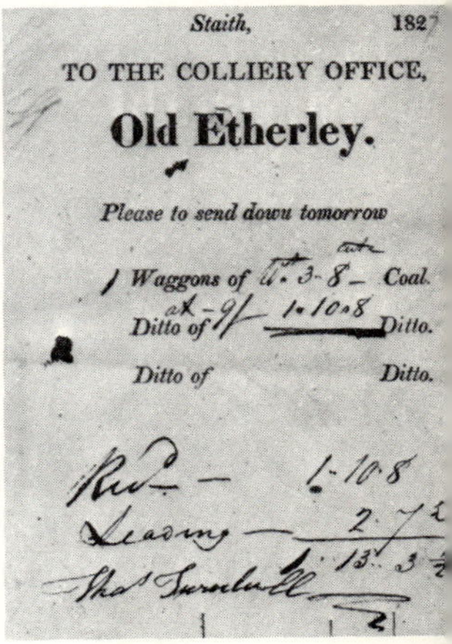

Staith, 182

TO THE COLLIERY OFFICE,

Old Etherley.

Please to send down tomorrow

1 *Waggons of* ... *Coal.*

Ditto of ... 1.10.8 *Ditto.*

Ditto of ... *Ditto.*

The first railways were built to link the coal mines to the ports: an invoice for coal sent from Old Etherley Colliery by the Stockton and Darlington Railway, 1829.

The growth of railway mileage 1840-1960 (in 1,000 miles)

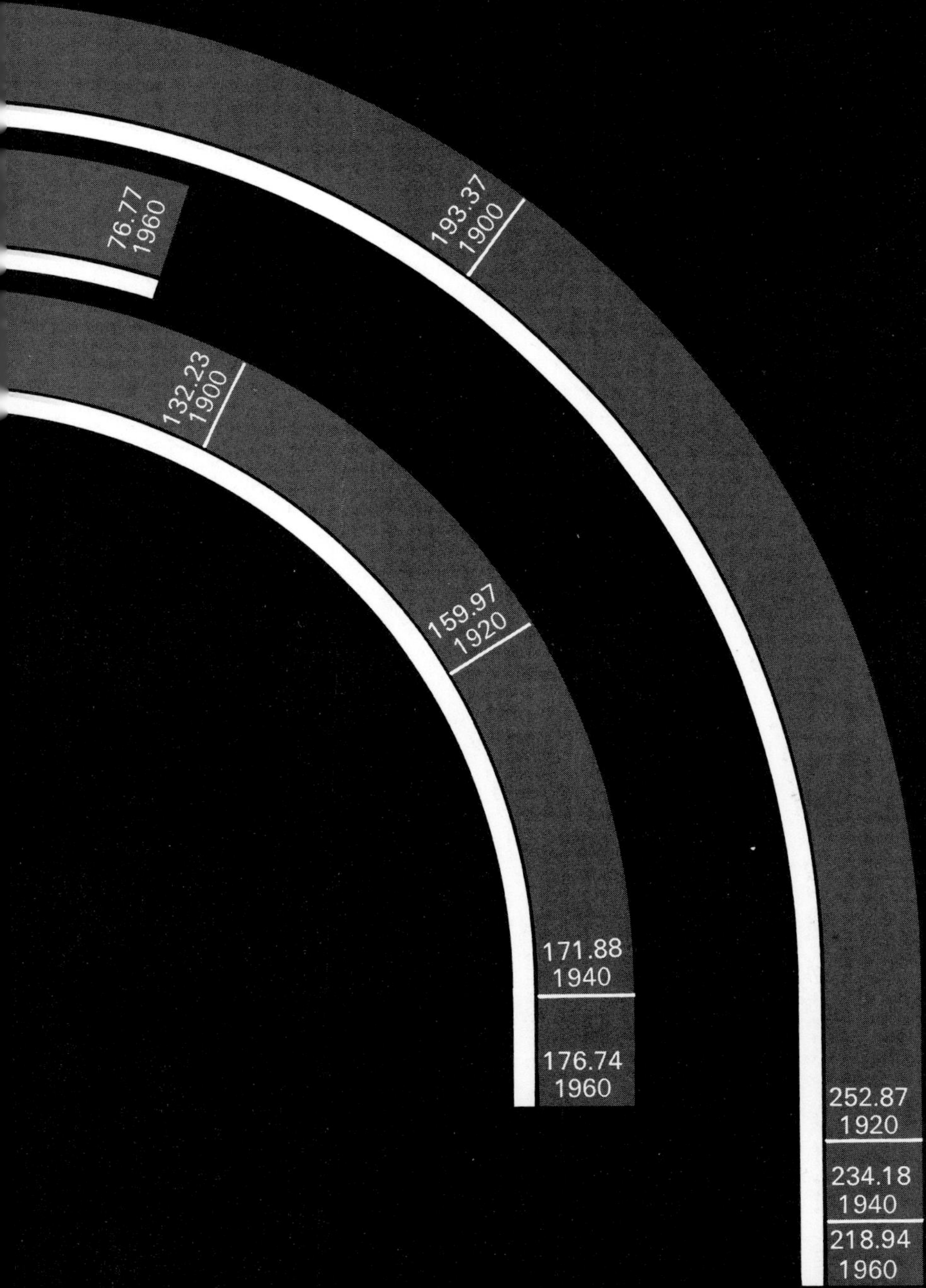

76.77
1960
193.37
1900
132.23
1900
159.97
1920
171.88
1940
176.74
1960
252.87
1920
234.18
1940
218.94
1960

The railway spread quickly to Belgium, France and Germany, though their route mileage was less than Britain's till the last quarter of the nineteenth century. America, however, introduced the railway only a little later than Britain, and there it spread even more quickly. By 1865 the American railway mileage was three times that of Britain. Also, the significance of the railway outside Britain was even greater (if that is possible) than in Britain. It was a unifying force: it helped to create a nation out of the United States, out of Germany and out of Russia. In America, by spanning undeveloped lands, it speeded up pioneering, hitherto virtually confined to areas near a great waterway. In Europe, where capitalism had not yet spread over virtually the whole country, as it had in Britain, the arrival of the railway helped to break down the isolation of local markets and to create national economies.

The spread of the railway in North America (for it was not widespread in Africa, Asia or Australasia till the last part of the nineteenth century) changed

An American poster of 1882 contrasting the speed and safety of the railway with the perils of road travel and the slowness of transport by canal.

An early German steamship, the 'Princess Charlotte', 1816.

the balance of world trade. It enabled the population of America, fed by huge emigrations from Ireland, Germany and England, to spread over the continent and enormously to increase the production of food and new materials. These not only permitted the growth of American industry, but by reducing the costs of production and transport the railway allowed cheap food and materials to flow to Europe. This ultimately transformed European (and especially British) agriculture, but, of more immediate importance, allowed the industrial population to be fed. Adam Smith's division of labour appeared to be working in a splendid way: the fertility of America reduced food costs, while European ingenuity led to an outburst of industrial production, spreading to more and more products, driving out the handcraft producers, reducing costs, standardising goods and killing the old society. The time was not far distant when the brassware of Benares would come from Birmingham.

To complete the transport revolution, the steamship became internationally acceptable. By the 1830s steamboats were chugging up the Mississippi and crossing the English Channel. After 1840 the iron steamship began to cross the oceans, making for far greater regularity (it had on occasion taken three weeks to cross the Irish Sea from Dublin to Holyhead), and the improvement of the screw propeller made it possible for the weight of the ship and its cargo to be much increased. There was a period when steamships still had sails (like the 5,000 ton vessel

Napoléon, built in 1850), and were still partly wooden-hulled. America was the great ship-building nation. But as all-iron (and later steel) all-steam ships came generally into use, British ship-building yards came to dominate the market and the British merchant marine to lead the world. It did so entirely because its costs were low and its reliability high, for the Navigation Acts, causing British trade to be carried in British bottoms, had long since been repealed.

Steam, then, made it possible for American food to come from the prairies, via railway, steamship and railway, to Birmingham, where it fed the workers who made the brass which the Indians sold to the English soldiers holding India. The capitalist circle was complete.

The railway mania

The railway transformed capitalism physically; it also transformed it financially and psychologically. The spread of the railway raised many, though not all, of the problems of early industrialism.

The railways had to be regulated by the government because, if they were to go across property, land had to be compulsorily purchased. The British railways were privately owned and managed. The shares were issued to the public on the Stock Exchange and attracted savings from all over the country. Because of large profits in the early days, high expectations were raised. Many companies were honestly and efficiently managed and paid regular dividends, but — inevitably in such a pioneering technology — some companies made losses, were badly run, or were plain fraudulent: in the boom of 1844 savings had flooded into the railways, and many families were ruined in the subsequent slump of 1845–7. Some dividends were paid out of capital, some companies were totally reconstructed, but after this temporary setback railway shares settled down as a secure investment. The government, of course, had to take powers to regulate railway charges and to safeguard railway safety. Transport had been completely changed: it had to be regulated. Such matters as a uniform gauge for railways, standardisation of techniques, a railway clearing house for travellers and freight routed through several companies, had to be settled. This was done partly by amalgamations and partly by agreements between companies. Usually a railway company was a local monopoly, because its costs were relatively so low that competing canals and turnpike roads went out of use and the companies owning them bankrupt. Governments had to regulate the conditions under which these monopolies conducted their business, to protect travellers, shareholders and workers.

Many overseas lines were financed by British capital, especially in Germany and the United States, and many of the European lines were built by British firms and engineers, the rails and equipment imported from England. America then developed its own rail-making industry and engineering works. The American investment was initially hugely profitable, since very favourable terms were obtained from the states — land and money grants especially — but in 1859 the initial boom collapsed and a series of defaults, even by the states, occurred. The American railway system, which stretched east-west, led to the victory of the north in the Civil War, and deflected the Mississippi north-south trade to the midwest and the north-east coast. From the vast development of railways in America sprang an American technological lead in engines and in associated work like the electric telegraph. Despite the heterogeneity of America and the large number of railroad companies, there were plans for working together on the grand trunk routes which the Civil War accelerated and formalised.

Much of Europe took a different path. The great

An Indian impression of the Punjab Railway in the 1880s.

stock market boom in railway shares which helped to establish London and New York as financial capitals for commercial stocks and shares typified the Anglo-Saxon devotion to private enterprise, and a demand for the nationalisation of British railways, after the railway mania, passed almost unnoticed (though it was later unearthed by socialist apologists). In Belgium, France, Prussia and Russia, the state either built the lines and operated the railways, went into partnership with private capital, or supervised the railways explicitly as public utilities. In Prussia the railways were selfconsciously part of the military system (it was later to be held that the First World War broke out because the railway plan for mobilising troops, once set in motion, was irreversible and lengthy). In many countries the strategic significance of the railways was regarded as most important. In France, for example, the state engineers constructed a national plan for railways radiating from Paris, avoiding the patchwork nature of the British railway system. In many countries the cost of constructing railways was far less than in England. Partly this comparison of costs was unfair — Prussia, for instance, was flat and barren, so railways were easily built, and landowners did not have to be given so much compensation. But partly it was because the lines were more efficiently if more slowly built under state auspices.

The railway, then, offered the opportunity for continental paternalist states to create public utilities, taking the 'exploitation' out of capital assets and running the railways for the public benefit. This involved

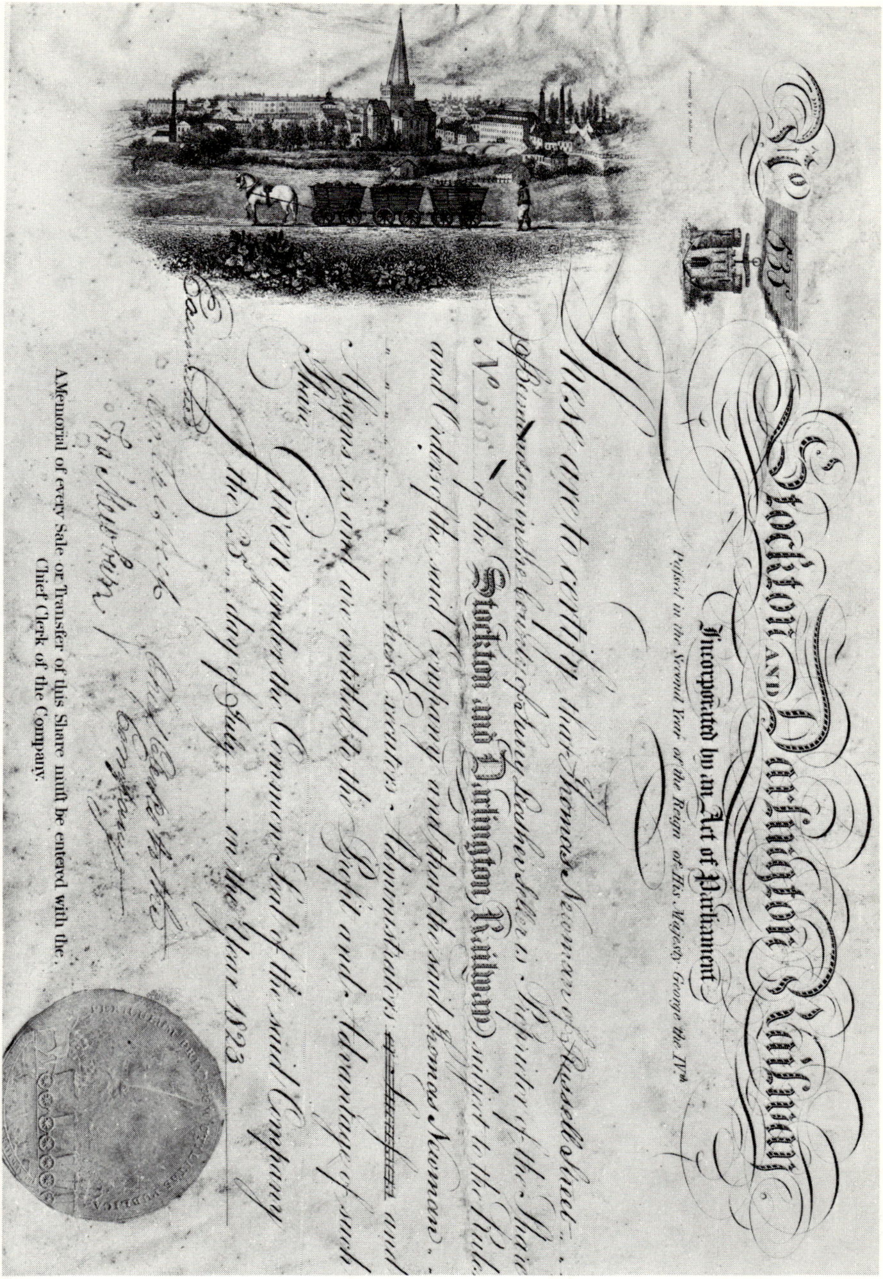
No. 535

Stockton and Darlington Railway

Incorporated by an Act of Parliament

Passed in the Second Year of the Reign of His Majesty George the IVth

These are to certify that Thomas Newman of Russell Street [illegible] is Proprietor of the Share No. 535 of the Stockton and Darlington Railway subject to the Rules and Orders of the said Company and that the said Thomas Newman [illegible] his Executors Administrators and Assigns is and are entitled to the Profit and Advantage of such Share.

Given under the Common Seal of the said Company the 23 day of July in the Year 1823

A Memorial of every Sale or Transfer of this Share must be entered with the Chief Clerk of the Company.

above: A share of the Stockton and Darlington Railway Company issued in 1823, two years before the line even opened.

deliberately constructing unprofitable lines for strategic reasons, or, as in Bavaria, to encourage economic development. The British were capable of taking this point of view, too, because in India the government not only guaranteed the interest on railway loans but covered some of the costs. Private enterprise built and operated the railways, but on very favourable terms, and the Indian people got the benefit of greater markets; the Indian government got a strategic network which the Indian Mutiny of 1857 showed to be essential for military control.

Yet in most cases state and private enterprise collaborated, since the profits gained by capitalists on the London and New York stock exchanges appealed to financiers in Paris, Vienna and Brussels. European businessmen wanted to get into the railway business, and capital creation on so vast a scale was beyond normal government financing. Russia was, as often, an example of private enterprise running into losses, being rescued by the state, and then being run extremely inefficiently. In Russia, so far behind the rest of Europe (except the Balkans), capitalism had penetrated very little, and the railway — the very symbol of capitalism — could hardly run as smoothly as in New York or in Lancashire. But in a very few years, after serfdom had been abolished, the railway in Russia was exporting Russian food and transporting the early products of Russian industry.

With the railway had come state intervention in capitalism, financial capital, booms and slumps on a large scale, and an irreversible and permanent technological advance that caused a tremendous fall in costs.

Textiles and consumer goods

The historical function of capitalism, according to Marx, was to equip the world with capital goods. To do so it had to extract the surplus from the workers and embody it in machines. These machines would have the capacity to produce goods on an immense scale which the workers *ex hypothesi* would be unable to buy. Certainly the railways, the smoking chimneys of the factories, the figure of the engineer, characterised the change that came over north-western Europe and the north-eastern United States in

Richard Arkwright's patent specification for his new loom, 1769. This was among the earliest of a series of technical innovations which led to the rapid growth of the eighteenth-century English textile industry.

the first half of the nineteenth century. But it was the great flood of consumer goods that represented as radical a change from previous centuries as the new capital equipment: and, certainly, the capitalists themselves pointed to the increase in output as the significant fact in the expansion of the whole economic system. True, in some parts of the world it was barely keeping pace with the rise in population, but that fact in itself showed what disasters would have struck if output had not risen. Ireland, stricken by famine, was a case in point.

Industrialisation first affected the Lancashire cotton industry. Cheap cotton came from America and the West Indies; Lancashire had water power, cheap labour, capitalists and technologists, and it had markets in England, Europe, Africa and Asia. Cotton textiles were the first mass-produced consumer goods, and were sold all over the world, changing the habits of dress and of decoration of whole nations. After cotton textiles, other goods followed. But cotton typified the whole capitalist process. First, bulk production rivalled the production carried on by hand manufacture. The standards of the handloom weavers fell catastrophically. Then, with technical improvements in the 1820s, handloom weaving went into its death throes. By the mid-nineteenth century cotton goods were manufactured exclusively in factories, in Lancashire and the United States. In the first sixty years of the nineteenth century, English production of cotton textiles increased over twenty-fold; in 1850 three-fifths of British exports were textile yarns and fabrics, including woollens. Lancashire cotton, and, after 1850,

A page from 'Knight's Cyclopaedia of the Industry of All Nations' showing various stages in the manufacture of textiles in 1851. **Bottom right**: making the punched cards to operate a Jacquard automated loom ; **centre:** Jacquard looms at work.

Yorkshire woollens, achieved a world dominance on which the English export trade was based for the whole of the nineteenth century.

Wool textiles, then, were a second industry that experienced enormous cost reductions as industrialisation developed. Australian and American sheep provided some of the wool — in fact a torrent of wool and cotton flowed into northern England from Amer-

Sewing machines in a factory at Netherfield, Kendal.

ica and Australia and other distant lands, to be exported as manufactures. Wool lagged behind cotton, partly because it was a fibre far more difficult to deal with mechanically and partly because the domestic industry was stronger and harder to displace. Also, the demand for cotton goods was extremely income- and price-elastic — as incomes rose and costs fell, the market rose inexorably. Less so with wool.

The process of industrialisation was patchy, and (as both cotton and wool illustrate) new and old techniques coexisted for long periods. The hand producers usually sank into misery, and increasingly their market shrank to that for custom-built, specialist and high-priced articles; but there was a lengthy period when the factory produced articles which were regarded as cheap and shoddy and actually were so. Old habits of production and consumption died hard and local markets for consumer goods persisted. But the tide of industrialisation was inexorable. In New England, for example, the boot and shoe industry was by 1860 predominantly a factory trade, despite a long struggle by the cobblers, who never entirely disappeared, a few remaining as shoe repairers, or high-class boot-makers. The availability of cheap boots and shoes was a major element in raising living standards.

The mechanisation of boot and shoe manufacture owed a great deal to the invention of the sewing machine, which also enabled the costs of clothing manufacture to fall. In fact, the clothing industry makes an interesting example of the capitalist transformation of a domestic craft. The old tailors and dressmakers were never entirely replaced by the industry producing 'off-the-peg' garments. But the price of textiles fell, and the sewing machine greatly speeded up the process of clothes manufacture. Therefore clothiers who could buy and hold large stocks of textiles, buy sewing machines, and market the cheap goods, could either assemble their workers in a factory or engage in the 'putting-out' system, which had been familiar for nearly four centuries from Jack of Newbury's time.

Pottery was another industry which was industrialised early. The Stoke-on-Trent potteries, which exploited furnaces, and enabled standard ware to be produced in bulk and sent down the canals to the ports, became the model for potteries which reduced the price of china to levels that ordinary people could afford. Wooden platters and pewter mugs became objects more of curiosity than of use. To the new cheap china could be added a range of domestic goods almost without limit. Inexpensive furniture began to be made in factories and workshops with new and improved tools. The cast-iron heating stove became cheaper and more important in western Europe and North America, as did the cooking range. On the cooking range could be found cast-iron pots and saucepans, replacing the tin kettles and vessels produced by tinkers. Ordinary cutlery, from Sheffield, was a result of the improvement of steel. So the domestic 'revolution' could be catalogued — textile manufacture altered curtains, carpets, furniture covering; cheap timber and new machinery affected furniture; heat, light (gas was widespread by the end of 1860 in most European and American cities) and sewage disposal were recognisably 'modern' by the early 1870s. The result was a dramatic change in the standard of living of ordinary middle-class and artisan life. There was a national, indeed an international, market for many of these domestic products, which ranged from pipe tobacco and matches to articles of clothing, boots and shoes, books and newspapers. The development of mechanical paper-making and mechanical printing, the invention of mechanical binding, the evolution of commercial glues — all this made the cheap book a possibility for all but the very poorest persons. After this development society was bound to change. Applied to products of all kinds, the inferences are obvious. The range of choice of the ordinary family was enormously increased.

Nowhere was this more evident than in the revolution in domestic architecture. Brick-built dwellings, spreading out into the suburbs which were made accessible by trains and trams, contained machined doors and door handles, window glass and frames. The bricks were made in bulk. Linoleum was a common floor covering. In the more prosperous homes, especially in America, bathrooms made their appearance.

The centres of these new construction trades were Britain and the north-eastern United States, though by 1870, technically and in adventurous pioneering, America was ahead of Britain and was, generally speaking, to remain so, continental Europe lagging further behind. Machine-baked bread and tinned foods are examples of goods that were common in England and America by the 1870s; till quite late on in the twentieth century they were rare in continental Europe. Partly this fact reflects the much larger peasant population of Europe; partly it is explained by the growth of mass markets in countries where proletarianisation had gone furthest. For when a mass market was created even middle-class goods were soon produced by mass techniques and hand labour went out. In the 1920s even the English aristocracy had bathrooms, instead of skivvies carrying up pails of steaming water from the kitchen to the bedroom.

Agriculture

Agriculture inevitably became a bastion of conservative attitudes and elderly techniques. The towns were the home of capitalism and of capitalist rationality, and the rural population was intensely suspicious of changes, understandably so since for them almost all change turned out to be for the worse.

Yet agriculture was where much of it had begun. The surplus from the land had provided some of the capital for early industrialisation. In England, as population rose, the development of new techniques and new forms of agricultural organisation enabled output to expand faster than the labour force engaged in agriculture. The surplus population moved to the towns, in conditions of hideous misery in many cases. But, at least for the most part, the townspeople saw some of the benefits from the rising agricultural output.

New ways of organising agriculture spread at about the time of the French revolution, and subsequently. In England, landowners organised their land into compact farms, run (for the most part) by tenant farmers and worked by agricultural labourers. In France and in some other parts of the continent, the revolutionary redistribution of land extended the areas controlled by small peasants, often with scattered strips and patches of land, to which his rights were inalienable, and subject to further subdivision under the Napoleonic Code of inheritance. In Russia, Prussia and Hungary, the landowners brought the waste lands into their pattern of extensive cultivation. In the United States independent farmers moved on to fertile free land and organised it on an extensive basis, unhindered by historical land-tenure patterns. (Of course, the pattern was not as simple as this, since each country had several types of organisation within its borders, but conceptually it is convenient to consider the question thus.)

Wherever industrialism spread fast, the market for food and raw materials rose, and despite intermittent depressions the spread of the market accelerated the radical organisation changes in agriculture and led to the spread of the area of cultivated land. Britain became a big food importer; Europe was, on the whole, a string of protected markets (since it never embraced wholeheartedly the laissez-faire faith); America's costs were so low that it hardly had to consider the question of food imports. The English, with the fastest growing industrial population, pioneered new agricultural techniques — draining the soil, feeding it chemically, selectively breeding stock and plants, applying machinery to ploughing, hoeing and (eventually) reaping, binding and threshing. In a part of the kingdom where the effects of the market were not directly felt, and where the landowners were especially backward — Ireland — population rose faster than output, though the area of cultivated land extended considerably. The result, when the crop

English farm machinery, c. 1861, from the 'Official Illustrated Catalogue Advertiser'.

failed in 1845, was a terrible famine which killed, directly and indirectly, one million people. This shows how great was the catastrophe which the new farming techniques avoided in England and elsewhere in Europe.

America took over the lead from England in the development of agricultural machinery. American farmers had abundant fertile soil. When it was exhausted they moved on, so they had no need to develop crop rotation, deep drainage and other techniques for preserving and raising the fertility of the soil. Moreover, initially, they had no big market for their supplies; they lived in a high-level subsistence economy, except for the cotton plantations where slavery was prevalent. After 1830, with the development of transport and the beginnings of large-scale industrialisation in the north-east, the wealthier agricultural workers could move west and found their own farms. Machinery was rapidly developed to save labour: John Deere developed a light plough with a steel blade, which formed the basis of a substantial agricultural machinery industry; Obed Hussey and Cyrus McCormick developed, in 1833 and 1834, mechanical reapers. Labour was scarce on American farms, and at harvest time it virtually vanished. Now large-scale grain production was possible since big tracts of land could be successfully ploughed and large prairie fields could be reaped. Other machines for threshing, drilling, harrowing and many other tasks were produced. By 1860 the United States had a large agricultural machinery industry which formed the basis of an export industry, and the huge crops were marketed in the growing American cities and in Europe.

No equivalent rise in productivity occurred in France, though there was a steady slow improvement of peasant agricultural techniques. In Prussia, however, the development of the chemical industry, the draining of marshes, and the ploughing up and improvement of sandy wastes, led to appreciable increases in agricultural output. The conquest of new lands was the chief Russian contribution to agricultural production, for the break-up of big estates and the settlement of the peasantry after the emancipation of the serfs in 1861 tended to hold back the possibilities of productivity growth. In Germany, however, the emancipation of the peasantry between 1830 and 1850 appears to have led to substantial productivity gains, especially in livestock production.

Denmark is an interesting example of a highly efficient grain-producing country whose peasantry was emancipated and which after 1860 increasingly turned to livestock production and to butter, eggs

The growth of industry and the decline of agriculture

Percentages of the total labour force occupied in industry and agriculture

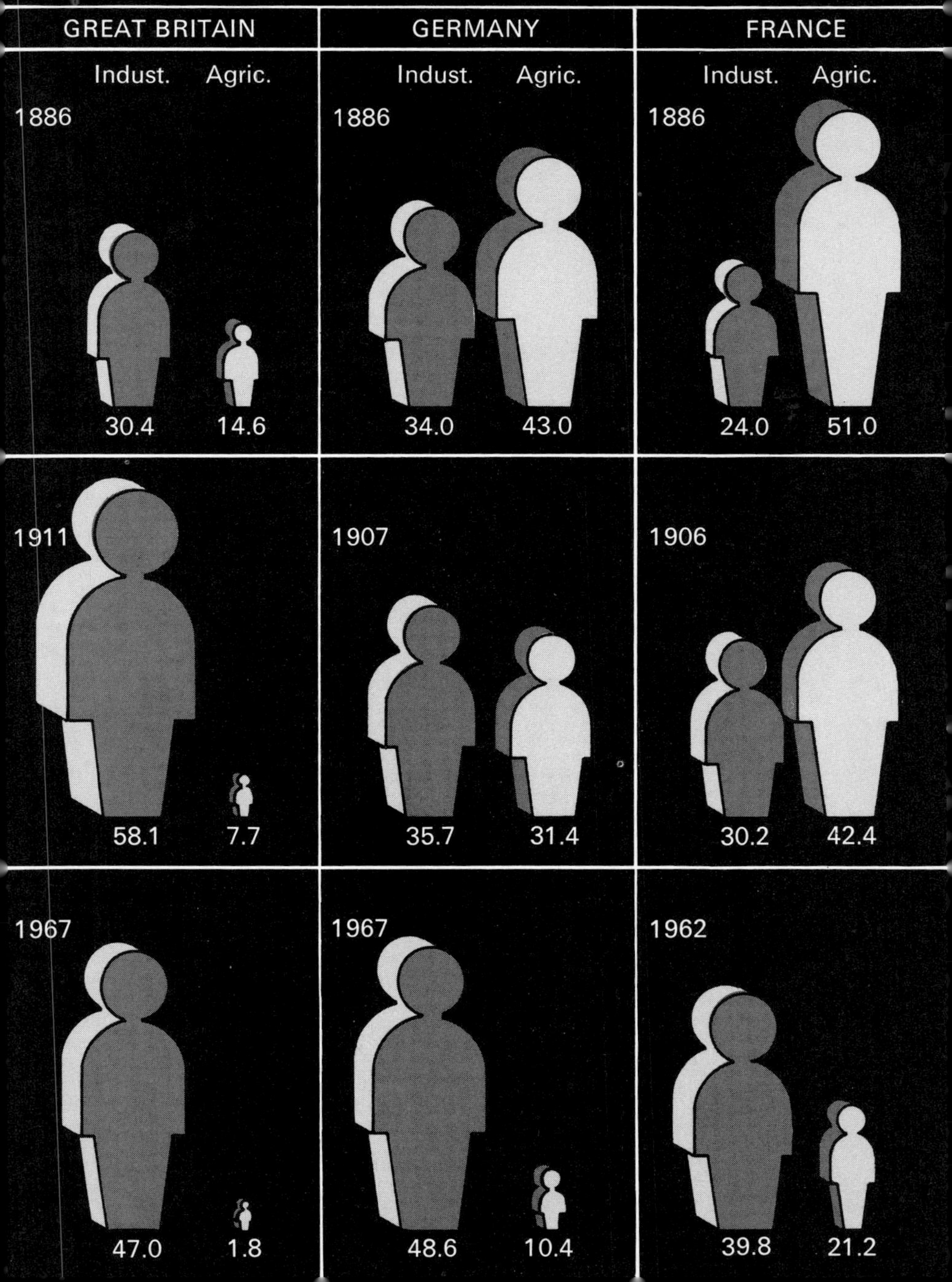

and cheese. The spread of rational techniques of livestock care and the processing of meat, eggs and butter spread throughout Europe from Denmark, and in the United States from Scandinavian emigrants (just as English emigrants had taken many of the new techniques there).

By 1850 or so the agricultural population in most countries in Europe had reached its maximum. Thereafter growth of output came from steadily increasing productivity gains; but in America the agricultural population continued to grow rapidly, and the western world was increasingly fed from American sources, and from the new farms in Argentina, Australia and South Africa. Their achievement was enormous. The European population (including Russia) rose from 190 million in 1800 to 400 million in 1900; America's population more than tripled between 1830 and 1870. By the end of the century the white populations of the world — well over 500 millions — had more than doubled since the beginning of the century and were, even so, much better fed (on average) than they had been.

The development of agriculture was accompanied, then, by an 'expulsion' of the 'surplus' population from agriculture, some of which moved on to the United States, in wave after wave, as the agricultural revolution travelled through Europe. First the British, then the Irish when their subsistence agriculture collapsed, then the Germans and Scandinavians, then the Poles and Russians, and the Italians — in all these countries population moved internally to the cities. In 1800 about four-fifths of the population of Europe and America were working at agricultural jobs; by 1850 it was down to about half and by 1900 to an even smaller fraction. At least three hundred million extra mouths were now better fed, by rather fewer hands, as a result of agricultural expansion. Even so, agricultural overpopulation was still common in Europe, especially in the southern and eastern countries, where the influence of the world market was weakest. In eastern Europe land was still relatively abundant, however, and population growth could still bend to the cultivation of new lands. In southern Europe rural poverty was widespread.

Indeed, America apart, the agricultural revolution which fed the world depressed the relative situation of the rural population. In north-western Europe, the age of the farmer was past; his reactions were to be increasingly defensive.

Technology, education and the transmission of knowledge

The capitalist spirit was a rational one. The capitalists were heirs to Galileo and Newton: see a problem, think about it, and adopt the most economical answer, and be damned to past practice and traditional theory. The capitalists, in England originally in large numbers but then in America and north-western continental Europe, applied this pragmatic outlook to the problems of assessing the market and solving their own production problems. Their initial response stimulated technology. The steam engine was the paradigm of a technological answer to a practical problem — how to use new sources of energy and apply them to machinery. Textile machinery was the first example of a rationalist approach to production problems in an industrial context. The railway was the supreme example of the coalescence of the solution of two problems: how to apply steam to transport, and how to make roads capable of bearing heavy weights.

In the eighteenth century Britain had, it seems, a relatively higher level of technical skill and ability to 'tinker' with things than elsewhere, though the natural sciences had advanced further in Germany. This interest in engineering was transmitted by British emigrants to the United States. The new professions of agriculturalist and engineer developed the capacity to solve problems. Out of their solutions — pragmatic solutions — problems were suggested to scientists. It was not the other way about. The science of genetics, for example, grew up to explain the processes of selective breeding already being applied by agriculturists.

The new industries went to great lengths to train a skilled work force, and people with advanced skills commanded high premiums. In Britain these skills tended to be work-based; on the continent they became institutionalised, in Napoleon's *grandes écoles* and the *Technische Hochschulen.* As the nineteenth century progressed the technical problems to be solved

Henry Bessemer's converter (**above**) made possible the large-scale production of steel.

became more complex. The movement from mass produced iron to mass produced steel is one example; the evolution of the chemical dyestuffs industry (based on coal tar) is another. The engineer, or his equivalent in other technologies, added to his trained experience in problem-solving a series of theoretical concepts which were necessarily linked to natural science and mathematics. It was this link that made technological progress irreversible. Even were some disaster to wipe out most of mankind and all of its artefacts, if only a few people remembered that it was possible to find out how to make things, mankind could never relapse into pre-capitalist modes of thought. Early engineering led to developments in the science of mechanics: iron- and steel-making affected metallurgy, and therefore chemistry; dyeing and other processes affected chemistry. Yet it was not till the later years of the nineteenth century that advances in the natural sciences directly affected technology. Electricity is one of the early instances, and led to physics succeeding chemistry as the major pioneering natural science. Faraday as the theorist and Edison as the practitioner were responsible for the fact that by the early 1880s electricity was a practicable tool for almost all its present uses. Geologists and chemists led the way to the great mineral discoveries of the late nineteenth century and to the exploitation of mineral oils, which formed the basis of the internal combustion engine of the 1880s.

Oil Creek, Pennsylvania, where the first successful oil-well was sunk by Drake in 1859. Within a year of the discovery the whole valley had been purchased or leased; this photograph shows it in 1865.

Thus, out of engineering and the other applied sciences or mechanised arts, came a fresh impetus in the sciences of chemistry, geology and physics. Biology and zoology, which developed later, owed a great deal to agricultural techniques. By the mid-nineteenth century a reciprocal relationship between the pure and applied sciences was already at work, and this led to the formalisation of the training of engineers and agriculturalists, perhaps best seen in the state colleges of the United States, which rapidly spread after the Civil War, and in the German technical high schools. It was these German and American colleges which gave Germany and America their industrial leadership in the late nineteenth century.

The relationship of these advances to education is a complex one. Most engineering-type skills were acquired on-the-job ; and apprenticeship was the normal mode of acquisition. Most advances in technology were extremely small : it was the cumulative effect of these apparently insignificant changes that led to the swiftness and the magnitude of the total advance in technology. It was only as the nineteenth centry wore on that a body of technical knowledge could be formally taught, and it was not till fairly late in the century that this body of knowledge could be directly related to scientific principles. An example of this is medicine : pragmatically, clinical and surgical techniques developed in the nineteenth century, but the theoretical basis of antiseptic practices, vaccination and anaesthesia could not be related to sophisticated scientific principles until physiology, bacteriology and pharmacology had solved the intellectual problems which clinical solutions to clinical problems gave rise to. Once that bridge had been crossed, modern medicine and modern medical education were possible. Thus the universities were products, rather than causes, of the capitalist technology.

There is little doubt that in the eighteenth century the general level of competence and skill of the British was higher than in other countries, and this was related to generally higher standards of literacy and education, which have in turn been linked to Protestantism. Certainly, obscurantist Catholicism was a major barrier to educational progress and so to a pragmatic approach to technical and economic questions. The high calibre of British emigrants to America (for it was mainly the skilled artisans who went) led to a rapid spread of high standards of education there; and by the early 1840s a doctrine of universal common education was accepted in most northern states. Napoleon adopted the principle of universal primary education for France; Frederick the Great did so for Prussia. The French had a setback after Waterloo, but Prussia developed its school system. Thus by the 1860s widespread primary education was common in France, Prussia, Scandinavia and America, and it was coming to be so in Britain. This provided a literate body of consumers and a labour force that could work in a rationalist capitalist environment. Out of this basic education, a few clever children could spring onto a platform of middle-level technical studies which enabled them to service the industrial machine and to act as clerks. Education for middle-class children, in Germany and America, also had a technological and scientific side, which provided the basis for their advance in high-level skills. It was the relative absence of this part of the education system in England which was much deplored by progressive opinion, and was held to be the cause of her relative falling behind in industrial advance after 1870.

New knowledge then, was developed by training and education. It was transmitted by a degree of population movement without precedent. Not only did millions of people, many of them highly skilled, cross the Atlantic, but large numbers of British engineers went to the continent, Frenchmen to Russia, and Germans to the Balkans, taking their skills with them. Trade carried the new ways wherever it went. The trader had changed his status. Feuer describes the Jewish pedlar—'this defenceless proto-bourgeois, this pioneer of trade, moving about through the uncertain apertures of closed, narrow, insulated feudal worlds, bringing goods, news, intelligence, himself an itinerant rationalist, observing people's superstitions in different places, this huckster, with his pack on his back, travelling in fear of his life, in dread danger...'. Now the trader was a man of power, bringing new knowledge to another tradition. He was helped by a world-wide postal service, the electric telegraph and the invention of high-speed printing. The trader now sent books, reports and news around the world. It was the immediacy of contact and the instantaneous reactions of thousands of knowledgeable and rational businessmen to it which instituted the world-wide market.

The immiseration of the proletariat

Capitalism created modern large-scale means of production. Its purpose was to increase consumption by raising output. Yet Marx held that capitalism would be unable to solve the problems of consumption, his evidence for this being the apparent deterioration of the standard of living of the working class. In the long run he was completely wrong: in any straightforward comparison of conditions in the industrial countries at the beginning and the end of the nineteenth century, there can be little doubt that consumption standards had risen, in food, clothing, housing, leisure, and in the general availability of goods, including transport and public services like education. Whether other sacrifices had been made, in working conditions, in political and social alienation, are questions that will be considered later; but it is doubtful whether those sacrifices (if there were any) outdistanced the gains made in consumption. Moreover, when it is realised that population in the white world more than doubled in a century, it is obvious that without the new means of production a terrible calamity, on the Irish scale, might have enveloped the whole world, as it still threatens to do in parts of Asia.

Initially, however, the impact of capitalism is not so clear, and controversy still rages about the period of initial industrialisation. The right answer appears to be that different groups were differently affected; almost any story can be told which fits some of the facts, while the whole truth is very complicated.

Let one thing be clear. The mists of time appeared to close on a bucolic and prosperous rural eighteenth-century past, which critics of industrialism glimpsed shining in the sunshine beyond the smoke pall of Manchester, Chicago and the Ruhr. Reality was very different. Before industrialisation there were patches of prosperity: New England was one; England itself reached, by about 1760, unprecedented prosperity on

Weekly budget of an upper middle-class family with three children (annual income of £1,000) in 1824

	£	s	d
Meat—52½ lb.	1	15	0
Fish and poultry		15	0
Butter—7½ lb.		7	6
Beer and other liquors	1	1	0
Vegetables and fruit		7	6
Milk and eggs		3	9
Coachman's wages		9	2¾
Footman's wages		8	5½
Cook's wages		6	2
House-maid's wages		5	7¾
Nursery-maid's wages		4	0½
2 horses	1	5	4
Rent, fuel, and sundries	11	16	0
	19	4	7½

Weekly budget of a semi-skilled worker with wife and two children (weekly income of 15s) in 1841

	s	d
5 × 4 lb. loaves @ 8½d	3	6½
5 lb. meat @ 5d	2	1
7 pints of porter @ 2d	1	2
½ cwt. coals		9½
40 lb. potatoes	1	4
3 oz. tea, 1 lb. sugar	1	6
½ lb. soap, ½ lb. candles		6½
Rent	2	6
Schooling		4
Sundries		5½
	15	0

the basis of its extensive commerce and the improvement in the manufacturing costs already apparent at the time. The general condition of the world, however, was one of grinding poverty, interspersed with famine or near-famine conditions. Even the accounts of the arrival of the Elizabethan English in Bengal, where they found an apparently limitless prosperity, speak more of the poverty of England than of the wealth of the prosperous classes of Bengal. So it would be hard to imagine that for the typical poor person conditions could deteriorate very much.

But they did for some. The skilled hand-workers who over a period of decades struggled against the falling costs of factory competition were groups who fell into misery and pauperdom. Some of the agricultural workers, similarly, lost their status in precapitalist agriculture and found no new place in capitalist agriculture. They lost rights which they had taken for granted, to graze their animals, to glean, to collect firewood, and there was no work. The third group who suffered were the paupers and the beggars — the dispossessed who had immemorially been in society; these were now regarded as pernicious wastrels who

'The backyards of London as they are', 1878.

Glasgow was noted for its slums even in the nineteenth century: Close no. 75, High Street, Glasgow in the 1870s.

had to be disciplined and who, in the words of the English Poor Law Commissioners of 1834, had to be reduced to the conditions of the 'least eligible labourer'. With wages almost by definition at subsistence level, this meant that their conditions were indescribably sad. Families were separated, their humiliation was endless. But whether it was worse than beggary is an exercise in comparative misery that it would be hard to establish.

People still died of starvation in the capitalist world until well into the twentieth century (as they died, of course, under communism in the 1930s). They did so chiefly in periods of slump, and slumps and booms, the eleven-year cycle of capitalist activity, appeared to intensify as industrialism spread. In bad years, therefore, in the 1840s for instance, many thousands were unemployed and, propertyless, without savings, with nowhere to go, found themselves homeless and starving. Only the Poor Law could provide for them. Again, these collapses were as nothing compared to the conditions in the pre-capitalist world where, as in Ireland, when the crop failed there was no social mechanism for providing relief. Despite the efforts of the government, there was no immediate means of providing relief for the Irish, except by emigration, or so it seemed.

The herding together of people into the industrial towns and cities caused a series of social problems. Infectious diseases spread easily. The absence of sewage and waste disposal facilities created conditions where dysentery, typhoid and other water-borne diseases were endemic. The death rate, especially among infants, soared. There is no doubt, either, that there was a serious deterioration in the quality of food: adulteration was common (not that it was unknown in the eighteenth century) and contamination was certain.

The towns, then, were less healthy than rural life had generally been. Food supplies were more regular, but poorer in quality. Illness was greater. In slumps, destitution was common, and destitution meant homelessness and starvation. For people with redundant skills, in dying trades, conditions were terrible. The afflicted were neglected, as the common assumptions of Christian charity were questioned in the name of efficiency and self-reliance. It was the treatment of those unable to look after themselves — the children, the old, the sick and the afflicted — which first seriously called into question the ethical standards of capitalism. The reactionaries, who looked back to an age where everybody knew his place, when it was a Christian duty to comfort the afflicted, joined with the revolutionaries, who looked forward to an age when poverty would be no more. Both condemned the conditions in which society wrung a surplus out of the industrial and agricultural workers to build the means of producing abundance.

The conditions of industrial work

Discipline was the clue to working under capitalism. Pre-capitalist countries had a rhythm of work and social behaviour which were dictated by the seasons and the weather, and which reflected a ritual interpretation of life, with fiestas and fasts, high days and low days. Productivity was low; the regularity of life was the regularity of the unconscious rhythm of a traditional society. Industrial society is different. The pattern and rhythm of life is set by machinery and team work. Everybody in a working group has to start together and stop together. If the machine speeds up, the worker speeds up; if it stops, he stops. The shift from one mode of working to the other is traumatic. This is the explanation of — though it is no excuse for — the conditions of the early factories. Discipline was harsh, dismissal was instantaneous, and the atmosphere was tyrannical.

The early workers had few rights. Ignorant, des-

Sweated labour, 1845. In some cases, such exaggeration was not so far from the truth.

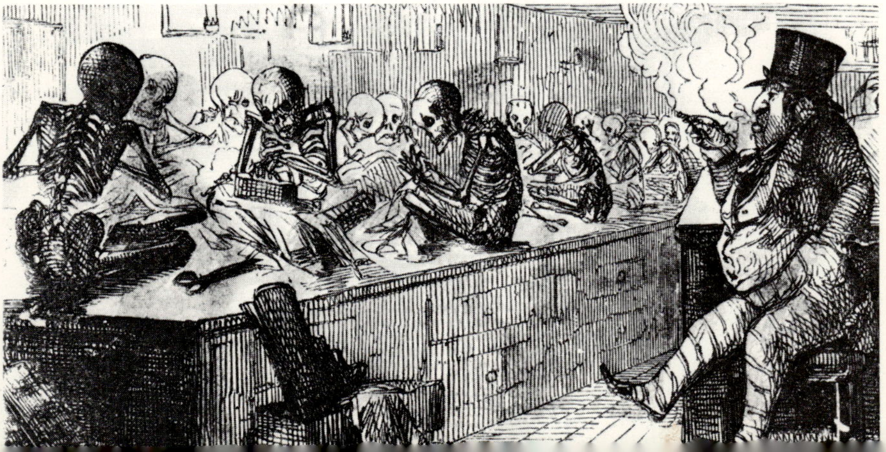

'He drew nearer to the extreme edge' – this engraving of 1840 interprets, in the Romantic style, the all too real deprivation of the child worker.

opposite: With the development of increasingly complex factory machinery, a skilled labour force came into being: English factory workers, c. 1900.

perately poor, and frightened, they depended on the factory masters for the bare conditions of life. Wages were at a minimum, and if they sought more there were others to take their place. If men were expensive, women could be used. Children worked — paupers of five or six were drafted into the factories. Hours were extremely long. Accidents were frequent. Life was cheap. In some factory barracks, or cheap lodging houses, successive shifts of workers shared beds; as one shift went on duty, their beds were taken by those coming off duty. Conditions in early industrialisation always seem to have been terrible: first in England (on the basis of which Marx and Engels wrote their reports), then on the continent and in America, then in Russia and Asia, the same experience of oppression and exploitation was undergone. There is a literature, from British official publications to Maxim Gorki, from Jack London and Upton Sinclair to Fidel Castro, describing the horrors of early industrialism.

It was the cruelty of the overseers and the callousness of the managers and foremen which were most horrifying. Conditions of domestic labour were physically little better: children probably worked as long and just as unhealthily in domestic trades as in factories; but were they callously bullied to the same extent?

These conditions lasted for several generations before amelioration set in. England began to develop a group of labour managers, industrialists who were interested in labour conditions, who realised that shorter hours and more sympathetic treatment might raise productivity, and so reduce costs, increase output and not lower it. In this respect they were soon overtaken by the Americans, where the supply of cheap labour (except on the slave plantations of the south) was continually replenished by immigration but frequently depleted by movement to the west. Labour prices were continually forced up and so it was essential to deal with labour as a scarce factor of production, and not as an abundant one as it was in Europe.

The labour force, as some of its members entered their second and third generations as industrial work-

ers, became used to industrial work and the discipline of working with machines, and therefore no longer needed to be dragooned. Machines became more sophisticated, needing more skilled people to operate them, and the general conditions of the labour force improved. Its educational levels rose perceptibly; it was composed of people aware, to some extent, of what was going on at their work and capable of working on their own initiative. Again, this was especially so in America where 'exploitation' became chiefly concentrated on vulnerable immigrant groups, the Negroes, and women. Yet 'exploitation' is an odd word to use, since the productivity of this type of labour was very low. The profits on highly paid labour employed in prosperous concerns were considerably higher. Marx was certainly incorrect in identifying surplus value with the degree of poverty of the workers.

After a time, of course, the workers began to combine in small numbers into labour unions. These unions sprang out of their growing sense of solidarity with each other. Initially, the unions in France, England, and to a small extent in America, had apocalyptic notions of a reconstruction of society on cooperative lines. The successful unions, however, were those of skilled and semi-skilled workers which could afford relatively high membership dues, engage in detailed negotiation with big employers, and seek to exclude new entrants to the trade unless they conformed to the wage conditions determined by negotiation. These bodies, similar to professional bodies, were closely allied to the concept of friendly societies and cooperative societies, which provided, in the one case, insurance against unemployment, sickness and burial costs, and in the other case reliable goods. In America, again, because of the generally higher level of the average citizen in terms of income and social aspiration, the spread of clubs, societies and communal activities was greater; the greater self-respect of the American worker was often noted both as a cause and a consequence of his higher standard of living and better working conditions.

In Britain the state began in the 1840s to regulate working conditions. The movement spread to other countries. There were safety provisions, limitations of hours, especially for children and women, and enforcement of environmental provisions for the health of the work force. Most of this legislation sprang from the enlightened middle classes; but increasingly the workers themselves demanded legal regulation of their working lives. This movement towards state provision was to become a significant feature of later capitalist society.

Profits and their spending

As industrialism spread, so did the size and importance of the profit-receiving class. The landowner and his rent (and tribute in kind) diminished in importance as the industrialist and businessman provided more of society's savings. This arose from two causes: first, an increase in activity, which had the effect of increasing the total level of profits, proportionately with rises in other factor incomes, and secondly, the depression of real wages which probably occurred in the price rise of the Napoleonic wars. After the end of the war, when price levels fell, profit levels probably fell as well, but as significant technical advances were occurring at the same time it is difficult to generalise.

With the coming of the railway, and the great expansion of world trade which followed the development of the British, north-west European and north-east American industrial complexes, more and more economic activity yielded a profit (as opposed to a landowner's surplus). It had two important characteristics: first, much of it was more a steady profit rather than a series of risky windfalls. Before 1840 it was customary to put money into landownership for security's sake. After the coming of the railways, holdings of railway stock became respectable. Throughout the nineteenth century, in country after country, this increasingly became the case. The London Stock Exchange, the Paris and Brussels bourses, the other continental and the American exchanges thus increasingly became the centre of a flow of capital seeking a safe haven. As the century wore on, a steady 5 per cent was expected. The nineteenth century, after the Napoleonic wars, was a period of

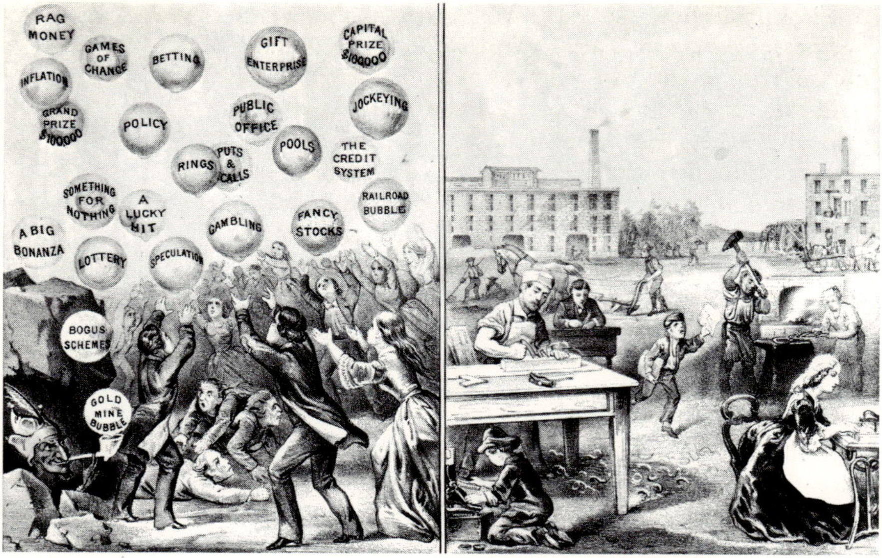

'The way to grow poor (**left**); the way to grow rich' **(right)** – American speculation, 1875.

steady (and sometimes falling) prices. Thus the rise of the joint stock company, and its regular payment of dividends, became the basis for a steady accumulation of savings, expecting a regular, safe return and prepared to seek it in business. Particular pools of local capital became part of a general flood of savings. Wherever returns increased, capital flowed. The international money market, helped by international banking houses like the Rothschilds, became a reality. The flow of British capital overseas through the City of London became prodigious. Much of American, European, Australasian, African and Latin American development was initially undertaken with British capital, which flowed out of British profits or came from the reinvestment of British overseas profits. Paris and Vienna followed suit; American capital generally found the vast opportunities of its own land sufficiently attractive to keep it there.

The second characteristic of the rise in the significance of profits was that more and more economic activity was directed to a profit-making end. The single-man business, the partnership, the firm — all of them thought increasingly of their surplus as a means of developing the market, of seeking ways to reduce costs by finding new ways of doing things.

Thus profit became a pool from which profit-making businesses took what they could usefully employ to increase profits, and those profits were returned to the pool where they were once more reallocated by the capital market. The generator of this activity was therefore the firm that increased its capital and raised its profitability. Everyone was looking for such opportunities. Railways offered them; the new mineral discoveries offered them, and capital flowed into companies in those sectors.

It would be a mistake to build up a picture of a frugal group of capitalists, reinvesting their capital with obsessive zeal. During the nineteenth century, ostentatious display like that of Louis XIV died out, even in Russia, but frugality was scarcely in fashion. The life of the great aristocrats continued, more comfortable, less violent, but still very expensive. To this was added the wealth of the new capitalist class. Some of the landowners became capitalists, by investing in industry, and some of the capitalists became landowners. There was intermarriage, especially at the edges of the classes. And there was a spread of solid comfort in middle-class lives. Houses still survive that attest to this, as do the hotels where they took their holidays, the churches, the libraries, and the universities that they built — best seen, perhaps, in the Paris of Napoleon III, almost perfectly preserved in its essentials (though the shop fronts have changed). But, even after the rising consumption of

Biltmore House, North Carolina, home of the Vanderbilt family.

the capitalist class has been taken into account, there was still, over the period of a trade cycle, a steady rise in savings to be invested. It was this disposal of the surplus that led to the further rise in profits.

Ricardo's prediction that the profit rate would fall was, generally, refuted by experience. The discovery of new lands and the development of new techniques kept profits up. The rate of realised profits may have fallen, as riskiness decreased in the main industrial centres, but the rate of loss also fell, so the average was kept up.

Money and banking

Credit oiled the wheels of capitalism. The nineteenth century saw many remarkable inventions, but none more remarkable than the growth of the banking system and the establishment and maintenance of the international gold standard.

Banking had begun in Italy and spread to the Low Countries, as goldsmiths lent out their gold on extended credit. Gradually the habit of financing trade by bills was extended and a complex system of discounting and rediscounting trade bills was built up. Local businessmen, extending credit to their customers, found themselves moving into banking. Out of this process of creating trade credit, banking on ordinary commercial lines developed and certain principles of behaviour were evolved. The credit extended by banks fulfilled some of the functions of money. Consequently, the state's regulation of the money supply was imperceptibly merged into a system of controlling the credit system.

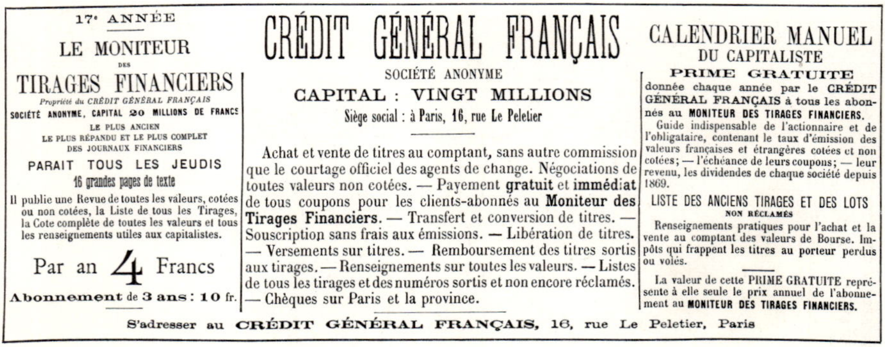

An advertisement of 1880 for the French bank 'Crédit Général Français'.

In England a network of country banks lent locally and financed local trade. Bankers learned to separate their banking operations from their original business as merchants or tradesmen, since a run on the one involved the collapse of the other. Gradually the Bank of England, which was set up to manage the National Debt, became a central bank. In the Bank Charter Act of 1844 its powers were formally determined in a way that set the pattern for financial stability in the capitalist world.

Banks had issued credit, largely by means of notes. The French *assignats* during the revolutionary period and the English inflationary note issue had shown how easy it was for a currency to be debased. Therefore the problem was to curtail bank note issue. The currency was defined as gold. The Bank of England Issue Department was to issue notes only up to its value of bullion (plus £14 million). The Banking Department was to carry on general banking activities. The right of other banks to issue notes was gradually withdrawn.

Unintentionally, by this process, not only was the gold standard established but the banks were driven away from note issue to the development of a full-fledged credit system (based on the cheque), whose extent was determined by the volume of credit extended to the banks by the Bank of England. For, so long as a bank could turn to the Bank of England and get credit (by rediscounting a bill, say), the Bank of England credit was — literally — 'as good as gold', and the bank could go on lending to its customers. But if the Bank of England did not extend credit, or

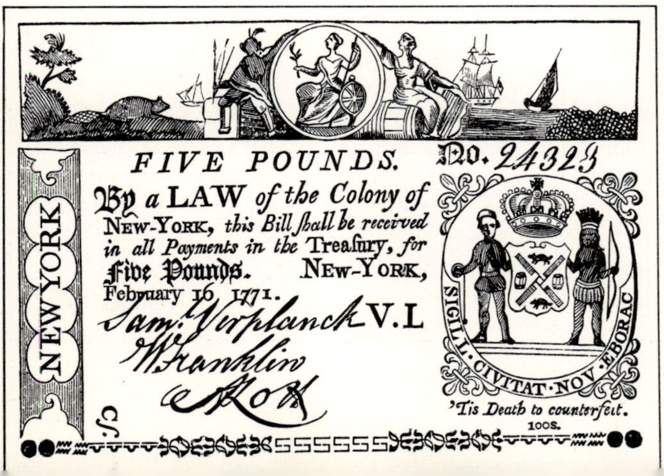

Paper money was an important development in the extension of credit facilities: an American £5 note of 1771.

Prospecting for gold in California, 1848. These miners are using the 'long tom', a wooden sieve for sifting alluvial gold.

did so only at a penal rate of interest, the bank itself could not extend credit to its customers. And when the Bank of England, managing the government debt, found that by selling securities it could contract the basis of credit, it had in its hands the weapon which enabled it to determine the level of domestic economic activity, for trade was based on credit, and contraction and expansion could be determined by the Bank of England as part of the process of managing the banking system.

These procedures were pragmatically adopted during the course of the nineteenth century, to be formalised by Walter Bagehot, the editor of the *Economist* newspaper. His principles were regarded as sound and were universally accepted. As London was the greatest centre of world commerce, the Bank of England was to a significant extent the arbiter of world economic affairs.

The principles on which it decided on expansion and contraction were relatively simple, though it is fair to say that they were interpreted with far less rigidity and far greater subtlety in the nineteenth century than they were to be in the twentieth century. The basis of the national currency was its stock of gold. If gold flowed out, the bank contracted the credit base; if gold flowed in, it expanded it. Gold flowing out was a sign that exports (including capital imports) were falling short of imports (including capital exports). It was a sign that the economy was overheated and was usually accompanied by other 'feverish' signs — full employment, rising prices and wages, and a stock exchange boom. The contraction was put under way in order, directly, to safeguard gold and, indirectly, to keep prices stable and at the same level (allowing for transport costs) throughout the world.

The same recipe, religiously followed, caused chronic deflation in the 1920s. It did not do so in the nineteenth century for three reasons. First, gold was repeatedly discovered — in California, Russia, Australia and South Africa — thus expanding the volume of bullion. Second, throughout the later part of the century, a flow of British capital exports occurred, which continually raised the ability of individual countries to import without worrying about their balance of payments. So long as Britain's gold reserves were maintained by the inflow of newly mined gold, the international credit system was primed by the steady outflow of British capital. Third, the Bank of England was most flexible in its control of the economy and rarely deflated for the sake of deflating. It was an expansionist age.

It was also an age of dramatic bank crashes. Things were less well regulated and so periodically there were financial crashes in which financial institutions went bankrupt. The great crash of 1866 was an example, and in America and the other 'new' continents the credit institutions were, of course, less stable than in Europe. Fortunes were made and lost; fraud, or

'The stoppage of the City of Gasgow Bank', October 17, 1878. Bank crashes were a frequent feature of the second half of the nineteenth century.

near-fraud, was common. It was only towards the century's end that the power of the financiers was to be seen as really sinister; and that was partly because the periods of contraction had become more frequent and more severe. Looking back, the golden age of banking was the middle years of the century.

In Europe, banking developed another side — investment in long-term capital projects — under state auspices in France. This was regarded by many bankers with deep suspicion, but the German bankers made a great success of 'mixed banking', and it was held that their practices were a useful guide to what banking should be like if national development needed to be accelerated. Both played their part in the growth of capitalism.

International trade

The growth of British exports of textiles, coal, iron and other industrial goods was a remarkable fact of the nineteenth century. It was balanced by a growth of British imports of cotton, wool, and, later, food. It was therefore apparently in the British interest (that is, the interest of those who were in the expanding trades) to promote the growth of international trade. The City of London's financial institutions progressively did so, as more and more world trade came to be financed by them; and British ships came to carry an ever growing volume of goods, not only between Britain and the rest of the world but between other countries. Britain also pioneered free trade.

Free trade had been Adam Smith's doctrine, for he looked forward to the international specialisation of factors and the division of labour. This was to replace a doctrine that the aim of policy was to maximise the trade surplus in order to import gold, and that a growing gold reserve was a sign of economic victory. This belief died hard; it never died in continental Europe, and was to become the basis of Gaullist economic policy after 1958.

The English Liberals, following the Scottish Adam Smith, argued the opposite. They wanted world trade to flow free of political interference. The conventional wisdom, then, for years was that trade barriers

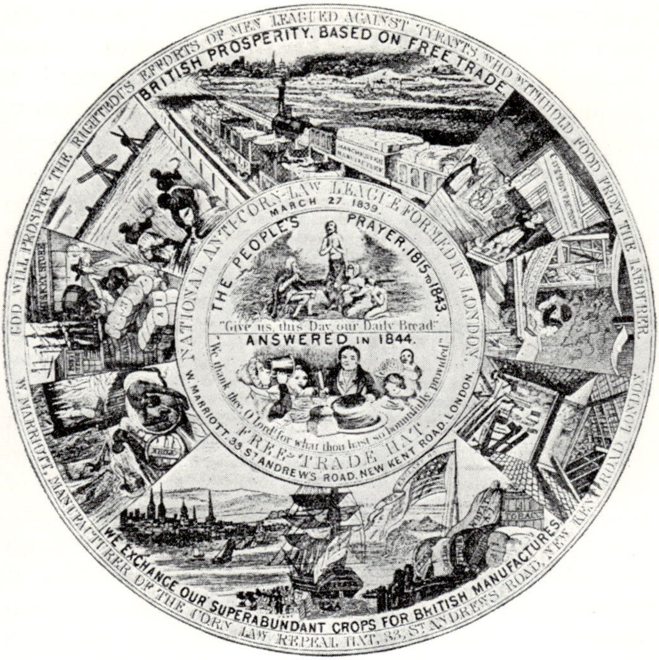

A print inserted inside the 'Free Trade Hat', celebrating the repeal of the Corn Laws.

must be dismantled. First to go were the Navigation Acts, designed to protect British shipping (for strategic reasons) by ensuring that British goods should be carried in British bottoms. Thus came a series of enactments allowing the export of British strategic goods, especially machinery, which could be copied or used by the foreigner to compete with British goods. The major victory, of course, was the virtual abolition of all import duties — first by Huskisson (later run over by a railway train, steam's first sacrificial victim, a political Anna Karenina), and then by Peel's repeal of the Corn Laws in 1846. This was a symbolic triumph. The duties on corn were intended to protect agriculture, so that Peel, son of a cotton manufacturer, was proposing a symbolic as well as a politico-economic act. His proximate cause was the Irish Famine : cheap corn and free trade, it was hoped, would enable the Irish to feed themselves by exporting and importing. In fact the reverse was true. The famine killed the old subsistence economy and brought a monetary, capitalist economy to the whole of Ireland, in which free trade could work.

The next era of British policy was to spread free trade through the world. In the Cobden Treaty with France, in 1860, they substantially reduced French tariffs. Other countries had a prior task: they had to abolish internal tariffs. The American Constitution had been strong on this point — the United States was a great free trade area. Germany became so after the Zollverein of 1834, and the foundation of the empire in 1870. Austria-Hungary progressively did so, and so did Italy after the struggle for unification. The British Empire was, of course, predominantly free trade. Yet America, Germany and Russia, among other countries, did not eliminate all their tariffs. This was for two reasons. Federal governments, especially, found that levies on imports were easy to collect, and often they had few other sources of revenue. The income tax was a newfangled invention; tax systems were extremely primitive. Even if the federal government in America had wished to reduce taxes it would not have been able to do so without bankruptcy. In addition, however, the free trade doctrine was not universally accepted. Bismarck had a group of 'historicist' economists who argued that national economies gave the state a separate economic well-being from that of the bourgeoisie, and that this well-being was closely allied to military power, together with a paternalist concern for the poor by the state. This Hegelian doctrine, expressed in England by T. H. Green, was to give a basis to non-Marxist socialism; but its immediate practical result was the protection of European agriculture by tariffs and the protection of 'infant industries'. The Prussians and the Americans were very concerned to develop native industries — iron, steel, ship-building, chemicals — which they felt they could best do behind tariff walls. There was, of course, an element of double-talk on this position, since powerful lobbies argued in their own self-interest; but there was also an element of truth. Tariffs undoubtedly helped the development of German and American industry, though after 1830 (since American industry was firmly rooted) American growth coincided with falling tariffs.

Thus, it was only in a relative sense that the capitalist world was a free trade world. Three things stand out. There was an extraordinary growth of world trade during the nineteenth century, in manufactured goods and primary products. It was based to a considerable extent on British capital and on sound currencies tied to the gold standard, whose basis was frequently expanded by gold discoveries. Next, the free flow of men and ideas was most impressive. Only backward governments required passports. Marx and other revolutionaries, and businessmen, could land at Dover without meeting an immigration officer; people could come and go to America (if they could afford the fare) without visas or explanations. Thus, to an extent incredible to those who began to travel after 1918, the whole world was open to travel without official intervention. It was this freedom which was the basis of the migration of peoples to the 'new lands'.

Thirdly, capital movements were virtually uncontrolled. British firms set up businesses in foreign countries; foreigners set up firms in Britain. The French built a considerable part of Russian capital equipment; the Germans spread out through the Balkans. Capital went where there was a profit to be made, and people were unashamedly unxenophobic about it. The free flow of capital was later to be identified by Lenin as the basis of imperialist exploitation. It was certainly a basis of imperialism, but in strangely international terms.

The state and the bourgeois

The state was an extension of the household affairs of the monarch, managed with futile extravagance in some countries, at some epochs, and at others (as under the Tudors, or Henri IV) with frugal care. Wars were the king's wars; charity was the king's charity, if it was not the responsibility of the church. The result was that it was impossible to say where the state began or ended; impossible to define its functions, or to rationalise its mechanisms. It operated by corruption (which was not necessarily viewed as corruption, but as an effective way of getting business done).

Looked at through the eyes of a capitalist, the

situation was terrible. The state got in his way with a series of laws and regulations, tax gatherers and licence-issuers, whose original purpose, if any, was lost in the past but whose present function was to derive an income from the exercise of useless powers. First of all, then, the capitalist had to remove archaic laws from the statute book and make government less arbitrary and tyrannical. The removal of internal and external tariffs, the reorganisation of government business, the removal of levies on transport, the repeal of laws against usury — all this represented a clearing of the decks which was to be found in America after the revolutionary war, in France in the revolution and the *Code Napoléon*, and in England after Bentham.

In this cartoon by George Cruikshank, 1829, the usual pyramid is inverted, with industry and commerce at the top and Church and Monarchy at the bottom.

The next step was to reform the machinery of state, to separate public business from the monarchy, and to put public business under some sort of regular supervision. This was achieved by the revolution in France, by the deposition of the Stuarts in Britain (in 1688) and the arrival of the dim-witted, unattractive House of Hanover whose affairs were managed for them, and, gradually, in other countries, either by revolution or a series of gradual changes. Even in Russia, where absolutism and meddling muddle lasted longest, by the time of the 1917 revolution the state was in fact separated from the monarchy.

Having limited and defined the power of the state and given it tolerably responsible government, the bourgeois was (until quite late on) content to leave politics mainly to the aristocracy (except in America, where the republic, once established, flourished without the hereditary principle). But, in Britain, till the 1870s, both Houses of Parliament were dominated by the landed aristocracy, though admittedly the aristocracy received constant transfusions of capitalists' blood and money. Even in France the aristocracy continued to be powerful. By the later part of the nineteenth century, however, the *haute bourgeoisie* was seeking office as well as behind-the-scenes power.

In so doing, there was a rationalisation of the machinery of government (itself a characteristically capitalist metaphor). The establishment of a *carrière ouverte aux talents* was extended to the army and the civil service. Governmental efficiency was encouraged by recruiting able people and paying them adequately so that they did not have to live by bribes. Especially important was the reform of the machinery of justice. Basic to all commerce, whether internal or international, was the enforceable contract — the shift to capitalism could be defined as the shift from status to contract. Thus, a series of clearly drawn contracts, speedily enforceable at law, required a judicial system which was incorrupt, swift and predictable. Two ways were found of providing this: the first was the evolution of the English system of Common Law, its gradual rationalisation, and the reform of the judicial system, which was finally achieved in

England in the 1870s; the other was the Napoleonic code — the systematic rationalisation of a code of law for a modern community — which Napoleon spread throughout continental Europe.

Behind both notions — the one proceeding from precedent to precedent, the other setting things out clearly — was a deep concern for the avoidance of arbitrary decisions and uncertainty. The key to the bourgeois concept of the state was that its powers should be clearly defined and that its acts should be lawful in the full sense. The most successful nineteenth-century nation, Great Britain, had no constitution, but Bagehot, in putting forward the paradox of the unwritten British constitution, argued that the constitution was in fact perfectly clear and lay on a basic foundation of total acceptability to the middle class. The consent of the governed to their mode of government and to the acts of that government was implicit in the whole way in which the community regarded its government.

What, then, did government do? It kept the peace. It saw that justice was enforced. If need be, it went to war to keep the peace or to secure the safety of trade. It 'kept the ring', as the community slogged it out by competition to get a living for itself. There was a residual poor law for the wholly incompetent. Eventually, it was thought then, the state should provide basic education. It laid down standards by which honest trade was conducted. That, in essence, was the Anglo-American view of government. The Prussians regarded their state differently. They did not renounce the principle of absolutism but continued absolutism with efficiency. Nor did they define the powers of the state to exclude powers over the economy. German industrialisation was fostered by the state, as was the creation of the railway system; and the state took a leading part in the creation of social institutions, ranging from education at all levels to social security. The German conception of the state, then, was far broader than the laissez-faire concept prevalent in Britain and America; and it represented a model that was to be widely copied once it was realised that the interests of the high bourgeoisie did not necessarily coincide with the interest of the whole community. For the anti-liberals had always argued that the state existed to protect the poor against the exploitation of the industrialists, and this aristocratic argument, which was (it seemed) accepted and successfully implemented in Prussia, became the basis for a working-class reaction to the limitation of the powers of the state.

The state and the worker

The concept of a working class, of a group of men and women working for wages, owning no property and having a common interest against their employers which could be organised politically, grew comparatively slowly. Political reform in the nineteenth century after the defeat of the Jacobins and Babeuf meant the tidying up and rationalisation of the state and the admission to some degree of power of those with property but no hereditary claim to government. In the elimination of the obstacles to progress, the aristocracy were usually able to protect themselves because almost all their assets, and some of their privileges, could be turned into cash and could be invested. Some of the greatest aristocrats became some of the greatest rentier-capitalists. It is no accident that Salisbury, Rhodesia, is named after Lord Salisbury, the British prime minister at the height of imperialism. The labouring classes, however, were in a different situation. Nobody would compensate them. Three times the Paris mob rose to seize power — in 1789, 1848 and 1871; each time it was humiliatingly defeated. The British workers did not rise, but they organised and agitated: in 1819, at Peterloo, they were defeated; in 1832, over Parliamentary reform, they were cheated; in 1848 their Chartist movement evaporated.

The great mass of the workers was an unorganised, seething group of people seeking a living and enduring such desperate privations that their thoughts could hardly be turned in a political direction. So long as the authorities could control the mob there was civil peace; when the control broke down, the mob got out of hand and the working class suffered even greater privations.

Thus the attitude of the working class as a whole

was essentially apolitical. Those who sought to give it a political role were small groups with many contradictory ideas and policies. Their attitudes to the state differed radically. The defenders of the old order, who became steadily more romantic about the old order as its reality faded into the distant past, saw the state as a paternalist institution, aiding the church to fulfil its role of Christian charity, where each class knew its place and played its preordained part. This was contrasted with the chaotic vulgarity of industrialist society. Ruskin and Pugin, the European Romantics, the great Russians, believed that industrialism was an aberration.

Another group were the anarchists — those who held that state power represented oppression in a new guise, and that by ending state power oppression would end. This was sufficiently close to laissez-faire in practice to make the idea seem more reasonable than it really was, for if the state did nothing except enrich those who corruptly had their fingers in the till, then by abolishing it social life would organise itself along peaceful cooperative lines, uninterrupted by the tyranny of repressive institutions.

The worker is free only as long as he obeys the guns of the police, who protect the interests of the employer: Kupka – 'La Liberté', c. 1905.

Thus the state could be seen not merely as an institution that was tyrannical in itself, but which was actively used by the dominant class to aid the exploitation of the powerless: in Marxist terms, the job of the bourgeois state was to aid the exploitation of the workers by the bourgeoisie, and to protect the bourgeoisie and their goods against the workers. For this reason, the early socialists wanted to overthrow the state rather than gain control of its institutions. By contrast, of course, the bourgeoisie wanted to take over the state and to curtail its powers.

The paternalists did not want to curtail the state's powers, which they saw as an essential bulwark against the remorseless exploitation of the workers by the capitalists. The early Factory Acts were introduced by Tories (that is, aristocrats) and were opposed by the supporters of laissez-faire. In England the reforms of working-class conditions brought about by state intervention were for a long period to be supported by the Tories and opposed by the spokesmen and apologists of the industrialists. Similarly in the United States the protection of the working class was left to agrarian interests who were instinctively populist and opposed to industrialism. Prussia was the supreme example of a paternalist state which both introduced industrialism and protected the workers by developing institutions for their benefit.

The radical groups in the working class gradually came, then, to take the view that the essential task before them was to extend state action, to limit hours of work, regulate conditions of employment, raise wages, and to improve social conditions by ameliorating the Poor Law, extending education, and moving into housing and health provision. The detailed construction of a welfare state began almost by accident, as the pattern established itself of some calamity being revealed (like an epidemic), its causes being investigated, and legislation being passed to remedy the conditions. The legislation was then found inadequate, a scandal would occur because it had not been enforced, and machinery would then be created for its enforcement. Once the bureaucracy had been established it acquired a momentum of its own, and a political lever existed which the working class and the reformers who were on the working class side were able to seize.

Working class activists came to see, then, that they had to achieve some say in state policy and take part in political affairs. The Tories in Britain and the absolutists in Prussia came to see that the top and the bottom were in a position to squeeze the middle. That, in essence, became the strategy. The working-class activists, having wanted to overthrow the state, came to see it as a weapon to be used against the bourgeoisie, and they sought to put back on the political agenda the issues that the exponents of laissez-faire had religiously removed from it. The state thus moved back into the regulation of conditions of work and into the field of social security, from which it had been excluded in the bibles of high capitalism. No conversion is more dramatic on this point than John Stuart Mill's. Having begun as a disciple of his laissez-faire father, James Mill, he ended, on the same philosophical Benthamite utilitarian principles, as a socialist — aligned with John Ruskin.

High capitalism

New lands

The early capital funds for the industrial revolution had been built up by trade, partly on the slave trade. The spread of steam-age capitalism involved more than trade. Permanent settlement took place, and the subjugation of coloured races. The Californian gold boom of the 1850s was followed by the rapid filling-up of the almost unpopulated spaces between the Ohio and the west coast; by 1910 'the Frontier' had come to an end, after three centuries. Australia, Canada, South Africa and New Zealand were other 'empty' lands which found people, partly on the basis of a new agricultural pattern and partly on a new basis of mineral exploitation. As England, and to some extent the rest of Europe, industrialised, so markets were created for North American grain, for meat, for wool, for dairy products — all of which were produced by the new lands. So, too, were minerals — gold, silver, copper, iron ore — which increasingly came from non-European sources.

South Africa was the country where a relatively populated area was colonised by the Europeans, and the Negroes driven northwards or brought into servitude. A similar pattern had prevailed in North America, where the American Indians were victims of genocide. But in tropical countries, some of which were fairly heavily populated, whites settled in only small numbers and colonialism meant trading and military outposts, from which plantation agriculture, under white ownership, spread through the hinterland. From the 1860s onwards the colonisation of Africa began. India had been absorbed by the British crown, which replaced the East India Company after the Mutiny of 1857. The French and the Dutch also conquered empires in Asia. By the end of the nineteenth century large parts of China lay under European semi-suzerainty.

The pattern of the 'new' world, then, was of large, English-speaking and sparsely populated countries,

Imperialism has done more than anything else to bring capitalism into disrepute. **opposite:** Native workers on a Congo plantation mutilated for not producing enough rubber.

like America and Australia; Latin America, settled by Spaniards and Portuguese, sometimes intermarried with Negroes and Indians, organised in nominally independent states but dominated by European capitalists; Africa, divided between Britain, France and Germany, with a European settled southern tip but for the most part consisting of European-dominated black colonies. Russia pushed across Asia to Japan, which remained one of the few states not dominated by Europeans. Only the Ottoman Empire stretched across Asia Minor, open to European penetration but not colonised till after the First World War.

This system of world domination, in which all the leading capitalist states took part — America in Cuba and the Philippines, Italy in North Africa and Ethiopia, Britain in Asia and Africa, France in Asia and Africa, Germany in Africa and the Pacific — was imperialism, and capitalist imperialism was the name given to the period of high capitalism.

What was the basis of imperialism? It was a dispersal of white people, some to settle permanently and to found new nations, like America and Australia, others to rule where on the whole they would not settle, as in India. It was a great dispersal of capital, to open up sources of raw material and food for the capitalist countries. According to the socialists this was because the profit rate was declining in the capitalist countries and the margin for exploitation was greater in the tropical lands. This is doubtful. Great profits were made overseas but they arose from the physically advantageous conditions of production in countries like America, where wages were far higher than in Europe. Apart from mineral exploitation, the profits from tropical crops were not extraordinary and the main area of capital flow was not the tropics but the temperate zones.

Undoubtedly, traders, settlers, missionaries and military expeditions tended to accompany one another, and as the capitalist states became efficiently organised so they began formally to draw boundaries round their colonies. After a time, in the 1880s, the 'unclaimed' lands began to run out and a competitive rivalry between European states began to assert it-

The European powers queue up for a slice of China ('the sick man of Asia'): a German caricature of 1900.

self, between Britain and France and between Britain and Germany, to add to the rivalries that had always existed between the powers with regard to the Ottoman Empire and was coming to exist with regard to the division of control over China. The rivalries of European states, which had persisted since the seventeenth century, underwent a change to rivalry in foreign lands, as the British and the French had struggled over America, Canada and India. The difference this time was the bitterness of the rivalry and the totality of the involvement, to which was added a real fear that industrial advantage would be lost if colonies were lost. Objectively this was absurd : Sweden, Switzerland and (effectively) America flourished without colonies. It was mercantilism revived — if trade were not conducted between the colonial power and its colonies, there would be a loss. This was a view that was reinforced by socialist views of the nature of empire. In truth, it was state rivalry and state competition seeking new forms. It was this rivalry which led, directly, to the First World War ; it was that war which ended capitalism as it had best flourished.

The spread of trade

The building of the Suez Canal by de Lesseps (and its subsequent purchase by Disraeli for the British government) and the building of the Panama Canal indicated how travel times to the Pacific and Indian Oceans were reduced by the steamship ; and indicated as well how fast traffic was growing between the colonies and metropolitan centres. By 1900 over half the food consumed in Great Britain came from overseas, including such perishable commodities as meat, vegetables and dairy products. The development of refrigeration helped to bring food to Britain, as did

'Imperialism is the highest form of capitalism' (Lenin)

European possessions in the Far East in 1914

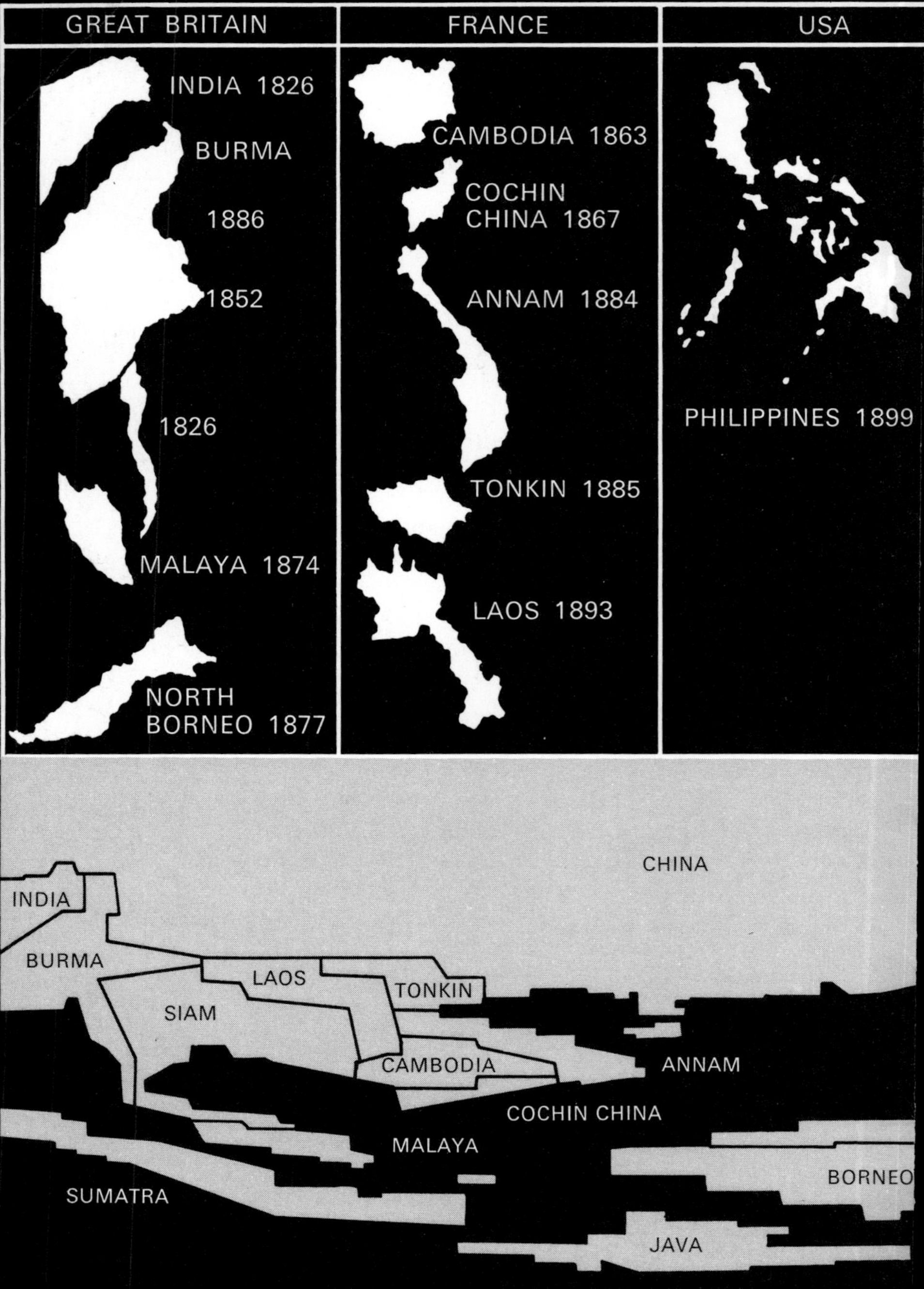

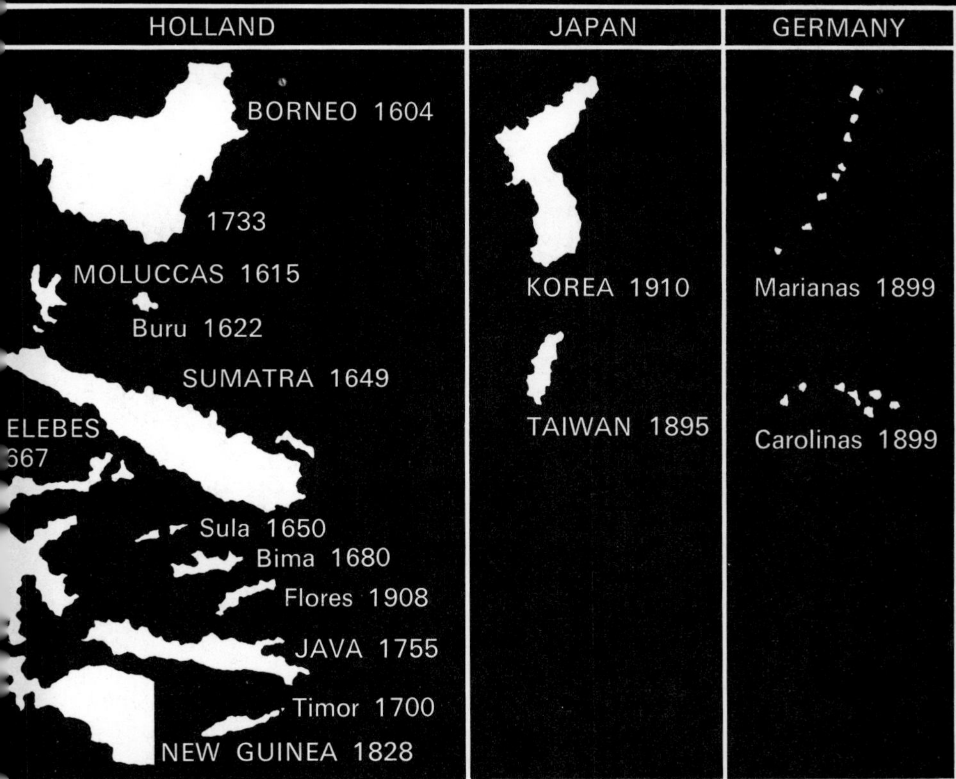
HOLLAND
JAPAN
GERMANY
BORNEO 1604
1733
MOLUCCAS 1615
Buru 1622
SUMATRA 1649
ELEBES
667
Sula 1650
Bima 1680
Flores 1908
JAVA 1755
Timor 1700
NEW GUINEA 1828
KOREA 1910
TAIWAN 1895
Marianas 1899
Carolinas 1899

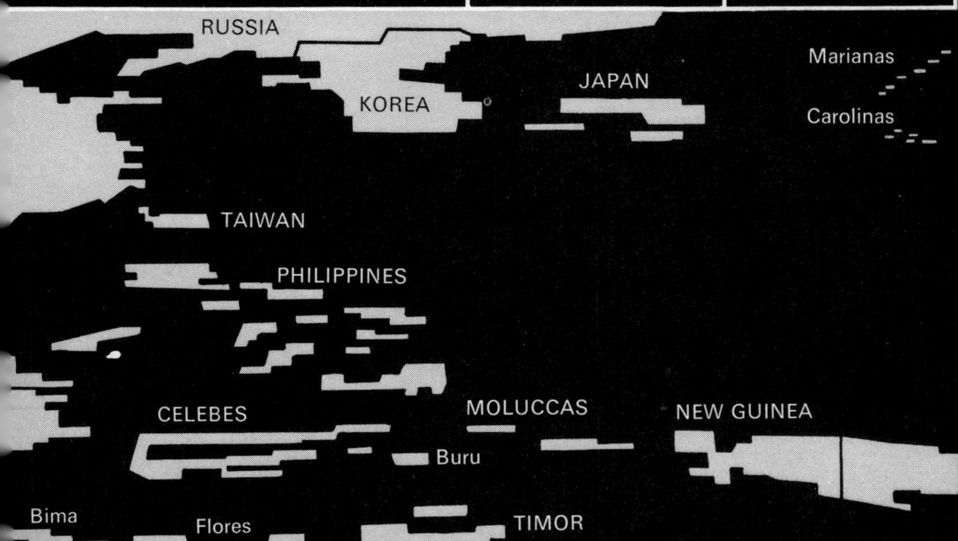
RUSSIA
KOREA
JAPAN
Marianas
Carolinas
TAIWAN
PHILIPPINES
CELEBES
MOLUCCAS
NEW GUINEA
Buru
Bima
Flores
TIMOR

Newly opened territories provided new markets for the manufactures of the capitalist countries; some unlikely products being unloaded in China in 1897.

the increase of speed of ships and trains. But the import of food was only one aspect of an increase in world trade which took many forms. Much of the transporting of goods was a two-way traffic, of raw materials from the colonies to metropolitan centres and a reverse flow of trade in manufactured goods from the metropolitan countries to the colonies. Increasingly, however, the trade pattern shifted to trade between industrial countries. As Germany and America became big manufacturing centres, so their exports went not only to the primary producing areas but also to England, France and Russia. The pattern of trade thus produced was a complex system, involving many-sided transactions. Many of these transactions were financed from London, which became an international financial centre in a new sense. A ship taking Japanese goods to America, American goods to Chile, and Chilean nitrates to Germany, might be chartered from London, insured in London and have its cargoes paid for by bills drawn in London.

Thus the great growth in world trade was accompanied by a complex international financial nexus which extended the role of bankers and financiers to an extent that the classical economists had not been prepared to imagine. The simple operation of the gold standard was now masked by a flow of international monetary transactions in credit terms which were only very loosely connected to the flow of gold and bullion on which, nominally, the gold standard rested. This was a paradox which ultimately led to the collapse of international trade in the 1920s and 1930s, because it was in the later nineteenth century that almost the entire world had moved on to the gold standard, often with serious internal opposition (as in the United States) to the severe monetary discipline that was implied by a gold standard mechanism operated through central banks, which came to dominate the domestic banking system in all the important countries.

It was the drawing of the whole world into a nexus of trade relationships, based upon a common monetary and credit system, that represented the apogee

The European nations saw their colonies as suppliers of cheap raw materials for their own use: a nineteenth-century print showing gutta percha growing in a British colony and being manufactured at home.

The growth of world trade 1750–1960 (in millions of US dollars) and the percentages held by leading trading countries

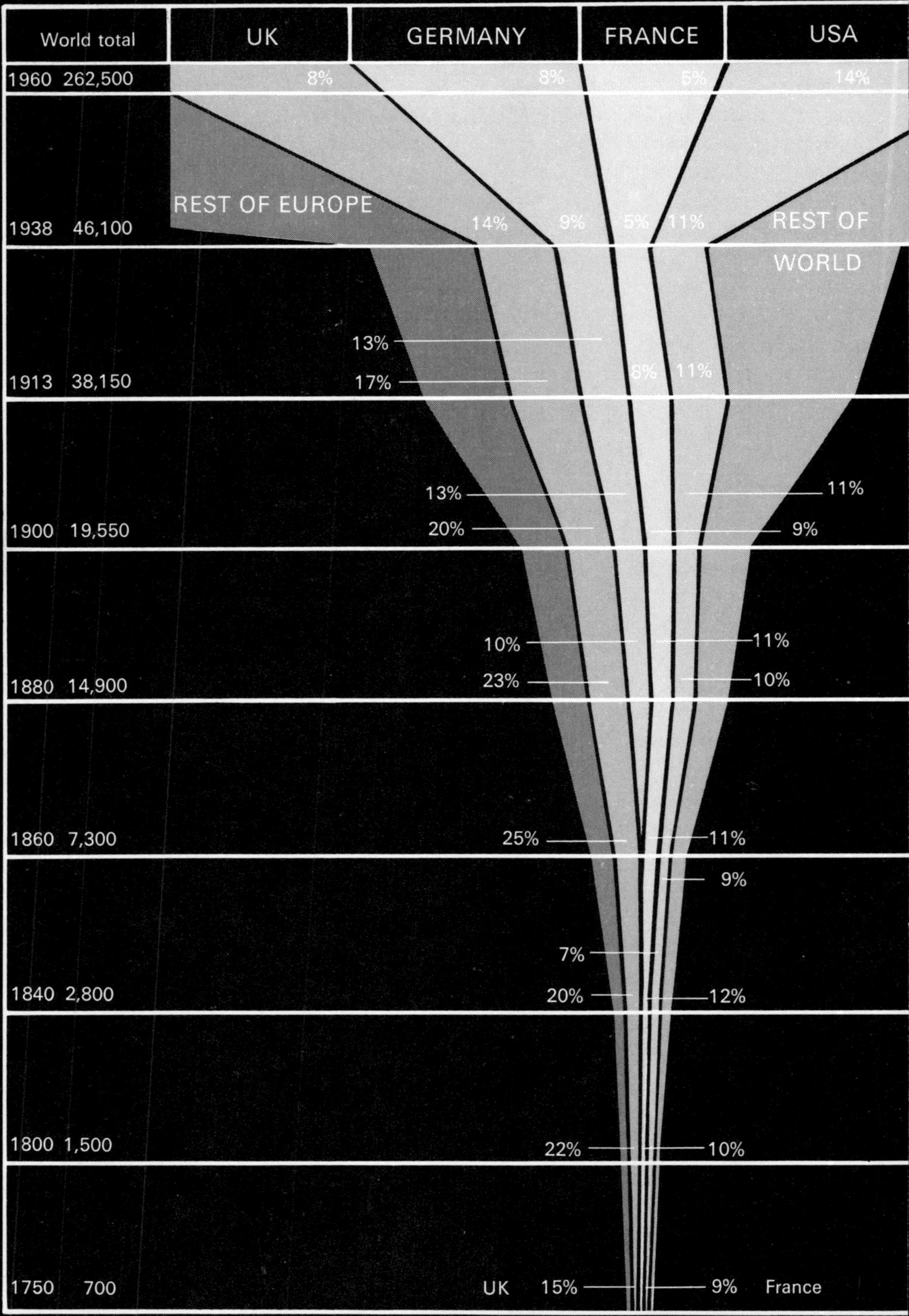

of high capitalism. After the First World War, Russia withdrew from the system and tariff barriers began to go up. With the virtual collapse of the gold standard in 1931, the elaborate structure of free trade and free monetary movements formally ended. Thus within twenty years, from 1911 to 1931, the system passed from its zenith to very nearly the opposite, and the financiers who were the heroes of one era became the villains of the next.

The positive achievements of this trading system were many. The first was internationalism, which allowed a free flow of men, ideas, capital and trade on a scale never before or since equalled. Even Russia, which every true liberal regarded with horror, allowed virtually unlimited travel by foreigners; and the beginnings of capitalist enterprise in Kharkov, Kiev, Moscow and St Petersburg received continuous stimulation from the inflow of capital (especially French capital) which occurred after 1870, as did the development of oil in the Caucasus and coalmining in the Ukraine and elsewhere.

The rise in trade certainly raised living standards in 'European' countries, wherever the white races were to be found. It did not do so generally for the other races, partly because their populations began to increase as fast as their national incomes. Indeed, some of this impact of world trade on developing nations was disgusting, both in terms of colonial violence and oppression (as in the Congo) and in terms of the disintegration of hitherto viable cultures, as in the Pacific and south-east Asia.

Nevertheless, the spread of trade also encouraged the development of local industries, often based on the local extractive or agricultural industry. India, for example, began a substantial cotton manufacturing industry (which was destined to knock out the British cotton industry) and an iron and steel industry. The 'white' colonies of Canada and Australia especially also began to industrialise. In this respect they were copying the European countries that had begun to overtake Britain and inevitably they began to chafe at the notion that their role was eternally to provide raw materials for Europe to manufacture. This chain of reasoning led, via nationalism, to tariffs and trade barriers which, in the case of those colonies which were not self-governed, were impossible to impose, and this became a powerful source of trouble. Irish nationalism, which became the model for nationalism elsewhere, derived a large degree of its impetus from the desire to make Ireland fiscally autonomous of Britain and to erect barriers to shelter infant Irish industry (dismantled after the Union in 1800) against British competition. That this argument was based on a false view of events before and after the Union, and that the Irish standard of living in fact rapidly improved after 1850 as a result of free trade, is irrelevant to the nature of nationalism. Once nationalism had begun to assert itself it was to be a potent force in dissolving free trade.

Nationalism and tariffs got powerful boosts during periods of trade depression, which occurred with increasing severity and were internationally felt as economies were so closely linked by trade. Primary production prices always fell during a slump, with disastrous consequences for primary producing countries, while the effects of the slump were somewhat mitigated in the industrial countries by cheaper food. It was a series of slumps, following the collapse of the international monetary mechanism in the First World War, that effectively ended high capitalism.

The migration of men and ideas

Over twenty million people must have emigrated from Europe to North America, Australasia and southern Africa between 1850 and 1900, and by the outbreak of the First World War in 1914 the total had reached over forty million. This is one of the great migrations in history, probably the largest that has ever occurred. It was made possible by cheap transport, settled government, and a liberal view of population movement which was, in turn, based upon increasing prosperity in the host countries. Outside the United States most immigrants came from Britain and Ireland, except for Latin America, which received Spaniards and Portuguese, and North Africa which the French colonised. The United States received wave after wave — Irish, Germans, Scandinavians, Italians, Poles and Russians (especially Jews) and, finally,

'In the land of promise – Castle Garden', an oilpainting by Charles Ulrich. Castle Garden, the immigrant landing station at New York, saw an enormous influx of European immigrants in the second half of the nineteenth century.

Greeks. All were received in America and, after dreadful suffering and generally vain attempts to maintain their own culture (as the French and Scottish migrants to Canada successfully did) went into the 'melting pot' of American culture.

America and other host countries continually drew highly skilled craftsmen from Europe, as well as engineers and other professional people to help manage the capital investment which was built with European money. But, after the Irish emigration in the famine, most American immigrants were poor and unskilled. The great achievement of American education and industry was that within two generations the majority of these settlers became educated and highly qualified members of the labour force, while their relatives who stayed behind made far less significant advances. It was the rapid improvement in the quality of the labour force which, together with the rise in the capital stock, explains the continued distance between American and European output per head. Initially it had been higher in America because the English-Americans were on the whole highly qualified and were working with plenty of capital in a rich natural environment. As poorly qualified immigrants arrived it became essential to raise their standards quickly; it was for this reason (among others) that America's

The cathedrals of the nineteenth century were its railway stations and exhibition halls, dedicated not to God but to progress and prosperity: the Crystal Palace at the time of the Great Exhibition, 1851.

open education structure developed so fast. In Europe, on the other hand, the education system remained élitist, even where — as in Germany — it had a very strong technical and vocational bias; in Russia and much of southern Europe the education system in rural areas was vestigial.

Nothing changed so much in capitalism as the reduction in these vast migrations after 1920. Even the colonial peoples had participated — Indians had gone to the West Indies and South Africa, Chinese had crossed the Pacific. But for the most part these migrations were confined to European stock. After 1920, Europe became far less significant as a source of new people in the mass, though the flight of Jewish intellectuals from Germany in the 1930s added a new dimension to the cultural injection.

The background, then, of free trade and great migrations of peoples, was based on an outflow from Europe, and an inflow to Europe of food and raw materials. This movement represented the creation of a new world-wide culture, based in Europe but in which America began to play a significant part. After the mid-nineteenth-century scientific achievements of Darwin and Liebig, there were two major developments. Pure science, based mainly at this period in Germany and Britain, developed an irresistible impetus of its own which led to ever more 'break-throughs' — ranging from Clerk Maxwell to Mendel, from Thomson to Pasteur. Science advanced boldly into physics, bacteriology, biology, statistics, and a host of new disciplines. Thus as universities were developed throughout the world — increasingly on the German model of the professor with his group of research students — scientific communication became a central feature of intellectual life, provoking discovery after discovery in an endless series of chain reactions.

Secondly, however, the new scientific knowledge became increasingly applicable to practical affairs. Pasteur, for example, was able to fight phylloxera, which was devastating French vineyards, and silkworm disease, which was affecting the Lyons silk trade, as well as helping brewers achieve a reliable product. The consequences of this for the acceleration of technological advance were notable; by 1900 the basis for modern 'scientific' industry already existed. Artificial fibres, new materials, electricity, the internal combustion engine, modern medicine, new agricultural techniques, were all developed as a result of science, reversing the order of events in which technology had posed intellectual conundrums which the scientists then attempted to resolve.

The impact of these ideas, together with the ideas of Marx, Comte, Mill and Darwin, on the conception of the world held by ordinary people, was profound. Though church-going continued to be a normal acceptable practice in Christian countries (except for the working class, whom the churches left on one side), the intellectual leaders of the capitalist world either overtly or covertly gave it up. When an idea is no longer entertained by serious people, when only politicians and the bourgeoisie hold to it, the position cannot be maintained. The central decline of religious beliefs, and their replacement by a belief in scientific progress, is one more distinguishing feature of high capitalism. This, and the rise of irrational nationalism, created the post-capitalist world.

Bourgeois culture

Despite the formal allegiance of all the white races to Christianity, high capitalism was the first secular and rationalist culture. It was also the first international culture in the sense that (despite the importance of English) no common language dominated the area in which it prevailed. Capitalism was a secular, polycentric culture, its eyes firmly set on this world and its own physical environment. Science was of growing importance in the *weltanschauung* and was related to rationalism, though it was by no means the same thing. (Voltaire was no scientist, and many scientists were exceedingly credulous outside their own fields.)

Within bourgeois culture there were always 'opposition' forces harking back to a non-rational era. The Romantics, the gothic novelists, the Victorian architects (the Houses of Parliament in London are a supreme example), all resented the counting, canting tone of a society revolving round money. But the dominant tone was realism.

It is always dangerous and nearly always wrong to argue from economics and society to the arts; but it does look as though the main trends in art have some relation to the ideas that are prevalent among dominant groups. For one thing, the market determines some at least of what will be produced.

Bourgeois culture was affected by the fact that more people owned more objects than ever before. The world filled up with people, and cities became full of artefacts. Many of these artefacts were manufactured and therefore set a new context within which the arts were carried on. The individual artist was increasingly an untypical member of society, producing objects for which there was no immediate resemblance in the objects that were not defined as art. Artistic objects ceased to have any connection with use and became reproductions — not of another world, of gods and goddesses, but of this world. Bourgeois art had a *motif* of realism even when it dwelt on historical or mythical figures. From portrait painters like Rembrandt through landscape painters like Constable, to pre-Raphaelite and high academy art of the late nineteenth century, there is a steady progression towards a conventional view of reality, seen through optimistic eyes. But then realism took a new turn, towards what came to be called sordid reality: so Goya's preoccupation with dark reality in his scenes of war found successors less in Delacroix's battle scenes than in the painters of the humble, and of poverty and distress, like Courbet and Daumier.

Art took a second turn. Following Turner, the impressionists affirmed that reality was what was seen, not what was conventionally thought to be seen. The impressionists and the post-impressionists carried realism to its logical conclusion of the visual rendering of sense data.

It is unwise to draw parallels between painting and writing, just as it is dangerous to regard either as having any direct relation to social relationships and conditions. But bourgeois culture's most characteristic products were reporting in newspapers, and the novel, rendering an imagined reality. The great

The Great Hall, Euston Station. High capitalism imitated Renaissance architecture in an attempt to secure for itself the cultural authority of what was viewed as the rationalist age par excellence.

mid-nineteenth century novelists — Balzac, Dickens, Flaubert — were all dedicated to intimately detailed descriptions of contemporary scenes. Here again there was a shift to 'sordid reality' — Zola being the supreme example — and to the detailed descriptions of minute by minute, second by second experience, internalised by Proust and Joyce.

Eddies and flows occurred; poetry certainly followed no similar pattern, though the theatre became increasingly naturalistic.

The highlighting of certain features of artistic activity enables some distinctive aspects of art under capitalism to be brought out. Art entered the market place. Artists became a consciously separate group of individual entrepreneurs, not a caste as in other societies, nor a group whose activities were related to other essential activities in society (like magic or religion).

The separation of artists and writers from any but a decorative role led many of them to adopt a critical or moralistic position which was profoundly opposed to some or all of the characteristics of capitalism. Though many of the most successful artists, financially, identified themselves wholly with the successful bourgeoisie, the most highly regarded

The realism of bourgeois art is exemplified by the conventional family portrait: 'The Hatch Family' by the American artist Eastman Johnson, 1871.

In the late nineteenth century bourgeois 'bad taste' was typified by its love of exotica: the 'Palais de l'Electricité' at the Paris Universal Exhibition, 1900.

artists — the writers' writers, the painters' painters — became the major source of articulate criticism of society as it was.

The artist as Job, crying woe on society, was not unknown, but it had never before become a dominant feature of an artist's position in society. As the church sank into disuse, as the working class failed to seize for itself the role that Marx had predicted for it, the main sources of opposition inside capitalism were the artists, writers, historians, social thinkers and 'intellectuals' whose ideas spread the more rapidly for the resentment they aroused.

There was scarcely a major artist whose work was not at one time or another looked upon with derision by some of the well-to-do bourgeoisie. The fact that many of these artists became rich, or (like Proust) came from rich families, or (like Joyce) were supported by the rich, and that the bourgeoisie bought their books and pictures, was forgotten, but the derision was remembered. The capitalist as philistine is a description that has stuck. It is not wholly fair.

La belle époque

The fact that this description of the capitalist as philistine was unjust may be clearly seen from the high point of capitalist society, which achieved a degree of civilisation that bears comparison with Greece of the golden age, or the age of Shakespeare. The last

A ball at the Hôtel de Ville in 1885. Paris was the playground of the late nineteenth-century capitalist world.

years of Napoleon III and the Third Republic up to 1914 — the years which embrace *la belle époque* — represent the consummation of capitalist society.

Great painters, great writers, great musicians, great scientists and great humanists congregated in Paris. They could also be found in Vienna, in London, and (to a lesser extent) in more remote capitals, but Paris was acknowledged to be the capital of civilisation, just as London was the financial capital. To look at Paris of the *belle époque* is to look, therefore, at capitalism's claim to be a great as well as a potent civilisation.

It was, for more people than ever before, a comfortable and safe city. The domestic arts, which now

Paris became the city of Offenbach, the Moulin Rouge and the can-can: a poster for Offenbach's 'opéra féerie', 'Voyage dans la Lune'.

included central heating, lifts, flats, gas and electric lighting, gas cooking, and fairly efficient sewerage and sanitary arrangements, enabled a society to flourish which encouraged good eating, good drinking and good talking. Apart from the submerged tenth — the distressing but almost unseen poor, who were witness to the other side of the story — the Parisians lived well. Comfort and safety, accompanied by improved medical care and a steadily increasing number of technically based amenities, provided the environment where cooking and drinking were raised to the level of art. From the point of view of domestic life, it would be hard to find a more congenial civilisation.

It was one where personal freedom flourished: not only the formal freedom to come and go without let or hindrance (not unimportant for an international capital full of foreigners) but also the personal freedom given to individuals in a big city to choose their own way of life. This freedom from conventional pressures — sexual, moral, social — was the more piquant since it took place in a society where the tight nuclear bourgeois family was at its most characteristic (and probably at its happiest). The texture of the culture was exceptionally rich, as the language shows.

What, then, brought *la belle époque* to an end? Militarism and nationalism, to begin with. The period saw two disastrous wars against Prussia — 1870 and 1914 — in which France suffered losses of men, loss of nerve, and loss of treasure (though it recovered from its economic losses with extraordinary rapidity). Prussia played Sparta's role to the French Athens. Prussian militarism was not only a desperate external enemy; its habits proved contagious and the French found some of their number prepared to copy the enemy.

Next, internal disruption caused by the gross neglect of the poor gave the achievements of French bourgeois society a hypocritical aspect. More and more of the articulate lined themselves up with the dispossessed, having come to regard the structure of the Third Republic as a façade erected by the middle class to expropriate the poor. With the distresses

In New York too the years 1880–1914 saw the heyday of capitalist affluence: a dinner given by Harrison Grey Fiske in 1900/1.

caused by the wars, the opposition developed a socialist ethos based on genuine social protest; and as the Soviet Union came into existence a model existed — based in part on the old and close links between French culture and Russia and partly on Marxism — opposed to the Third Republic.

Third, there was the rise of illiberal absolutism, partly in response and opposition to socialism. It showed itself in various ways: a credulous and nasty Catholicism of a Jansenist type, antisemitism (as revealed by the Dreyfus Case), admiration for the inviolability of the army (again in the Dreyfus Case and during the First World War) and, above all, a loss of confidence in political and bourgeois institutions.

At this stage — and what is cause and what is effect it would be dangerous to say — art turned to abstraction and writing moved into a phase either of committed Marxism or of dissociated consciousness. The Third Republic lived on after 1918 as a consciously hollow shell — its frock-coated politicians openly despised, its bourgeois comfort rejected, the bourgeoisie loathing the opposition and the opposition loathing the bourgeoisie. When Prussia struck again, in 1940, the bourgeoisie turned openly fascist and the intellectuals and some of the workers joined the resistance as communists. The compact of enjoyment, the treaty of comfort, known as the *belle époque*, which had allowed bohemianism to flourish, broke into open class war.

The spa enjoyed a vogue among high society at the turn of the century. This photograph of 1905 shows sports week at Baden-Baden.

The great boom

The period from the end of the American Civil War to the First World War marked the high point of high capitalism. It had its problems — problems which were to become almost insuperable from 1915 onwards — but the problems were masked by the achievement of what, in retrospect, seems to have been the greatest secular boom in history, surpassed only by the boom of 1947 to 1967. Both booms covered much the same general area of the world; both had similar causes and similar effects.

The bourgeois comfort of Paris, Vienna, New York, London and the other great capitalist cities rested upon the advance of technology, revealed in an increasing flow of improved goods selling at lower prices. These lower prices, which occurred mainly in a period known as the Great Depression, were due partly to lower costs and partly to depressed profit levels. It was the response to lower profit levels which accelerated the tendencies towards large monopolistic and cartelised organisations, seeking to keep the profit rate up, and which also provided much of the impetus for the export of capital from the industrialised countries, because higher profit rates were hoped for (but rarely attained) in the underdeveloped regions of the world.

The fall in costs was due in part to improved communications and to a dramatic fall in transport costs. That brought down the cost of food. But changes in

The motor car heralded a new age of mass-production: a poster for the motor show at Olympia, 1905.

manufacturing techniques were also important. Veblen discussed 'the technology of physics and chemistry' because, for the first time, science led technology, rather than technological advance providing problems for science to solve. The widening of the market, caused by falling transport costs and rising incomes, enabled mass production techniques to be adopted. These mass production techniques involved massive investments in capital-intensive equipment, which in turn required big companies to operate them, with sophisticated and complex managerial systems. It was in this field especially that the Germans and above all the Americans were able to overtake the British, to become the industrial giants of the early twentieth century.

The developments on which the mass production age rested were, first, cheap steel. Bessemer, Siemens and Gilchrist were examples of scientifically trained

The first magneto assembly line tried out by Fords at Park Plant in 1913.

technologists who between them reduced the cost of steel by a factor of ten or more. The rise of a cheap steel industry led to the growth of a machine-tool industry, which could manufacture steel into machinery, on a large scale, by the use of interchangeable parts, and which was capable of a high degree of precision. The machine-tool industry, from the time of Eli Whitney on, became an American speciality, owing its origin to the need to produce many thousands of rifles for the conquest of the west and for the American Civil War.

Henry Ford, who began to turn out motor cars in large numbers just before the First World War, used cheap steel and machine tools on an assembly line. But the assembly line was first used for meat packing in Cincinnati, about eighty years earlier. By Henry Ford's time it was a procedure that had been widely adopted in American industry.

To operate the new processes electricity was a great help, since it eliminated the complex arrangements for belts, pulleys and shafts that were entailed by steam power. Here again, America and to a lesser extent Germany dominated the world.

The effect of all these changes was dramatic. It reduced costs of production in all metal-using industries where bulk markets could be brought into existence. It reduced costs in all industries that used machinery. It shifted the balance of world economic power away from Britain towards America and Germany, and also began to shift the weight of industrialism away from textiles and coal to steel and electricity. And it boosted the engineering industry, and the importance of science, technology, and the highly skilled workers.

Applied to transport, for example, the speed and cheapness of the railway and the steamship were profoundly affected. Frozen meat was transported across America and across the Atlantic in refrigerated vans and ships.

Farming in the United States began to be mechanised on a large scale. Elsewhere, especially in Britain, the fall in farm prices and the rise in incomes produced a notable shift towards horticulture and animal products. Agriculture, too, began to see the application of natural science on a wider basis than ever before.

The great boom, then, was a mass production boom, based on steel and electricity, with consequences for almost all other industries, including agriculture. The invention of the internal combustion engine, the arrival of the motor car, and the growth of the oil industry, completed the boom. Modern consumer capitalism had arrived.

The rise of the consumer society

The joint stock company and the international cartel represented the capitalist entrepreneur's response to the challenge of falling costs, falling prices, falling profits and the great growth of markets.

The spread of markets, and the growing prosperity of the lower-middle and upper-working classes all over the capitalist world, formed the basis of the great boom (which, paradoxically, because of falling profit rates was labelled the great depression). This host of small but increasingly prosperous consumers represented for the ambitious entrepreneur a market with several characteristics that were notably different from those which had gone before.

One characteristic was that market forces were mediated through a complex retailing and wholesaling structure, in which department stores, chain stores and mail-order houses began to play a significant part. Thus the retail structure itself began to determine the manufacturers' production pattern. The manufacturer, interested in steady runs, began to integrate forward into the retail market. An interesting example was the English brewers' purchase of public houses in the 1880s and 1890s, where survival as a brewer depended upon control of a retail market whose extent was limited by the number of drink licences extended by magistrates.

Manufacturers were interested in long runs of their products, which meant standardisation, which meant a development of advertising to create a steady market for the standardised product. The retailer, far from being a man who consulted his customers' tastes and then ordered for them, was a man who tried to convince his customers that the manufacturer's products

The Paris department store 'Au Bon Marché' in 1880, shortly after its opening.

were what they wanted. Consumers' tastes and needs were now manipulated and even invented. This represented a striking break with the system about which Adam Smith had written and about which the neo-classical economists were writing, in which 'consumer sovereignty' dominated the productive process and directed the pattern of output.

The third shift in the market was towards manufactures. The rise in consumers' incomes and the fall in agricultural prices meant that proportionately less was spent on food, liberating more and more purchasing power for manufactured goods of all kinds. The improvement in domestic comfort — better houses, better lit and better heated — meant that more time was spent at home, especially as the hours of labour were falling rapidly. Better education led to more sophisticated tastes. As a result there was a shift towards more books, more newspapers, more furniture, more equipment of all kinds.

More was spent on travel, on holidays, and on entertainment. The market was therefore established for wide-scale provision of service trades of all kinds, and the extension of retailing was one indication of this.

Society, as it existed in the industrialised countries in 1914, had in it the very rich – a small but obvious class, with huge houses, special trains, racing stables, steam yachts — and the very poor, a large but unseen class; but the prevailing tone was set by the middle and upper working classes. They had servants (a skivvy in an artisan's house, several of them in a middle-class house); they had a growing quantity of manufactured goods; and they had political weight. It was they who lived a life that was recognisably modern — their hours of work were short, they had Sunday and possibly part of Saturday off, their children went on to a secondary school, they read daily newspapers and took regular holidays, and many of them practised birth control. The 'emancipation' of women had begun. The world of H. G. Wells, of the silent movies, of the early Gide had arrived.

The emphasis on consumption rather than on work carried with it a profound cultural and economic transformation. The function of capitalism had been to accumulate the means of production by keeping the standards of consumption down while an increasing part of the national income went into the construction of capital goods. Mass production meant that the trickle of factory-made consumer goods now became a torrent. Food was processed and manufactured; household goods and clothes — virtually every commodity — was enmeshed in the mass production process. This meant that an ever wider range of industry was dependent for its existence on constantly expanding markets, which enabled costs to fall as the economies of scale were reaped: the consumer market had to be created. The direct end of capitalism now became one of creating enough consumption to absorb the ever growing production.

The increasing severity of cycles of economic activity meant that in some years there was a serious slacken-

The development of advertising pointed to the contradiction within capitalism of workers producing consumer goods which they themselves could not afford to buy. **above:** A caricature of a Pears' soap advertisement.

ing of activity and acute unemployment. Thus the paradox of crises of under-consumption, of poverty in the midst of plenty, became apparent for the first time. For if it were true that technology, by mass production, could steadily produce goods at an ever decreasing cost, then it must follow that it was technologically possible to produce enough goods to give to the working class, and the 'submerged tenth', a more middle-class standard of living. The rise in the real incomes of the artisans in steady employment (a rapidly increasing class) created expectations in the less prosperous groups which could not then be fulfilled. The immediate power of mass production to solve all production problems was exaggerated, though its long-run potentiality was not.

Allied to the submerged industrial proletariat, also excluded from these benefits, were the remnants of domestic labour and the agricultural workers and small peasants. These people thought of themselves as the victims of the mass production system, and mass-production came to carry with it the revolutionary consequence that it both raised expectations as to its technological power, and provoked fear and distrust, since it seemed to impoverish those who were outside its scope; periodically, too, those who worked in its factories were thrown out of work.

A consumer society, then, laid emphasis on a steady, rising level of demand, manipulated by manufacturers and mediated through retailers. It generated exaggerated fears and hopes. And it raised the question: who was to consume its products and who was to control its power to create abundance? At the same time it created organisational forms and managerial skills which threatened the logic of free competitive capitalism. How could the doctrine of consumer sovereignty survive advertising, which treated the consumer as a victim? How could free trade coincide with a desire for orderly, steady markets? How could poverty be reconciled with the means of achieving plenty? And, ultimately, mass production, which virtually began with the manufacturing of rifles for the first modern war — the American Civil War — created the means of mass slaughter, in the European war of 1914–18, the war which signalled the end of high capitalism.

'Muscular strength, physical endurance and staying power – Cadbury's Pure Cocoa is recommended by the Medical Profession as an agreeable article of healthy diet for all classes.'

The great monopolists

Individual businessmen were the dominant form of capitalist enterprise throughout the nineteenth century, but the railway joint stock companies formed the model on which mass manufacturing industry came to be based. In the relationship there were stockholders, usually a transient body of people buying and selling on the stock exchange; directors, increasingly a managerial body; workers; and customers. But the early joint stock companies were usually dominated by one man or by a family who had a large block of shares. It was men of this type who created great commercial monopolies, or combined with other industrialists to form combines and cartels. They came to have increasing political power, and were to be increasingly identified by socialists and social populists as the source of evil in capitalism, trampling on workers and consumers alike in order to amass great fortunes.

The early monopolies and cartels arose out of severe cut-throat competition. Vanderbilt, Jay Gould and Jim Fisk, American railway kings in the area between Chicago and New York, engaged in a ferocious war to reduce freight costs. In 1877 they joined in a pool, raised rates and shared revenues. Cartels developed in electrical goods, in meat-packing, in tobacco and in other trades. The pool, which could be broken, was succeeded by the trust, which had legal force. Standard Oil was the major example of a trust; and it enriched the ruthless Rockefeller family, who have been expiating their guilt ever since by philanthropy and by seeking and even occasionally filling public office. Oil was a rapidly developing industry, first for kerosine for lamps and cooking and then with gasoline for cars. Profits were enormous; and the power to create a monopoly, based on difficulties of freight and limited access to the oil fields, was enormous.

So rapid was the growth of trusts and so ruthless their business methods that the United States Congress passed the Sherman Anti-Trust law (1890) which prohibited combinations in restraint of trade. The law was virtually a dead letter but it signified the apprehension which monopolists caused even in legislatures where they had great influence. The Act was followed by more trusts, and a growth of mergers: Carnegie's US Steel Corporation, Duke's American Tobacco Com-

Rockefeller (king of gold and oil): 'Sir, don't think that it is only the Orientals that are idolaters; we are too, and our idol is money.' A French cartoon, c. 1910.

pany, and many other great combines, often in the new and growing industries, where large amounts of capital were required and where big plants operated under conditions of decreasing costs. The big financiers aided the process of amalgamation, especially when mergers were involved. By 1904, it has been estimated, 40 per cent of the American manufacturing capital was controlled by mergers and trusts with a capital value of $1 million or more. The world of 'big business' had arrived, with one big company, or at most two or three, dominating an industry, setting prices and determining the pattern of consumption.

In Germany the cartel was the dominant arrangement in big business. The coal cartel, formed in 1893 into the Rhenish-Westphalian Coal Syndicate, ended competition in the German coal industry by setting prices and regulating production. It did so behind a tariff barrier.

The *Stahlwerksverband* (steel union) did the same for steel; another cartel limited competition among potash producers; and a further series of cartels led to IG Farben's dominance of the chemical industry, and AEG and Siemen's control of the electrical goods industry. These giant concerns, like that of the arms manufacturer Krupp, had big banking interests behind them.

Monopolies and mergers were less prominent in Britain than in America and Germany for two reasons: Britain stuck remorselessly to free trade, so that there was always the possibility of foreign competition, and Britain was relatively backward in the developing industries like electricity and steel since so much of its capital was invested in the older staple industries which were still extremely competitive. Nevertheless, Lever Brothers in soap, the Salt Union and the railway companies provided examples of big businesses which exercised near-monopoly powers.

The monopolies were intended to safeguard profits, which they did — when they were successful. They were also intended to stabilise output and safeguard regularity of employment; the evidence is that they did not do so — if anything they were a de-stabilising influence. What they did do was to substitute for the power of market competition by price, the rivalry of product development. If one firm controlled the railway industry, there was an incentive to develop motor cars as the alternative means of transport, rather than to build a second railway. The great companies which were dominant in America and Germany by 1900 became major sources of technical innovation, in rivalry with each other, especially in third markets. Technical innovation depended to a great extent on the corporation.

This was inevitable. The very size of the enterprises associated with heavy technological investment required massive organisational forms. They employed thousands of workers and commanded thousands of dollars of capital. To control these enterprises complex managerial skills were necessary.

The development of the giant corporation, increasingly international in scope, raised acute problems of control. Most of the shareholders were virtually anonymous; and the men who directed the enterprises — Krupp, Rockefeller, Lever, Vanderbilt — were powerful in a way that no capitalist had been before.

Some of them — Lever for example — controlled tracts of Africa, where they virtually ran the government. Others — Krupp was the supreme instance —

A late nineteenth-century American cartoon showing Monopoly and Labour in unequal combat.

made the arms for the growing military forces of the world. Inevitably, the expansion of capitalism through imperialism was interpreted as a thinly veiled attempt on their part to use their power in the state to enrich themselves by conquest. Inevitably too they were accused of fomenting war, or fear of war, to enlarge the markets for their own wares. The old aristocracy was involved with the big businessmen in every way it could find — investment, marriage, assimilation. It even overcame its antisemitism if the profits were large enough. It was not known in detail but well enough known in general that monopoly capitalism represented a coalition between those with political authority and the rich industrialists. Thus the new technology erected industrial empires which yielded a vast output of consumer products. But it raised acute problems of control. Lenin and others saw in monopoly capitalism the coalition of business interests, faced with falling profit rates, to exploit the colonies and to repress the proletariat, whose growing demands for some of the proceeds of capitalism threatened the industrialists' existence. The picture may have been highly coloured, even wrong, but it had some verisimilitude.

The trades unions

As business coalesced, the workers formed their own groups. Faced with monopoly buyers of labour, it seemed inevitable that the sellers of labour would also seek to become monopolists of what they had to sell.

The early trade unions were British, and were limited in objectives, weakly organised and primarily political. Robert Owen's Grand National Consolidated Trades Union of the 1820s is an example of an unfocused union, with no staying power and chiefly concerned with constitutional reform. In the 1850s a number of craft unions were formed in Britain — like the Amalgamated Society of Engineers — which negotiated wages and conditions for skilled workers and provided social security benefits for their members. They were in many respects analogous to professional bodies. They were small, relatively rich, and well organised, but the mass of individual workers were outside their scope.

In France some of the workers were loosely organised in political revolutionary groups but there was no parallel development of trades unions in the British sense. In America the early unions were broken in the 1830s, as the Owen union in Britain had been; and in the 1850s a craft union movement spread which was parallel to that in Britain.

Unions, then, which had been illegal in the early days of capitalism, were now tolerated, but they confined themselves to the skilled and more prosperous workers.

In the 1880s and 1890s the trades union movement spread to the ordinary industrial workers. In 1867 the British Trades Union Congress was formed; in 1869 the American Knights of Labor. Both marked a step forward in class consciousness among the working class and both were followed by a marked rise in union activity.

This rise was followed by severe industrial unrest, and in America especially by employers' attempts to break the unions. In America the Knights of Labor fell apart (as an organisation they were too big, with objectives which were vague and apocalyptic) and in 1886 the American Federation of Labor was formed, on an almost exclusively craft basis. The craft unions in Britain in the 1850s and 1860s, and the American Federation of Labor, accepted the framework of capitalist society and negotiated on a limited basis for small (but genuine) improvements in conditions.

The new industrial unions in Britain in the 1890s marked a transition to a completely different basis of trade unionism. First, they encompassed the unskilled workers; secondly, they provided few, if any, social security benefits for their members; thirdly, they were militant; and fourthly, they believed in the formation of a trade union political movement, which was rapidly to become an explicitly working-class socialist party. In Britain this movement took place against a background of growing political and legal freedom for trade union activity. In France (after the legalisation of trades unions in 1888), the movement was weakly organised and more explicitly socialist and syndicalist than the British movement. Elsewhere, as in Germany, the socialist commitment was strongly

MAKING COMMON CAUSE

"When it comes to putting down Socialism we have to join hands"

Democracy and Republicanism (both bearing the label 'Capitalism' on the collar) unite to fight Socialism: a late nineteenth-century American cartoon.

Marxist, but when after 1890 the German trade union movement was legalised, its weight moved the socialist movement to the right and Bernstein's revisionism (far more akin to Fabian socialism than to Marxism) became the official doctrine. The German unions, in contrast to the British, were big and were earlier politically influential, though in a context where state absolutism limited the potentialities of their power.

Thus, the growth of capitalist enterprise called forth organisations of working people. These organisations spread their activities from negotiation with the employers to outright opposition to the system in which they were all involved. Members of trades unions were still a minority of the working class.

Rural workers and peasants were unorganised, as were women (especially domestic servants, who formed up to one-tenth of the urban labour force in western Europe) and the casual transient members of the working class amongst whom poverty was endemic. The trade union movement, therefore, was not a movement of the really poor but of those who were above the poverty level, and it was strongest among those groups who came nearest to the lower middle class in incomes, aspirations and outlook. Their concerns were with the detailed negotiation of conditions affecting their work and with wider political participation for the working class. The industrial leaders tended to be politically cautious, even conservative, because their main activities were negotiations with employers; to gain one cent or a few pennies an hour meant a great deal for their members and provided the justification for the continuation of the union. The political leaders, on the other hand, tended to be secularists, rationalists, conservatives — serious, puritanical figures, with a small following and a 'scientific' creed and outlook. They were part of the growing army of the intelligentsia, those rootless, fanatical 'half-educated' (according to the bourgeois classical canons of the time) men who sought the overthrow of society.

In America the trades unions were small and their influence among the working class negligible: the American dream still held sway, and the continuous influx of immigrants enabled employers to dismiss 'trouble-makers'. In Britain the trades unions were influential industrially, but the socialist movement was relatively unimportant. In Europe the socialist movement was more significant, the unions less so. Socialism in Europe built upon the revolutionary tradition of 1789, and had a hard intellectual edge which led it frequently into schism, purges and disorder. In Britain the unions and the politicians came together, forming a pragmatic social democratic party to represent the working class — inside the capitalist order. Thus socialism had two faces: one seeking amelioration, the other seeking revolution. Which was which the socialists themselves hardly knew; the capitalists detested and feared them both.

The bourgeois state

Gladstone stripped down the state to its bare essentials. It kept order, kept a minimum army and navy for foreign affairs to be conducted, and it had a residual poor law. It would have been hard to discover anything else that the government did. By 1914 the state's functions were greater than ever before and its role more significant than it had been since Tudor times. What caused this transformation ?

First, growing technological development in war *matériel* meant that armies and navies were considerably more expensive than they had been, and on top of this growing international rivalry led to an increase in the requisite armed forces. The American Civil War and the Franco-Prussian War both marked significant advances in fire power. As a result, by 1914 the cost of armaments was substantial: rifles, machine guns, steel battleships, big guns and the very earliest aircraft were all bought in substantial quantities. France, Germany and Russia had large conscript armies, while Britain and America had small professional forces. Thus the revolution in steel manufacture and in machine tools raised the cost of war preparations to unprecedented heights.

A change of an equally profound character occurred in the Poor Law — the invention of social security. Most countries had spent a little on education in the nineteenth century; by 1900 compulsory primary education was universal in all industrialised states (it had been earliest in Germany and the northern United States and latest in England). Secondary and higher (especially technical) education was beginning to spread and significantly to affect the quality of the labour force and the rate of technical progress. Education thus formed a significant part of public outlays.

Bismarck started in Prussia a system of compulsory health, old age and unemployment insurance, making that country — despite its authoritarian political character — a greatly envied nation by the militant working classes elsewhere. Britain followed in 1911 with the Lloyd George schemes for sickness and unemployment insurance, and old age pensions were introduced in 1908. Thus the stage was set in the industrialised world for a significant step forward in social security.

The causes of this were manifold. Society was more prosperous and the claim of the poor to share in the prosperity was becoming increasingly hard to resist. Growing cyclical unemployment threw groups of workers out of employment through no fault of their own. The decline of the extended family left the old socially independent and therefore needing independent financial support. Medical advances raised the cost of medical care. Above all, the Germans had never accepted the basic tenets of laissez-faire and had never thought that the growth of social vigour and economic welfare depended upon the virtual absence of social services for the poor. On the contrary, the Prussians took the view that it was the state's duty to protect its people and to encourage their physical and mental development by whatever means came to hand, and those means certainly included the use of a highly developed state bureaucratic apparatus.

A third aspect of the modern state was a growing intervention in industry and commerce. In Germany many of the railways were publicly owned. In America there were laws against monopolies and trusts. Workmen's safety acts, factory acts, acts against adulteration of food: a whole host of laws giving powers of intervention in the working of the economy were passed. And they were much more ably enforced, as there had also been over the last decade or so a notable advance in the efficiency with which the state was conducted. There were technically qualified inspectors in many fields and the officials in

One product of the new concern for social welfare was housing estates for workers, like the Shaftesbury Park Estate shown here in 1874. Estates like these were to become slums in the twentieth century.

Britain and Germany were impartial and incorrupt. Taxes were collected, even in France and Russia, and the growing use of the typewriter and the telephone made rapid communication possible. Thus the bourgeois state by 1914 was bigger and more efficient than would once have been dreamed possible.

This professional bureaucracy also faced in most advanced countries a government of semi-professional politicians, no longer wholly drawn from the aristocracy and relying now upon a mass male electorate. The extension of the franchise had been achieved in the last half of the nineteenth century in America, France, Britain, Prussia, Italy and — to some extent — in Russia. This meant that the character of politics had changed. Politicians depended for office on the response of a mass electorate, many influenced by the press, and consisting partly of workers organised in trades unions and in Europe already to some degree committed to socialist ideas. It followed, therefore, that there was pressure to define politics as the use of the new bureaucratic machine to satisfy the demands of the poor. This led to a concept of radical imperialism — a concept which powerfully influenced Germany and Britain and — to a lesser extent — France and America.

The radical politicians supported imperialism for a mixture of motives. One was patriotism. Another was a desire for cheap raw materials to reduce costs and prices. A third was to find places for the poor to emigrate to. But imperialism, combined with social reform at home, became immensely popular. It led to the growth of the state's power by increasing expenditure both on armaments and on welfare services. The poor, far from being internationalist, were excessively patriotic. It was their patriotism as well as their manifest needs for state help that provided the basis for the modern state.

The Edwardian compromise

When Edward VII succeeded his mother, Queen Victoria, to the British throne in 1901, the classic phase of capitalism was drawing to a close. Britain, which had been the centre of capitalism, was already declining. It had missed the greater part of the new

A German interpretation of British involvement in the Boer War; among the bones John Bulldog is guarding are the Kimberley Mines. 'Bark as much as you like, — none of you is biting!'

technological revolution which was transforming America and Germany, mainly because its inadequate education and training system did not provide the necessary technologists to initiate change, and also because there was a severe lack of capital prepared to risk new ventures. Edwardian capitalists wanted something safe, preferably abroad, to put their money in.

Britain was engaged in an imperialist war in South Africa, against the Boers, in order to gain control of the Rand gold mines. It nearly lost the war. The Germans and the French were also engaged in imperialist expansion, which nearly led to war in 1911 over Agadir. The Russians and the Austrians were near to conflict over the Balkans. The Russians were defeated by the Japanese in a naval war in 1904. The atmosphere was becoming increasingly warlike.

The doctrine of free trade and laissez-faire was on the retreat. Germany and America were building tariff walls. Government intervention in commerce and industry was growing. Industrial competition in international trade increasingly took the form of competition aided and abetted by government support. The most clear example of this was in subsidies to shipping, and in colonial rivalry, but in many fields of activity it was possible to perceive a rivalry of governments as well as a commercial rivalry between countries.

The 'social question' came increasingly before the public. Poverty was diagnosed, by Charles Booth in London, by Rowntree in York, and by professional

Free trade was a big issue at the 1906 General Election: a poster issued by the Liberal Party supporting free trade.

social workers elsewhere. The Webbs, and Bismarck, proposed machinery for its treatment. Unemployment was a social disease which defied treatment, but it was apparent that capitalism unaided would not be able to cope with it. The condition of women was a matter of intense social conflict, and in all countries women were seeking education, civil rights and the vote. Thus the Liberal government of 1906 in Britain faced serious social problems, which it attempted to deal with by social insurance legislation and other social legislation for health and welfare. It faced and failed to deal with the women's suffrage issue. It faced and failed to deal with increasing industrial strife, with strikes and with lockouts.

And, on top of all this, nationalism was becoming a central question of the age. The unification of Italy had become a great liberal issue in the mid-nineteenth century. The unification of Germany under the empire had been widely welcomed. In the early twentieth century the Irish, the Hungarians, the Czechs, the Serbians, the Poles and many other nationalities began an agitation for national self-government which raised new issues. Liberal-minded people supported movements for independence. But the nationalists themselves were backward-looking, supporters of tariffs, anti-industrialism, sometimes revivers of dead languages (like Irish), and militaristic.

The Edwardians tried to keep afloat on this sea of troubles, which all the time was becoming increasingly stormy. They increased taxes to pay for more arms and for more social security but did not seek to reduce the great wealth of the rich. They tried to give home rule to Ireland, and they did give it to the Boers in South Africa, but they did not assuage nationalist passions, which were increased as victory grew nearer. In Germany, nationalism became increasingly identified with the notion of military grandeur. In France, French nationalists and Catholic reactionaries looked forward to a military revenge for the humiliations of 1870 and 1871. Even America, under Teddy Roosevelt, became an imperialist, nationalist power, as de Tocqueville had predicted it would. The age of democracy became the age of nationalism.

As George Dangerfield argued — brilliantly — the glittering façade of Edwardian society suddenly cracked. The European aristocracy had married the American plutocracy, and it kept up a hideously vulgar and expensive life. The King of England, the Emperor of Germany, the Czar of Russia and the other royalties, were all related to each other. The appearance of a unified, stable, international society, presiding over an economy with a rapidly advancing technology, was maintained. But nationalism threatened the empires; democracy threatened the aristocracy; unemployment and strikes threatened the economy; and socialism challenged the capitalist assumptions on which it all rested.

After King Edward's death the new reign saw a period which was manifestly drifting into war, and in which Irish nationalism, women's suffrage and the rise of the Labour Party showed, almost conclusively, that the attempt by the Liberals to modify the laissez-faire capitalist system by extending the suffrage, giving limited self-government to national minorities, and extending the social security system, was doomed to failure. There was an air of increasing violence and social tension that showed itself in social relations and in art. Freud, with his hypothesis of the unconscious, Trotter on the herd instinct, Graham Wallas on human nature in politics, the early D. H. Lawrence, Guillaume Apollinaire, the Cubists, all showed an increasing distaste for the superficial rationality, the simple-minded notions of cause and effect, which were the hallmarks of Liberalism. It seemed that the world was full of dark forces which the rational, liberal-minded businessman was ill-equipped to understand and wholly unable to appreciate. Of these forces, it was to be seen, the most devastating was nationalism, and the war to which it gave rise.

The First World War

The First World War brought capitalism almost to its knees. It broke out, it seemed, almost by accident, and once having begun it was waged with a cold ferocity which confirmed all the fears of dark forces in man's soul and showed up liberal internationalism as a sham. An even greater surprise was that almost all the socialist movements proved as nationalistic as the bourgeois political parties.

The war disrupted international trade. It bankrupted Britain, hitherto the prime source of capital for many countries. It led to currency inflations. It led to massive government intervention in industry and trade, culminating in food rationing, import restrictions and government control of whole industries for war production purposes. It thus achieved, in four short years, many of the measures for which socialists had been arguing for years.

The destruction of property was small. But the loss of life was enormous and has never been accurately assessed. It was sufficient to weaken France for a generation.

The chief effects of the war, however, were political. Four empires collapsed — Germany, Austria-Hungary, Russia and the Ottoman Empire. Two major industrial powers — France and Great Britain — were gravely weakened. Three of the empires were succeeded by many weak nationalist states — Czechoslovakia, Poland, Iraq, Transjordan, Hungary, Estonia, Latvia and Lithuania were only some. This gave rise to grave political instability and led to further nationalist demands which were eventually to dissolve the British and French empires.

In Russia the régime collapsed in 1917. The decision of the liberal successor to continue the war with Germany led to a further collapse of the régime in November 1917 (on the unreformed calendar, October) and to a successful *coup d'état* by Lenin and the Bolsheviks, who declared peace with Germany. A major Civil War followed, which the Bolsheviks won. This led to the expropriation of most private capital, including foreign capital. In one of the major states of the world capitalism had been overthrown.

In Germany the collapse of 1918 was followed by a revolution, and a situation developed in Berlin in which it seemed that in Prussia, too, the communists might take over power. A counter-revolutionary rising succeeded in preventing this, and a social-democratic republican régime was established. This republic, called the Weimar republic after the town where it was set up, began life under the twin handicaps of a military defeat which was attributed to internal subversion, and a severe food shortage which was due to a continuation of the naval blockade of German ports after the armistice was signed. For fifteen years the republic staggered from crisis to crisis, unable to pay its debts, surviving a massive inflation, a further foreign occupation and massive unemployment, until it was finally brought down by a majority vote for Hitler and the fascists in 1933.

In France the Third Republic looked at times as though it would be overthrown, but it continued, though gravely weakened internally by the rise of left wing and right wing parties who rejected (for opposite reasons) its ethical and political basis.

The United States saw two opposite consequences of the war. The first was that it became manifestly the richest and most powerful country in the world. Power moved from the City of London and the continental bourses to Wall Street. The boost to demand offered by the war resulted in a great burst of investment which continued through the 1920s, especially in the new technological industries, the automobile, engineering goods of all kinds, chemicals and synthetic fibres. But, at the same time that Wall Street became the financial capital of the world, the United States recoiled from the political involvement which was entailed by world power. The American Senate refused to ratify the Treaty of Versailles and the United States effectively withdrew into isolation.

The consequences of this withdrawal were catastrophic. Laissez-faire capitalism had flourished during a period which was predominantly peaceful. The peace had been kept by the balance of power and the effective naval dominance of Britain. Economic growth had been ensured by the gold standard, which

The United States emerged as the most powerful nation: a German cartoon of 1922 showing Uncle Sam holding the scalp of the Old World.

in turn was maintained by the continuous outflow of capital from Britain and other European financial centres to support new ventures overseas. America, the centre of financial and political power, refused both these roles. In this situation, France and Britain behaved with growing foolishness.

The First World War revealed a political bankruptcy which amounted to an intellectual weakness of an extraordinary kind. It seemed as though capitalism must have grown old, tired and timid in the face of new ideas. The continent which had produced Napoleon and Wellington now threw up a group of generals of limited intelligence and sympathy, whose one idea was a static war in which millions of conscripts were slaughtered. The continent which had produced Pitt and Talleyrand, Disraeli and Bismarck, Cavour and Metternich, now produced people like the drunken Asquith who, having blundered into war, could not end it, and when it finally petered out, like Lloyd George had no idea how to settle it. Faced with financial problems, unemployment and serious social unrest, all that the businessmen could think about was Bolshevism.

The new position of Wall Street as financial centre of the capitalist world was demonstrated during the slump: a French cartoon of 1933 showing Britain, Germany, Italy and France looking angrily on as the dollar falls at the fence.

The feeble wits of the governing classes had become manifest before the war and could in no way be attributed to the loss of able young men during the war. It was an unwillingness to accept a world which had changed that was to render them impotent before the world financial problems and the rise of authoritarian régimes.

The First World War then, apart from the immense suffering that it caused, led to a complete recasting of international politics. It accelerated technological change especially as it affected the automobile, aviation, wireless, and chemicals. It led to social upheavals that ranged from a new political and social status for women in the west, to a Bolshevik dictatorship in Russia. It accelerated the nationalist movements throughout the world — after seven centuries, the Irish, on Britain's doorstep, became virtually independent. Above all, the First World War completely upset the monetary apple-cart. In face of the consequences of this upset, socialism became the number one question of the day.

The disruption of world trade

How was the monetary apple-cart upset? First, by government intervention in a growing number of money and commodity markets throughout the advanced countries, which meant that the network of communications that had been established informally over the years was broken or disturbed, with consequences that revealed themselves in shortages, sudden price adjustments and all the signs of a severely maladjusted system.

Next, by a flow of gold and currency reserves from the European combatants — especially Britain — to America and the neutral countries, the basis for the gold standard was destroyed. European currencies were separated from their gold basis and (as had been seen in Britain after the Napoleonic wars) the return to gold was certain to involve serious deflation.

The exporting trades of Europe were diverted mainly to home production, and consequently many overseas countries received a boost to their own industrial development which ended forever the neat reciprocal flow of manufactured goods and raw materials; future trade patterns would require to be far more complex. Thus not only did Britain especially lose markets, it also gained competitors in the old staple trades on which its prosperity had been based.

In addition to the loss of currency and reserves, the European countries became saddled with external and internal debts. The external debts, owed chiefly to the United States, were intended to be repaid by Germany, but Germany's economy, disrupted by the war and particularly by the loss of large parts of its coalfields owing to territorial adjustments, was unable to meet the cost of reparations to the victors. In addition, the victors, facing unemployment, were unwilling to receive the goods with which Germany would have had to finance its reparations (which would have meant a continuing German surplus on current account). To replace the outflow of British and (to a lesser extent) French capital, there was a chronic intergovernmental indebtedness, which required each country to earn a surplus on its balance of payments. This could only have been financed by a massive outflow of capital from the United States, which would in turn have required a massive United States trade deficit based

German banknotes being pulped during the inflation.

upon a large and steadily growing propensity to import. This, of course, was impossible both because the United States had no tradition of importing and also because the United States tariff situation was such as severely to discourage imports.

Thus there was a fundamental imbalance in world trade patterns which it was impossible to cure until the Marshall programme of 1948.

In addition to the problem of external debt, each country in the war was faced with the problem of managing the public finances. Germany financed only 6 per cent of its war effort by taxation, the rest having been raised by borrowing — and the price level rose by 250 per cent between 1914 and 1918. The situation was as grave in France and almost as bad in Britain. Britain, determined to return to Ricardian orthodoxy, attempted to service its National Debt through a budgetary surplus, causing the chronic deflation of the interwar years. In Germany, the borrowing by the government which had financed the war was continued in the peace to service the debt. As a result, there was a continuous printing of bank notes which led to a continuous and accelerating fall in the value of money.

Thus, internally, a major industrial nation experienced the inflation that had been experienced in France during the revolution. The fear of inflation haunted Europe. It caused a continuous fall in the value of the mark on world markets, leading to still further international troubles but above all to the expropriation of virtually all fixed-interest saving and the ruin of the older members of the middle class. At the same time businessmen were converted into 'profiteers', people who lived on profits from inflation rather than on the profits of production. The detestation of the militant working class and the dispossessed intellectual middle class for the capitalist system was enhanced by this experience, especially when, in the deflationary situation which followed the return of monetary stability, the horrors of unemployment succeeded the miseries of inflation. The humiliation of Germany, until 1917 a nation full of patriotic imperialist fervour, was very genuine, and formed a basis for the nazi appeal for national regeneration by clearing out profiteers — whom they identified as Jews.

In the midst of this mess, the rapid advances in technology continued, partly accentuated by the growing prosperity of large groups of Americans, who created a market for consumers' electrical goods, for automobiles, and for the light engineering products of the rapidly growing mass production industries. Not only was Europe badly suited to adopt this technology, since its chaotic monetary and fiscal system prevented the steady development of rising demand for new products, but Europe's heavy investment in older industries left it with an apparently chronic problem of overcapacity.

Britain suffered most because its industrial capital was the oldest. British output records in many trades — coal, ship-building, textiles — were achieved in 1913. Thereafter there was a decline, which was directly due to the growing difficulties of international trade but which was also indirectly due to Britain's growing obsolescence in capital equipment.

Thus, the radical effect of the war was the disruption of the international pattern of trade and of the monetary mechanism. But there were two other major consequences. The first was the growing difficulty of emigration from Europe to America: the American immigration laws stopped the great tidal waves of emigrants from crossing the Atlantic and there was no longer a European safety valve. There were still big population movements but they were the result of persecution, like that of the Greeks in Smyrna, or the Armenians, and the victims moved to neighbouring European countries.

This growing illiberalism was connected with an extension of governmental powers which coincided, however, with an increasing fragility of constitutional institutions. Russia, Turkey, Germany, Austria, and the successor states, all suffered civil war or near civil war after their change of régimes. In some cases there were military *coups d'état*. Even Italy, for so long the hope of liberals, suffered the indignity of becoming the first Fascist country, in 1922, and Mussolini, himself a direct product of the social distress caused by the war, became the archetypal European

Inflationary conditions in Germany led to severe hardship: troops guarding grocers' shops against looters in Berlin.

dictator. The liberal era of capitalism was, it seemed, over, wrecked in those trenches which its third-rate generals had caused to be dug.

The communist revolution

The Russian secret police were right after all: the tiny clique of Marxist revolutionaries, riven by schism, reading manifestos to each other in the Parc des Martyrs in bourgeois Geneva, were the most dangerous men of the century. Lenin had been one of the most *difficile* men imaginable, continually splitting the communist movement (which was tiny), by metaphysical distinctions that only de Valera (in another context) could rival. He had continually declared his minority a majority, until he had convinced people it was.

Whether or not he was sent to Russia in 1917 by the Germans, his arrival in St Petersburg was the most devastating blow Imperial Russia ever received. Within six months he had successfully engineered a *coup d'état*. A year later and Trotsky had organised the Red Army. In the midst of intolerable suffering, the Bolsheviks clung to power and extended the power of the state throughout Russia. Despite foreign intervention, the White Army of Czarists was defeated; the Poles were thrown back from much of the Ukraine; and the communist party established itself throughout Russia, except for the Baltic states which were taken from it by the Treaty.

Lenin was helped by Kerensky's lack of ruthlessness. Kerensky refused to sue for peace, so that he lost the war and could not cope with the consequences. Had he denounced the allies and gone over to the German side, not only would the Germans have won the war but Russia would have been saved for liberalism. Ke-

A Soviet propaganda train, showing peasants and workers attacking capitalists.

rensky also refused to accept the seizure of land by the peasants. He wanted to compensate the landlords. All he succeeded in doing was getting most of them shot, except for those who escaped to drive taxis in Paris.

Lenin ended the war and shot the landlords. It was scarcely surprising that the rest of Europe trembled in its shoes. The spectacle of the successors of Cromwell and the French revolution weeping for the death of the Romanov-Hanoverian Czar, Nicholas II, was as ironical as it was indicative of the loss of nerve that the capitalists had suffered.

above: Europe was terrified by the spectre of Bolshevism: a German poster of 1918 with the slogan 'Bolshevism brings war, unemployment and starvation'.

Lenin broke all the rules. Communism did not come to power where industrial monopoly-capitalism had failed but in the country where it would next have been tried. (The closing of Russia to capitalist investment was a potent force in reducing the scope for profitable outlays of savings and so accentuated the deflationary conditions in the west.) The revolution was carried through against the opposition of the peasants, and Lenin mobilised the industrial workers during the period of war communism to fight them — an enemy identified in Marxist theory as the bourgeoisie. By 1921 the economy had virtually collapsed and the workers were fed only by the forcible seizure of food from the countryside. Then anarchy and distress added to the horror with which communism was regarded in western Europe. The failure of communist revolutions in Berlin and in Hungary ensured that a worldwide revolutionary movement could not centre on the industrialised countries; if communism were to succeed, it had to survive in Russia.

A German cartoon of 1931: Stalin is bringing capitalism in through the back door with the words 'Come along, you can come back in, but for the time being only by the tradesmen's entrance'.

In order to do that the economy was revived by passing, in seven years (1921 to 1928), through a period which resembled in some respects a crash course in the revival of capitalism. The New Economic Policy restored the market, which brought food into the towns and revived the small capitalist enterprises which had been multiplying rapidly in the early years of the twentieth century. The big enterprises were nationalised but even they were sometimes leased to capitalists. Foreign capital was briefly encouraged. The production levels of 1913 were never restored until after 1950 but the economy revived enough to give some hope of rapid economic growth.

The communist challenge

Comparative growth rates of industrial output for the United States and the Soviet Union

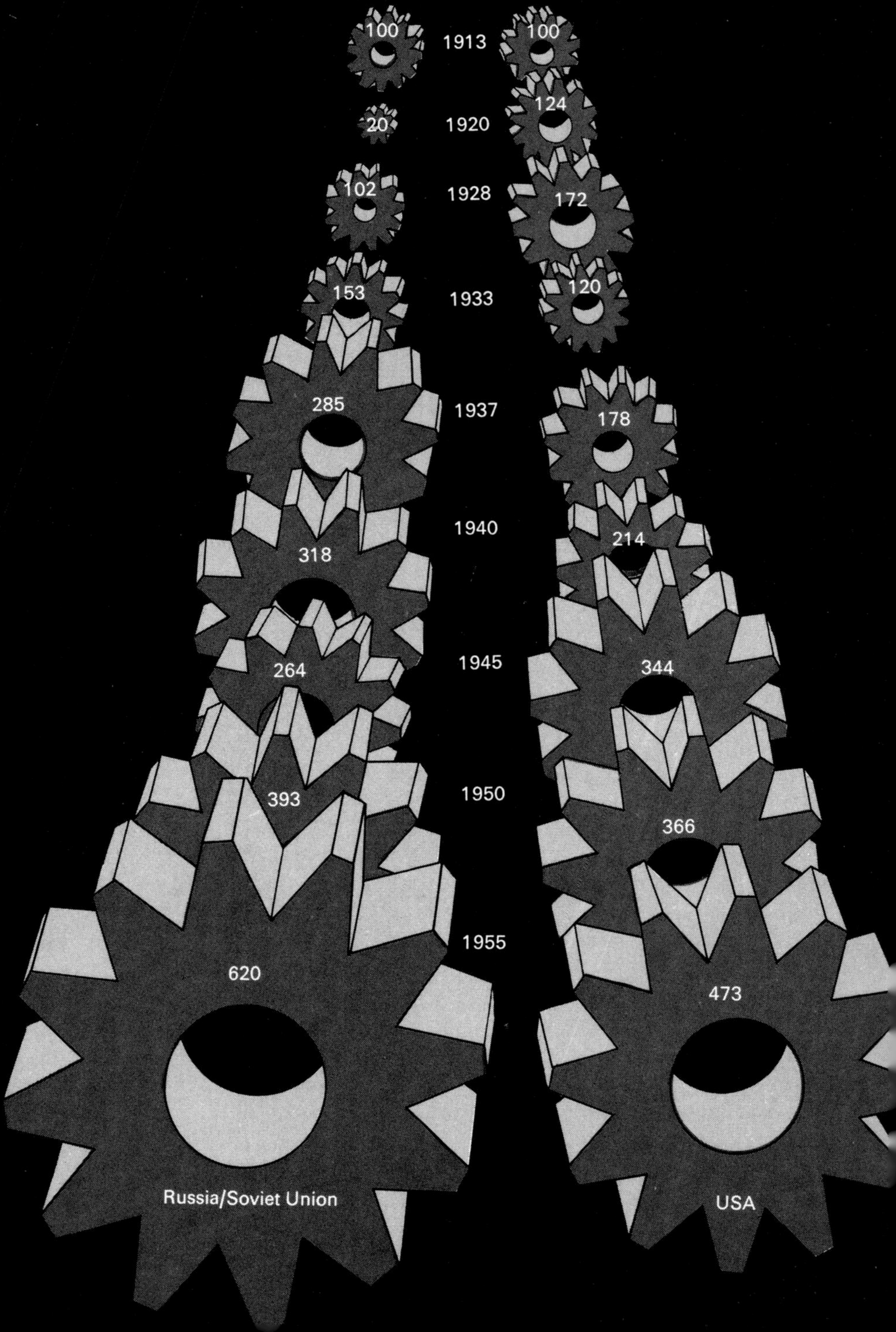

The communist party took control of the state and ruthlessly destroyed its opponents. It used this power, first to make a great leap forward in education, at all levels, and secondly to introduce electric power on a wide scale. The decision was also taken to plan the economy centrally. After Lenin's death and the struggle for the succession, Stalin seized power and in 1928 inaugurated the era of five-year plans, which accomplished the industrialisation of the Soviet Union by ruthlessly driving down consumption standards and using the surplus to build industrial plant. At the same time a proletariat was created by collectivising the farms and driving many of the peasants off the land. Agricultural output fell catastrophically; a terrible famine raged in the Ukraine and millions of people were executed or sent to labour camps, but industrialisation was successfully carried through.

The significance of this experience was that communism survived. Despite the abundant evidence of starvation, suffering and persecution, when western capitalism was going through its worst years, in the 1930s, socialists and communists were able to point to the Soviet Union and say that a post-capitalist society was functioning. Capitalism was no longer the 'natural' form of society: it was one of two forms. The suffering was either ignored (Russia was more than ever a society where secrecy was universal), or explained as the parallel to the sufferings of the industrial revolution — only that in 1840 it had been the English working class who had been the victims, while in Russia it was the working class who were benefiting and the 'useless' classes who were suffering. And, certainly, if that comparison was regarded as valid, the Soviet emphasis on education and social welfare represented a positive advance in civilisation.

When widespread unemployment chronically afflicted Britain, America and Germany, Russia apparently had none. Against this economic suffering, and the manifest benefits of communism, was political liberty a serious counterweight? It would be wrong to present this view too starkly: the majority of people in the capitalist countries remained anticommunist and, except occasionally, antisocialist. But capitalism was now on trial as it had not been before.

On the defensive

Unemployment

Britain, where industrialism had begun, suffered continuous unemployment between 1920 and 1940; its statistical measurement is disputed but it hardly fell below 12 per cent of the labour force and on occasion probably rose to something like 25 per cent. In Germany, as well as the inflation, unemployment again never fell below 11 per cent and on occasion rose to over 40 per cent of the labour force. According to Svennilson, about one-quarter of the potential European labour force was out of work. In 1932 and 1933 one-third of the labour force in America was unemployed.

Unemployment represented a chronic incapacity of the capitalist economy to use its productive resources to achieve high consumption, because those terrible years of unemployment were accompanied by dreadful poverty. One-third of the British working-class families were clinically undernourished. Agricultural incomes throughout the world collapsed and there was widespread underemployment and suffering in the great primary producing countries like Canada and Australia, and in the peasant economies of Europe.

What caused the unemployment ? Why was it not remedied? The most obvious cause in Britain, and to some extent in Germany, was the decline of the old staple industries like coal, shipbuilding, cotton textiles — the first industries to be revolutionised by capitalist technology. This unemployment tended to be heavily localised in the coalfields — especially, in Britain, in Northumberland and Durham, south Wales, Scotland and Lancashire.

But, more generally, as profits fell and confidence in the future sank ever lower, the level of investment was far below what it could potentially have been. Thus unemployment was severe in the investment goods trades — steel and engineering especially — with consequent effects on the demand for raw materials, particularly coal.

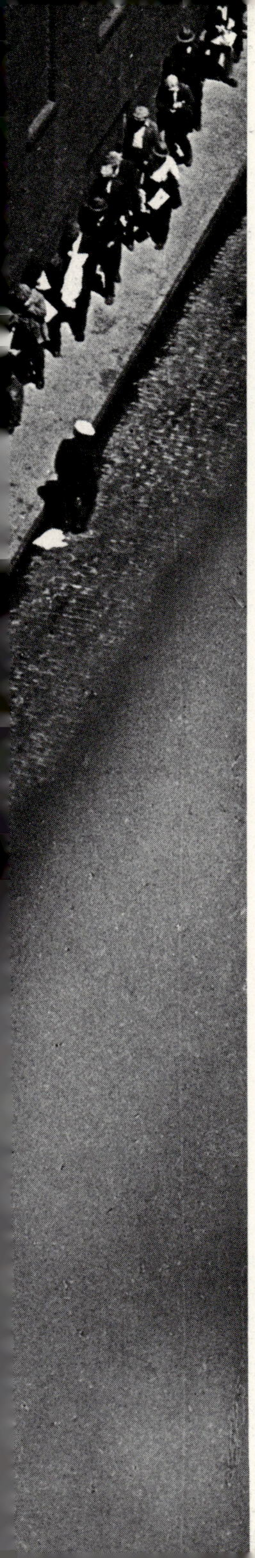

International trade also declined. As incomes were stagnant in the industrialised countries, the demand for food and raw materials was also stagnant. Productivity in agriculture rose, therefore more agricultural output came on to a stagnant market, to face collapsing prices. As farm incomes fell, the demand for industrial imports fell. The process of declining incomes became cumulative and was accentuated by growing efforts to protect home markets by tariffs and quotas. Therefore all industries selling on the international markets found themselves in jeopardy, and the big exporting nations faced special problems with their exporting trades. Shipping also suffered severely.

The general decline in investment goods trades, exporting industries and older industries, cut consumption by impoverishing the workers in those trades. This had a multiplier effect on consumption, and consumption goods trades, especially those catering for the working-class market, also declined. Whole regions fell into a state of chronic depression — the Ruhr, Pittsburgh, the Belgian coalfield — and were, as it were, cut off from the rest of society. These working-class communities were isolated from the main financial and governmental centres of capitalism, where the severity of the disaster was not fully appreciated.

The actions of governments made things worse rather than better. The attempts to pay off debts and to balance budgets caused chronic deflation throughout capitalism. The peace settlement was followed by rapid disarmament, which removed one possible boost to the steel and engineering trades. Some countries had social security systems and there, despite government wishes, public expenditure rose as payments were made to the unemployed. Had these payments not been made there would have been revolution. America had no system of benefits and at the time of Roosevelt's inauguration, in 1933, the breakdown of society was narrowly averted. In Germany the Nazi electoral victory in 1933 was followed by the end of democratic republican government. In 1926, Britain in the Gen-

The breadline in New York, 1932.

Hunger riots in London, 1932.

eral Strike appeared to be threatened by revolution, and in 1931 the normal party system collapsed.

The predominant economic theory was weakened by the migration of many of the best intellects into socialism: they had given up the analysis of capitalism as a useless task, since it was obviously in its death throes. Neo-classical economic theory taught that world trade could only revive with a return to the gold standard and orthodox budgetary measures, which meant (in 1925) a devastating blow to the export trade in Britain by an upward revaluation of the pound sterling, and in 1931 a blow to the poor by cutting social security benefits. Orthodox theory taught that unemployment was caused because the price of labour was too high: if wages were reduced, then employment would increase, just as the sales of apples would increase if their prices fell. The implausibility of this argument was that it rested upon the hypothesis that unemployment could never in fact occur. Say's law taught that supply created its own demand, so that if the supply potential of the economy increased, the demand would automatically rise to the required level, provided that the price system was allowed to work. The fallacy was that if wages fell, consumption also fell, thus creating more unemployment. The Swedish economists, and later Keynes, taught that the only way out of the vicious cycle of unemployment and poverty was to increase demand by raising government spending and reducing taxation, and flying in the face of all orthodox reasoning about state finances, which said that the state had (like any businessman) to balance its books.

The most fantastic thing about the situation was the intellectual stranglehold that incorrect and implausible reasoning had on businessmen and politicians. Even socialist economists and politicians could not refute the orthodox arguments, and when they achieved office, as they did in Germany, or in Britain in 1923 and 1929, their behaviour was exactly the same as their most diehard opponents on the right. This failure to understand was allied to an almost fatalistic acceptance of bankers' reasoning. Montagu Norman, the neurotic and ambivalent Governor of the Bank of England, behaved as though his sardonic silence in the midst of economic collapse betokened a deep understanding of mysterious processes which would lead to even worse happenings if the banks were touched. In fact he knew nothing, even during his relatively sane interludes.

Why were people so gullible? Partly they were frightened of communism, of violence, and of financial panics like that in Germany which had brought about the collapse of the currency. Partly, large sections of the population were benefiting from the growth of new industries and the fall in the price level. If a man had a job or a secure private income, the fall in prices and the steady technological improvement in the goods that he bought raised his standard of living continually and agreeably. Partly because it seemed that — Keynes and the Swedes apart — the solutions to the crisis of capitalism were apocalyptic. In Russia there was communism. In Italy and Germany, Mussolini and Hitler offered new dictatorships, and they found imitators in every country, from Mosley in England to Salazar in Portugal. Only Franklin D. Roosevelt seemed able to burst out of the strait-jacket with the New Deal, and even that, it seems, was based on an incorrect understanding of orthodox reasoning. Capitalist political institutions and capitalist thinkers were quite unable to save capitalism. Only war did that.

New industries

Technological development continued its headlong progress. The 1920s, in contrast to Europe, saw a boom in the United States. The car, electrical goods like refrigerators, cookers, radios, improved housing, aircraft, telephones — the whole complex world of durable consumer goods — all became part of everyday life for ordinary middle-class Americans. It was at this period that virtually universal secondary education was introduced; that the film industry became the great entertainment industry; that mass production of high quality cheap clothes became common; that the five and ten cent retail store became a model for retailing; and that America — as the movies revealed it — became the model for the desirable way of life. Even communist Russia set itself the task of catching up with America, and by America it increasingly meant Hollywood.

The biggest 'new' industry in America in the 1920s was housebuilding, and all the other construction work associated with it. The boom occurred in Britain in the 1930s. This movement into housing affected the whole nature of American and British civilisation, which became increasingly suburban and home-centred. Taken with the emancipation of women, birth-control, and nuclear families, the pattern of life perceptibly changed, now radically differing from the way of life of the poor (and, in America, especially the Negroes)

Hollywood was to become part of the capitalist image: an American movie palace in 1931.

with their extended kinship system, high birth-rate, and densely urban style of life. Allied with this shift to the suburbs was the extra mobility generated by the automobile. By 1928 four million cars and lorries were being produced annually in the United States. This meant a boom for the automobile firms and their suppliers, a boom in road construction and a boom in oil supplies. The internal combustion engine formed the basis, too, of a revolution in agriculture, with the tractor; and a revolution in the art of war, with the aircraft and new long-distance ships and submarines operating on diesel oil.

Electricity was the other boom industry of the interwar years. Except during the worst years of the slump, electricity generation continued to grow, as did all the industries which were related to electricity. There was a perceptible shift to light engineering, to chemical-based industries (including the beginnings of plastics), and to all new consumer goods.

The basis for this 'revolution' in industrial structure was the pronounced shift in the demand pattern. The rising middle class, without capital, was spending its increasing income on the goods and services which made use of the new technology. Paradoxically, throughout the depressed interwar years, technology leaped ahead. This meant that productivity rose in the new industries, and as it did the numbers of people employed per unit of output decreased, thus intensifying the problem of unemployment. Electricity generation, for example, was a far less labour-intensive industry than coalmining had been. The chief characteristic of the new industries was that they were labour-saving. They also tended to be located near the great suburban consumer areas which provided their markets — New York, California, London, Paris — rather than in the old industrial areas. This meant an internal migration of population, which intensified the depression of the badly hit coalfield-based industries.

The new industries tended to be controlled by large corporations, and were heavily dependent upon substantial advertising. The workers in these industries were only slightly affected by the trade union organisations that had developed in coal, steel, railways and the other older industries. Typically, a new factory employed a transient force of unskilled and semi-skilled workers (many of them women), with a much higher proportion of skilled engineers, technologists, research workers and sales people.

The major new industry, quantitatively speaking, was distribution and the service trades — retailing, hairdressing, laundries and dry-cleaning — because as less of the consumers' dollar was spent on essentials (like food), more was spent on personal entertainment and the consumer satisfactions that sophisticated retailing existed to foster and meet.

The new industries marked, then, a clear break with the heavy industry phase of capitalism (the period which the Soviet Union was entering) and entry into a period of a consumer-oriented society, based on the satisfaction of non-essential needs, where advertising and fashion played a part out of all proportion to the role they had previously known.

Had demand been higher during the period 1920 to 1940, and had unemployment been avoided, there is little doubt that the growth of the new industries and service trades would have been far quicker. The period from 1950 to 1967 in Europe indicated what could happen under full employment, for the rate of accretion in the national incomes of western Europe was faster than that of America between 1920 and 1940, yet America in 1920 and Europe in 1950 were not too dissimilar in industrial structure. Thus it might have been expected that the relative growth of the automobile industry, of home construction, of consumer durables and of service trades could have been faster, and (the other side of the coin) the contraction of the older industries more rapid. Thus, during the 1950s and 1960s European railways, coalfields and cotton textile industries were drastically run down. They were, too, between 1920 and 1940; but their former employees remained idle for the most part, and governments went to great lengths to try to reconstruct the industries, to protect their markets, and to bolster them in every way possible. In this process they were most unsuccessful and their lack of success was another nail in the coffin of liberal, democratic government. For if government could not achieve even the limited ends that it set itself, what could it do?

[t]he new distribution and service industries

[St]ructure of the non-agricultural labour force (in 1,000s) of the United States in 1935

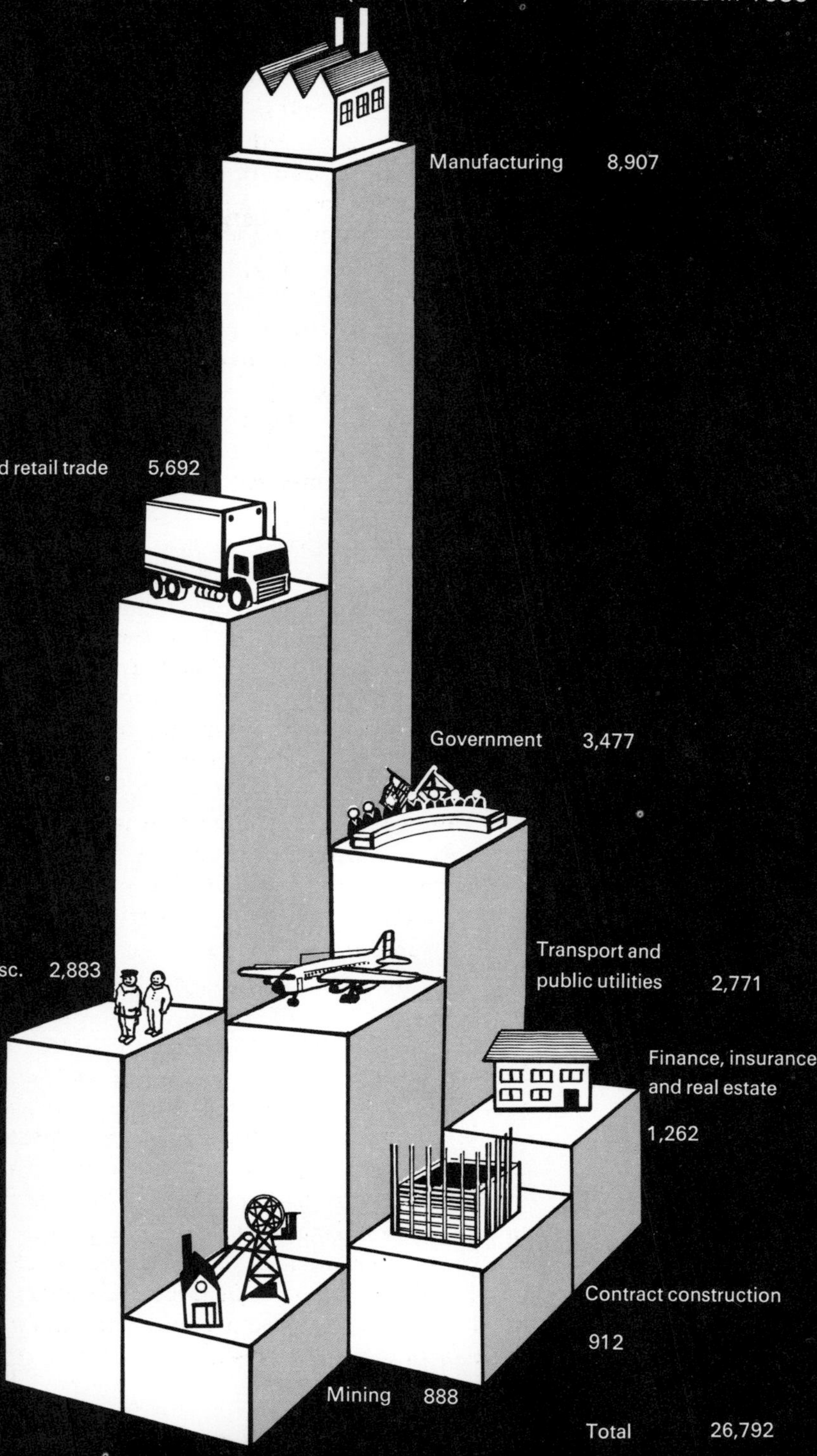

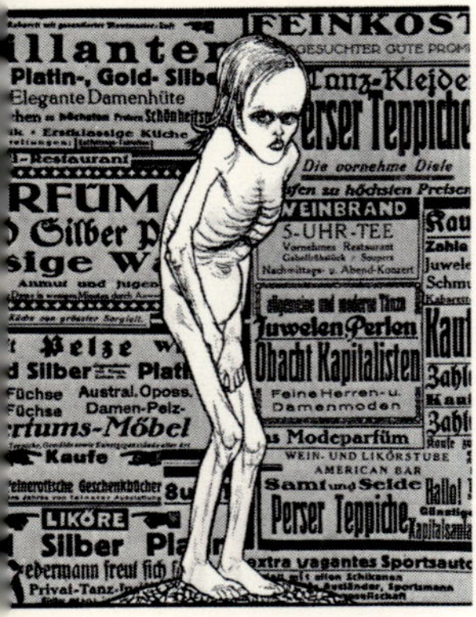

Speculators of the world, remember the starving children – a German cartoon of 1921 attacking the consumer society.

The decline of the heavy industries and the rise of the light industries had two consequences which were of immense importance. The first was the development of credit institutions for consumers, which was one of the main bases on which the new industries stood. Mortgage corporations and building societies for new housing, hire purchase and consumer credit for durable consumer goods and cars — all this meant a great growth of credit institutions. These institutions led the way in the erection of a structure of credit which collapsed in the Great Depression, but which (once revived) formed the basis of the post-Second World War capitalist era.

Secondly, and connected with the credit developments (which lend credence to the view that bankers were at the heart of the mismanagement of capitalism), the shift to 'light' from 'heavy' industry implied, for many critics, a basic frivolity in capitalism. While the many went hungry, the affluent bought 'toy' machines; in Russia, on the other hand, steel works, dams and electricity plants were the order of the day. When the Second World War demanded more heavy industrial output, the frivolities of capitalism were to be blamed for a state of military unpreparedness against fascism and Nazism. This was an unfair charge, but for many people, by 1940, nothing that capitalism did could be right.

New techniques

From 1920 onwards the scientist-technologist assumed a key role in economic and social change. In medicine, for example, the pharmacological advances, based on biochemistry, meant a steadily accelerating rate of improvement in medical sciences, progressing through sulphonamides and penicillin to the powerful drugs for treating mental illness and other serious diseases. Parallel advances occurred in anaesthesia, surgery and almost all other aspects of medical practice. The consequences for society were obvious: a continuous rise in the cost of medical care, a continuous fall in the death rate, a diminution in the number of crippling diseases.

Medical science is a good instance of a general tendency for scientific advances to be transferred into the economy by technology with much less of a time lag than formerly. The advances in energy generation, culminating in modern power, make another example, as do aviation and chemico-plastic processes.

The growth of the physical sciences had three interesting characteristics. First, their discoveries were neutral with respect to the form of the society that adopted them. Capitalism had come into existence to accumulate capital, ultimately in the form of steam engines or their equivalent. Other forms of society had found it difficult to accumulate useful capital without adopting capitalist modes of operation. Science showed itself fruitful under communism and capitalism, and it doubtless would have been so under nazism had so many distinguished scientists not been Jewish.

Secondly, to an increasing extent the scientific and technical procedures which led to significant advances were supported by government. A government enclave, as it were, produced the basis for economic and social progress. A special example of this was the fact that the Second World War, and the succeeding Cold War, led to significant advances in fields primarily relevant to defence, but which came rapidly to have peaceful applications: radar, micro-circuitry, nuclear power, computers were but some of the fields that owed most, if not all, of their major development to defence appropriations. Thus the state, whether in capitalist America, social-democratic Britain, or communist Russia, adopted an almost wholly new role in society. It would be almost impossible to think of a privately financed rate of scientific and technical advance which would come anywhere near that achieved with state support. According to neo-classical capitalist criteria, this devotion of resources to technological advance was a misappropriation of resources, since it rendered obsolete capital that was fully able to function adequately to meet consumer needs, and it was certainly arguable that the world would have been capable of giving its people a higher standard of living if it had not devoted so much of its surplus to scientific and technological development.

But that argument was strikingly irrelevant, because the third feature of scientific advance that was especially noteworthy was that it had become a headlong

The employer: 'One sign from my mighty arm and all wheels stop turning' – a German cartoon of 1928. With the development of the large corporation, the employer acquired an even greater importance.

process, with a logic of its own; one discovery led to another; one hypothesis confirmed raised doubts about another hypothesis; and the insistent demand of science and technology for more resources could no more be resisted than could the demand of the nation-state for armaments. There was a long series of major scientific discoveries, many of which had direct and indirect technological implications.

There were also major innovations in the fields of management and industrial organisation which were in their own way just as significant. The growing use of 'scientific' management techniques, derived from the social and behavioural sciences, was allied to the spread of mechanical aids — culminating in the computer — which enabled management and organisation to become a procedure far less dependent upon whim and genius, and far more 'rational'. It was this 'rationality' that gave big corporations and state bodies a significant advantage which overcame the inherent infeasibilities of large-scale organisation. Capitalist competitive economic theory had been based upon the fact that for most purposes a small organisation was more successful than a big one, and that the consequent diffusion of power among many units was both economically and politically desirable. It became obvious that economically this was no longer so. The economic justification of the small-scale unit had largely gone in many fields; and the political justification, far from being rooted in economic reality, now seemed a romantic one.

The slump and the collapse of the gold standard

The 1920s were a period of boom in America and slump in Europe. On 'Black Tuesday', 29 October 1929, the American boom ended in a stock market collapse, when the ill-regulated credit system seized up. The confidence of investors in the situation suddenly drained away and share prices collapsed. Probably nearly \$30 billion of paper value were lost in two weeks or so, and many rich and middle-class people were ruined.

Why did this loss of confidence occur? Partly because the upward speculation was bound to come to an end, as prices had got quite out of hand (they reached a spectacular height on 3 September 1929). Underlying the end of upward speculation was a realisation that profits were ceasing to rise; this was because investment was becoming less profitable, as the market for the goods that the investment was producing had suddenly ceased to grow.

Businessmen were slow to realise that this was the cause, and buoyed up by spectacular technological inventions which were continuing to appear, they assured the government and the public that record sales were in the offing. When the sales were not made, the shock to confidence was even greater. The first trades to be depressed were the investment goods trades, when a few businessmen prudently postponed extending their plants and installing new machinery. Credit began to dry up. And as that happened, the sales of consumer goods began to plummet.

Unemployment rose rapidly; it doubled in a year. By 1931 it stood at about eight million; eventually it reached well over thirteen million. Between 1929 and 1937 the national income was halved; industrial production was halved; and investment became negative: capital, far from being extended, was not even replaced.

The process of downturn was cumulative. Stock exchange prices fell repeatedly. That helped to knock the bottom out of credit institutions, and so did the collapse of their debtors. Farmers, for example, faced with astonishing falls in the prices of farm products, found themselves quite unable to pay their mortgages and the interest on their bank loans. Thousands of banks and credit institutions in the rural states went bankrupt — as did several of the states themselves — and this in turn spread to the cities, where many mortgage companies and consumer credit institutions were also faced with similar problems.

The effects in America were dramatic. But the slump spread throughout the world, bringing down the depression in Europe to new and catastrophic depths. In the brief stabilisation period of 1927 to 1928 the gold standard had been restored in full force. This stabilised exchange rates in terms of gold and meant that when a deficit occurred in a country's balance of payments, and gold began to flow out, deflationary action had to be taken by cutting the money supply, and internal prices had to fall. But internal prices proved exception-

'The politicians took so long breakfasting that they were eaten for breakfast'. The slump took the capitalist world by surprise: a German cartoon of 1931.

ally sticky, as Britain discovered upon returning to the gold standard in 1925 under Mr Churchill, when it attempted to cut coal miners' wages, leading to a General Strike and a lockout and to apparently interminable labour troubles. When the American collapse began, international trade took a turn for the worse and deflationary policies were intensified throughout Europe. The first major casualties were the overseas primary producing countries, as primary products (food and raw materials) dropped to catastrophically low prices. The primary producers severely reduced their purchases of European goods. At the same time, the American banking collapses cut off the supply of American money which had come across the Atlantic to Europe for investment.

The European countries most badly affected were the heavily agricultural countries of central Europe, whose bankers were chiefly in Berlin and Vienna. Berlin and Vienna were major financial centres but, in turn, their credits came from London, Paris and New York. Thus when financiers in central Europe were

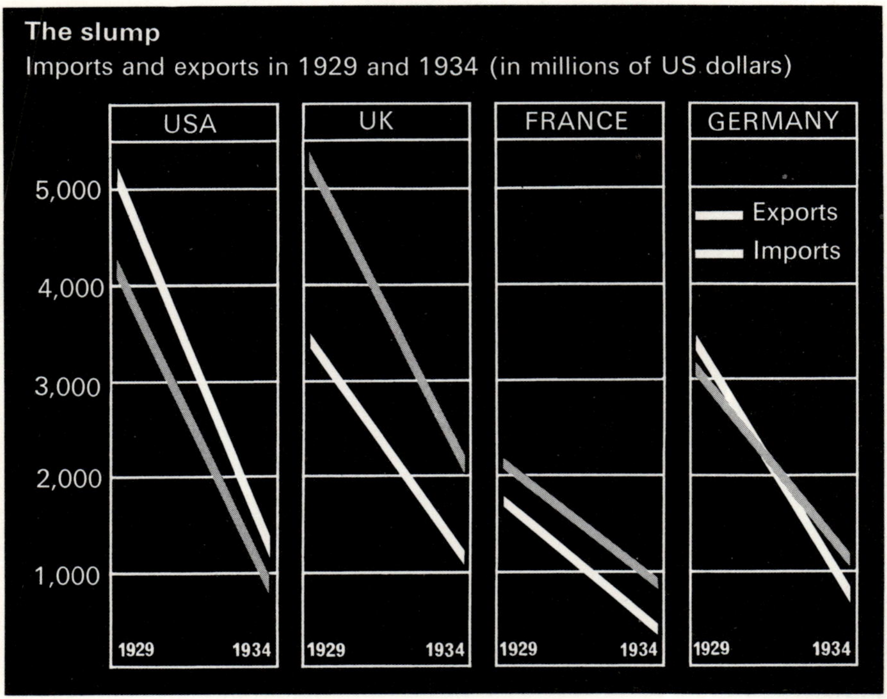

badly affected, their difficulties were transmitted immediately to London and New York.

1930 was a year of relative calm, while things got steadily worse. The 1929 panic passed. Bankruptcies mounted, unemployment rose, investment plans were cancelled, and trade fell. More and more countries adopted policies to restrict international trade. More and more firms joined defensive alliances, cartels, groups, mergers and monopolies to try to preserve themselves in a world of falling demand, falling prices and vanishing profits.

In May 1931 the central European bankruptcies caused a crisis in Vienna — a city already gravely weakened by the dismemberment of the empire of which it had been the capital. The biggest bank, the Creditanstalt, collapsed. As a result, Germany, to which Vienna was closely linked, experienced a further collapse. The stock exchange closed in Berlin, and the discount rate rose to 15 per cent. By July Germany had ceased to make foreign payments, and what it owed in London and elsewhere became a sheer loss on the books of its creditors. This caused a run on the London credit institutions and gold began to flow out of Britain at an astonishing rate.

The Labour government in London, under Ramsay MacDonald, had no idea of what was happening. A committee it had appointed now reported that the loss of confidence was due to high government spending (which was partly and superficially true). The party was deeply split on this issue, and disillusion had rotted its heart, as MacDonald had failed to deal with the economic problem and, notably, unemployment, which was growing weekly more intense. MacDonald went to the king and formed a national government, a Conservative dominated coalition, the rump of the Labour Party going into opposition. MacDonald's government was set up to save the gold standard; within three weeks the gold standard was abandoned. The international credit system collapsed. In the general election the Labour Party was virtually annihilated.

The collapse of the Labour government had widespread consequences. For all its faults — and its merits could be written in large characters on the back of a postage stamp — it was a social democratic government, drawing its support from trades unionists and non-communist intellectuals. It was revealed to be ineffectual in the face of international monetary convulsions, and to be completely devoid of intellectual resources. When the neo-classical economists trotted out their dogma that the only way to cure unemployment was to cut wages, the Labour Party intellectually accepted the arguments; even its honest leaders (who were few enough) like Hugh Dalton had no effective policies to propose which differed, in essence, from those of the bankers. Thus, by the collapse of the Labour Party in 1931, social democracy was widely discredited and there was a retreat either to authoritarian solutions (whether communist or fascist) or to ineffectual liberalism, vaguely waiting for the economic storm to pass.

Oddly enough, after the collapse of the gold standard in September 1931, Britain managed to insulate itself from the worst of the storm, largely because the national finances were exceptionally well managed by Neville Chamberlain. This did not mean that things got better; they did not, however, get very much worse. Unemployment remained in the millions, and whole areas were on the verge of starvation. In Germany and America, however, things went from bad to worse. The flight into gold continued. Credit declined rapidly. Unemployment mounted. Government crisis succeeded government crisis on the continent, while in America it seemed as though the very constitution itself was irrelevant to the crisis through which the nation was passing. President Hoover, who said in 1930 that 'prosperity is just around the corner', was utterly powerless.

France and America, which stuck to gold, suffered the worst loss of exports in 1932, and the loss of gold that America suffered caused still more credit contraction and further collapses. By the time that Franklin Delano Roosevelt was inaugurated president in March 1933, the economic system had virtually come to a stop. The banks were shut. Roosevelt promptly broke the link between the dollar and gold. This marked, for all practical purposes, the end of the gold standard. It also marked the beginning of the New Deal and of the United States' recovery.

A Conservative election poster of the depression period campaigning for an end to free trade.

The slump, then, marked the end of many stages of capitalism. It meant an increasing disillusion with democratic, liberal politics, and a growing attraction to authoritarian régimes of the left and of the right. It meant an abandonment of free trade and the gold standard. Great Britain's reversal of policy was the most dramatic. For a century Britain had been the central advocate of free trade, and its nineteenth-century prosperity and political reputation had been indissolubly linked to free trade. By the events of 1931 Great Britain not only cut the link with gold, but it went over to tariffs, and (to a marginal extent) to exchange controls. Germany, which had always been a protectionist country, went over to exchange controls — or autarchy — rejecting international trade entirely, save as a means of obtaining products that could not be produced at home. The concept of international specialisation was rejected and as an inevitable corollary the search began for territories which could be militarily conquered and which could supply what Germany could not produce.

The disillusion produced by the slump also marked the end of the belief that the system could work spontaneously. From the spokesmen for the unemployed to the manufacturers, the call for government intervention was almost universal and was irresistible. No government, whatever its dogmas, could sit by and watch its economy be paralysed. The trouble was to know what to do. Lloyd George and Keynes moved to the concept of deficit financing — that government should take up the slack in the economy and put the unemployed to work on useful projects. The Swedish government, advised by its excellent economists, managed by monetary and fiscal policy to insulate Sweden from the worst of the depression and to embark on a programme of social amelioration. Roosevelt tried a

No one was prepared to take the blame for the depression – an American cartoon of 1932.

pragmatic policy: he attempted to guarantee agricultural incomes, to develop industrial combines, to raise prices, to increase relief payments. The bankers reconstructed a system of international payments based on mutually acceptable exchange levels, and reserves held in the major currencies (the dollar, the franc and the pound). The American banking system was reconstructed.

Out of this chaos of ideas and initiatives two things stood out. One was that totalitarian countries somehow seemed to come through. The other was that Roosevelt's New Deal seemed to begin to work. Thereafter it was a race between the New Deal and totalitarianism.

The rise of authoritarian politics

Lenin seized power in St Petersburg in 1917. In 1922 Mussolini marched on Rome. In 1928 Salazar took office in Lisbon. In January 1933 Hitler won the German election.

Lenin's successors remained the only communist government in the world, but the working-class organisations in many countries turned increasingly to communism as their political philosophy, and their pattern of behaviour came to be rigidly controlled by the Communist International (the Comintern) in Moscow. Thus, for capitalist governments in many countries, the real opposition seemed to be the Bolsheviks, acting as agents of Moscow. In France, Germany, Italy and Spain, for example, the communists came to control important working-class organisations which henceforth were treated as outside the normal political process. To the capitalists, moderate socialists were often identified with the communists; to the communists, on the other hand, the socialist parties seemed the worst kind of bourgeois lackeys. In the crisis of 1932, in Germany, the communists fought the socialists, taking the view that the nazis — in their view the party of monopoly capitalism — would be succeeded by communism. Thus left-wing politics were rent by schism.

Fascism and nazism had dissimilar roots but increasingly they had common policies and a common ideology. They were nationalist, and arose from a sense of national humiliation that became widespread as

Hitler being shown round the United Steel Works by Fritz Thyssen (second from right) and directors.

governments appeared increasingly impotent in the face of international financial movements. They identified as the enemy international finance, which they labelled Jewish; the nazis regarded German Jews as rootless aliens and agents of international finance. Some of the Jews, however, it was held, were agents of Bolshevism. Both cases were aided by the fact that many international bankers and some international communists were Jews — so also were some bakers, furriers and boxers.

Nazism asserted the supremacy of the state, as embodying the true will of the people: its members were prepared to use the state to run the economy, achieve full employment, regulate wages, and remove poverty. The liberal institutions were swept aside. But nationalism and state power meant, also, strong armed forces and territorial aggression. A virile nation would have a big army, and would use that army to conquer territories in the colonies and among inferior peoples, which meant, first, the Balkans, and secondly Africa. The campaigns against Ethiopia, Poland, and Russia followed inevitably.

His Master's Voice: Hitler harks to the tune of the industrialist Krupp — 'My dear Führer, I absolutely approve of your kind of pacifism'. A Belgian cartoon of 1933.

Both nazism and fascism dissolved the trades unions and formed them again as expressions of national unity (a process also adopted in Russia by the communists).

Totalitarian régimes, as their name implies, wanted unity rather than diversity, and sought to unite all people of one race (whatever that might mean) into one national unit. Hitler rejected religion, though he tolerated it. The fascists, Salazar in Portugal, Mussolini in Italy, and Franco in Spain, were blessed by the Pope. In some respects fascist practice embodied Roman Catholic doctrine. The corporate state, in which all people in one trade cooperated rather than competed, in which free thought and expression were forbidden lest they lead to disunity and godlessness, represented the culmination of the counter-revolution and a return to pseudo-medieval modes of thought. It was an utter repudiation of 'godless capitalism' no less than of 'godless communism'. Pope Pius XII, who blessed German troops fighting against the Allied armies to liberate Europe from nazism, was right to regard fascism as an embodiment of his philosophy (which was subsequently repudiated by Pope John XXIII and the Second Vatican Council).

Yet, ironically, fascism and nazism, which represented the repudiation of the philosophical basis on which capitalism was built, received virtually unanimous support from the business classes. Krupp, for example, was to be sent to prison by the Allies for war crimes, so keen was his support of Hitler. The businessmen prospered because of rising demand caused by increased public expenditure, because genuine trade union activity was forbidden, and because their capital assets and gains were not taken from them.

It seemed as though the communists had a case, and that nazism and fascism (which they lumped together generically under the label of fascism) were the political embodiment of monopoly capitalism. The régimes enjoyed the support of big and small business. They made trades unions illegal. They threw the opposition into jail and killed the more active. They talked, openly, in imperialist terms.

But, in fact, what they did was so much the antithesis of capitalism as to render the terms 'monopoly-capitalist-fascist' a total paradox. The businessmen under capitalism had sought profit wherever and however they could. The nazis (especially) took control of the economy. It was, moreover, inefficient control, save in the one aim of building up military strength swiftly. The nazi régime ran an economy tied hand and foot by government regulations, and the prosperity of the German people, up to almost the point of collapse in 1945, was due to the systematic looting of the occupied territories. Private international trade was virtually abolished, in the sense that trade was conducted entirely by government permission and increasingly through government agencies. The intellectual freedom, freedom to travel, rights of free speech and of assembly, which were all abolished, had been essential concomitants of capitalism and had followed it wherever it had gone. Capitalism had been defiantly internationalist and had reluctantly recognised national boundaries. The spirit of xenophobia and the cult of aryan blood were directly antipathetic to it. Capitalists had had a rationalist, pragmatic, scientific spirit. Nazism was inspired by Nietzsche and fascism was blessed by the Pope.

Indeed, almost the only evidence for the charge that fascism was increasingly capitalism in jackboots was the fact that it persecuted socialists, communists and trades unionists. But as it also persecuted liberals, Jews and democrats, that proved nothing.

In the Spanish Civil War, which was fought from 1936 to 1939, both sides sought foreign assistance. Out of the complexities of that conflict two points emerged. The first was that the communists would turn their weapons as quickly on democrats, anarchists and Trotskyites as on fascists, and that their main aim was power, not the cause of the working class (except in the purely tautological sense that they identified their own interests as by definition those of the working class). The second was that fascism, in any of its forms, was a cult of violence and irrationality that was totally alien to the forms of government and the independence of thought which had characterised capitalist régimes. Further, it was to be seen later that capitalism was not only capable of reforming itself, but that it could defeat nazism. But the question remained — whether the successor societies to the devastation that occurred in the Second World War could be called capitalist at all, or whether some other name might not better describe them.

The New Deal

Franklin Delano Roosevelt, the wealthy poliomyelitis victim who was four times elected president of the United States, has many claims to be one of the greatest figures in American history, surpassed only perhaps by Lincoln and Washington. This is not mainly because of his contribution to the Allied victory in the Second World War, important though that was, but because he presided over the recovery of the American economy and the consequent revival of faith in American political institutions. It was the transformation of economic, social and political attitudes and institutions, which came to be known as the New Deal, that transformed capitalism. Taken together with the effects of the Second World War, a new social order was created which was so unlike capitalism — while having some common features — that it deserves a new name.

The New Deal was a confidence trick. 'The only thing we have to fear is fear itself' was Roosevelt's opening shot in the battle to revive confidence, and he succeeded in reviving it by a series of unorthodox measures. He took America off the gold standard and altered the basis of the currency and credit system, so that it was a managed currency — exactly the opposite to the system that Ricardo had recommended in England one hundred years before. Congress also passed laws to protect the reserves of the banks and to establish a proper central banking system. Thus the credit structure was able to resume activity, insulated from foreign crises. At the same time Britain and France had managed currencies, and Hitler (with his financial expert Schacht) had isolated Germany. International trade therefore depended upon a triangular arrangement between the banking systems of America, Britain and France, each economy successfully insulated by high tariff walls and import quotas.

The effective characteristic of the New Deal, and especially its first year, was hectic activity. It was as though governmental activity proved infectious. This reversal of the situation of before the First World War, when the less government activity there was the more business felt confident, was astonishing. What the New Deal actually did was to implement a number of policies, many of which were mutually contradictory. Roosevelt substantially increased expenditure on social security and welfare. The Public Works Agency increased its expenditure and was replaced by the Civil Works Administration and the Works Progress Administration which eventually, by the end of Roosevelt's second administration, employed one-fifth of the American labour force. The government also set about afforestation, soil conservation and other agricultural projects.

The National Recovery Administration effectively abolished the anti-monopoly laws and established codes of behaviour for different trades and industries. This policy was based upon a fallacy : industrial reconstruction could not succeed in reforming business when demand was so low. If demand picked up, organisational structures would change. This fallacy affected policy measures in Britain as well. But the Act, though it was soon declared unconstitutional, first embodied the principle of collective bargaining between trades unions and employers in American legislation. It also provided a body of administrators who were able to mastermind the rearmament programme which brought America into and through the Second World War. This defence programme became the basis of the post-Second World War Atlantic economy.

A similar fallacy was implicit in Roosevelt's Agricultural Adjustment Act, which sought to control agricultural production and so to raise prices. Once more, although state regulation may have been necessary, since technological advances led to continuously increasing crops, and demand for food could not rise at the same rate, the juxtaposition of restricting output and hungry people represented a paradox that Roosevelt need not have accepted. Increasing demand would have revived agriculture and provided jobs in industry for surplus agricultural labour, as the experience of the Second World War showed.

Roosevelt's Social Security Act of 1935 marked a fifty-years belated conversion of America to Prussian social arrangements. It became a basis for modern society, because social security benefits provided a floor below which demand could not fall.

The clue to the New Deal, then, was in reviving public confidence rather than in its detailed measures. Its two successful measures — substantial public investment in public works, and a budget deficit, were not meant to be permanent and the latter — the deficit — was, indeed, unintended. Between them they boosted demand. This led to a tremendous revival of the economy. By 1937 output was above 1929 levels, investment was rising rapidly, unemployment was falling and prices were rising.

It was in 1937 that the test of New Deal pragmatism came. The recovery suddenly faltered. A great many of the New Deal Acts had been declared unconstitutional; the first *élan* of the administration had begun to wane and orthodox finance began to make itself felt again. Government receipts began to exceed government expenditures. Almost immediately unemployment rose again, prices fell, and investment (especially investment in stocks of raw materials) began to fall very quickly. By March 1938 it looked as though the depression might return in full force.

'New York Daily News' 1936: 'Looks like the boys will have to find a new wailing wall'. By this date the New Deal had proved most of its critics wrong.

The international position was different, however. Germany was rearming at an increasing rate and had almost solved its unemployment problem. Britain had had six years of recovery and was also rearming. The international situation was tense, with Civil War in Spain, Germany preparing to invade Czechoslovakia, and the Italians threatening their neighbours. Japan was advancing rapidly across China. In these circumstances, with an international currency situation that was tightly controlled, financial panics were now part of history rather than of present reality. The forces of inertia and inaction were no longer on the side of orthodox economics; they were on the side of countries that had decided to put foreign policy and armaments first.

Roosevelt decided to act, as he had acted in 1933, without closely considering the ultimate implications of his activities. He adopted deficit budgeting as a policy. He asked Congress to authorise a further big spending programme. The National Recovery Administration, and many other attempts at detailed intervention in the economy, were forgotten; Roosevelt decided to spend his way out of depression. This was the new orthodoxy. It was embodied in John Maynard Keynes's work, *The General Theory of Employment, Interest and Money*, published in 1936. Keynesian economics and armaments rivalry, together with scientific progress, underlay the new civilisation. When Roosevelt began to rearm, early in 1940, he had an ideology at hand.

Keynes

John Maynard Keynes was a Cambridge mathematician and economist, a pupil of Marshall and Pigou, the great neo-classical economists. He was a member of a distinguished group of philosophers, writers and artists (Russell, Wittgenstein, Virginia Woolf, Lytton Strachey), the lover of Duncan Grant the painter, and the husband of Lopokova the ballerina. He dabbled in government, was an amateur of the arts, and was a brilliant journalist. He wrote some of the most distinguished economics of the century and some of the best prose. His worst book, *The General Theory of Employment, Interest and Money*, became the bible of the new society.

The thesis that Keynes propounded, from his book on the Versailles Peace Treaty which ended the First World War — *The Economic Consequences of the Peace* — to his last essays on world monetary questions, in 1945, was in essence this. Capitalism was not an ideal system. It would be a mistake to raise to the level of eternal moral principle the doctrines which enabled it to operate successfully. What capitalism had done was to provide the means by which scientific and technological progress could be incorporated into machinery, equipment, and capital goods of all kinds. The ends to which this productive capacity could be put were a different consideration. Abundance was technically feasible, within a reasonable span of time, and at that point the real issues of what life was to be lived for would be discussable, because the struggle for existence would be at an end.

Keynes, 1934, in the Philadelphia 'Inquirer'

As a matter of pragmatism, it had seemed that private initiative was the most successful system for achieving high economic and technical progress. As a further matter of pragmatism, free trade, generally speaking, also was the most successful way of arranging the international order. All previous systems — feudalism, slavery — had been inefficient, and Keynes regarded the totalitarian systems of communism and fascism as hopelessly inefficient and inflexible. Thus, at the level of tactical decision, as it were, Keynes held that decentralisation, by response to the price system, worked best, and that centralisation did not really work save in grave emergencies where one end was dominant. Since the economic problem was to reconcile diverse ends, centralisation could not last long. But government had a strategic role. Left to itself, capitalism had reached the stage where it was in danger of chronic deflation, partly because of the way the international monetary system worked, but also because the most urgent of man's needs were satisfied in the industrial countries, and people tended to save extra income, thus not spending enough to create the demand to keep the advanced technological resources of modern capitalism fully employed. The government's task was to generate this demand, by deficit finance, and (on an international level) for all governments to continue to take a collective policy to make international trade once more what it had been in the nineteenth century, a force for economic expansion. It was this strategic role of government that marked Keynes' second major break with capitalist philosophy. Not only was market economics not a moral principle, but a pragmatic one; government was important as a strategist rather than as a policeman.

His third break with the past was his view of personal liberty. Keynes was a libertarian (of a somewhat stuffy Cambridge kind) in sex, art, morals and politics. In his view, capitalism had interfered less with people than any other system, past or present, for ordering society. It therefore was to be commended as a system that accorded with a moral absolute, that people should be allowed to go to heaven or hell in their own way, because only in that way could they achieve the harmonious personal relationships, and the cultivation of taste, which formed the basis of true civilisation. For the purpose of economic activity was the good life. The good life consisted of making love to beautiful people, talking to intelligent people, reading books, seeing plays and painting pictures, in a free society. To do this, affluence had to be available for all. Keynes, as the apostle of hedonistic affluence, could not have been more in conflict with the puritan philosophers on whom the capitalist system had rested its case. Their defence of capitalism was that it maximised savings; Keynes', that it taught people how to spend them happily. Their defence of capitalism was that it encouraged people to work; Keynes looked forward to the only work that was done being done for pleasure. They regarded discipline and morality as synonymous. Keynes was a moral anarchist.

Thus the entire philosophic defence of a free society moved on to a different ground. Keynes held that society could be so arranged that people could be free and prosperous. The New Deal and the postwar North Atlantic economy proved that this was so. Keynes argued that totalitarianism was both inefficient economically, and, once adopted, very difficult to shake off. Soviet Russia showed this to be the case. Keynes argued that in a free society the government's role was limited to seeing that the economy functioned and to providing welfare services; beyond that, business would solve the economic problems.

This hypothesis was never to be tested. The whole of Keynes's case — which reads like a philosophical justification of much of Roosevelt's New Deal — was swept aside by the Second World War and the Cold War. A new society came into existence which was based, in part at least, upon war. Keynes's techniques allowed the western allies — Britain and America — to survive the war (though the war was almost certainly won by communism); but the world that followed was one that was of a very different character from what might have been expected. For not only did communism survive, but it spread to China. Communist doctrine proved extremely attractive to the poor countries of Latin America, Africa and Asia. America and its allies undertook vast expenditure on arms. Governments regulated their economies to a degree that would have seemed impossible in the 1930s. Above all, scientific endeavour, subordinated to the arms race, transformed the world. Keynes was proved right that governments could avoid the curse of unemployment. But the society which was created — scientific armaments, for embattled alliances, in a framework of social democracy — was utterly unlike the good life of artistic endeavour that Keynes had hoped for.

The Second World War

The war between France, Germany, Poland and Britain began in 1939. Northern Europe and Italy joined in during 1940. In June 1941 the Soviet Union was invaded. By December the United States and Japan were at war. With few exceptions, all countries and continents, except Latin America, were involved. The loss of lives was horrifying — up to twenty million in Russia, six million Jews murdered by the Germans, and three million Germans killed by the allies. Whole countries — the Ukraine and Byelorussia, Italy, Germany, Yugoslavia, for example — were extensively damaged. Trade was deeply divided and semi-starvation conditions prevailed over whole areas of the world, especially at the end of the war in 1945.

The progress of the war illustrated the thesis that peace was indivisible, a thesis enunciated by Litvinov, the Russian Commissar for Foreign Affairs, in the abortive negotiations to prevent war. Its outbreak clearly refuted the hypothesis that war was an extension of monopoly-capitalist imperialism. The war was between communists and nazis, capitalists and fascists, democracies and totalitarian states, with alliances formed accidentally between those attacked and those doing the attacking. The only common features in all these combats were the expansionist aims of the three countries, Germany, Italy and Japan, which had militarist-fascist dictatorships, the inability of other states to join together in defence, and the rivalry between the communists and the democrats, seen most strikingly in Spain, and then in the German-Soviet pact of 1939. There was more in common between Hitler and Stalin than between the capitalists in Germany and the capitalists in Britain. To describe the war as a struggle between monopoly-capitalists is a fantasy.

Yet the war completed the end of traditional capitalism. It led, first of all, to the end of the traditional international monetary system. The British, especially, sold some of their overseas assets (during the year that they fought alone, from June 1940 to June 1941) and accumulated large overseas debts. The Americans, on the other hand, became creditors on a massive scale. Thus the conditions for recommencing international trade after the war were, first of all, an international system of payments started *de novo*, at the Bretton

Woods Conference, with the establishment of the International Monetary Fund, and secondly the use of the American surplus to extend credits to other trading partners on a systematic basis, which occurred through the Marshall Plan. Thus international trade ceased in any sense to be regulated by an automatic mechanism.

Internally, even in countries of extreme laissez-faire philosophy, the anti-slump measures were developed, in the process of rearmament and of total conflict, into an almost all-embracing system of governmental control. In Britain, where this process extended furthest, there was direction of labour and consumption affecting almost the whole labour force, control of prices, rationing of consumer goods, allocation of raw materials, and government determination of the final output pattern. The war was financed on Keynesian principles, partly by saving but mainly through very high taxation, so that the inflation was very small. Interestingly enough this enormous increase in government intervention led to little diminution in the standard of living. Full production and full employment were achieved, and for many working-class families adequate incomes were received for the first time. The capacity for output at full employment seemed, by prewar standards, prodigious. At the same time what came to be known as 'the welfare state' was in fact invented. Whole sections of the population became entitled to welfare benefits and medical care to which they had previously not been entitled.

The situation in America was even more astonishing. By 1943, ten years after Roosevelt's inauguration in conditions of economic collapse, American output levels were higher than ever before, levels of real income were higher than ever before, and the output of war *matériel* and the size of the armed forces were without parallel. Thus government control plus the capital equipment and skilled labour force of a post-capitalist economy could achieve extraordinary output levels. The same was even true of Russia, the country that suffered most from the war. Despite the 'scorched-earth' policy, which destroyed virtually all capital equipment in the areas captured by the Germans, despite millions of deaths, output levels in the Soviet Union remained surprisingly high, and though there were grave shortages of all kinds, some sort of economic existence continued. It looked as though Keynes was right and that the problem of production was solved provided government intervened sufficiently and ensured that demand was high enough.

Managed international trade and managed economies therefore followed logically from the war. So, too, did the welfare state. Once it was seen that the output capacity of the economy was such that none need be paupers, and that government support could supply the necessary income in cash and in kind, the European countries moved over to comprehensive social security programmes and systems to provide free or heavily subsidised health care. Britain lagged behind Europe and the United States in social security (largely because of its extremely conservative trades union movement) but it led with its free comprehensive National Health Service.

The political consequences of the war were tremendous. First, the new international alignments, following the destruction of German and Japanese power, were centred on America and Russia. The postwar era was to be a Cold War, occasionally hotting up, between these two systems of alliances. The old empires which had survived the First World War — the British, French and Dutch — collapsed, the most notable event being the independence of India in 1947. To an important extent the capitalist assets and political interests of the imperialists in the colonial territories were taken over by the United States, lending some verisimilitude to the Russian charge that the 'liberation' of the colonial territories was merely an episode in an inter-imperialist struggle. On the other hand, the Russians succeeded to the imperialist heritage in the Balkans and eastern Europe and took far more open political control there than the Americans did anywhere, except in South Korea and South Vietnam. A power struggle between military alliances was a more plausible description of what was happening than an inter-imperialist conflict.

Within these new alignments, socialism and communism had a new status. Communism as a world power, based on Russia and China, might be tyrannical and inefficient, but it obviously worked well enough

The orientation of the present-day United States economy around the scientific-military establishment is leading capitalism into a new phase: a poster celebrating the tenth anniversary of the National Aeronautics and Space Administration.

to threaten the military conquest of the world. Socialism was a vague and often contradictory creed (like most creeds), but it was the accepted creed of many postwar governments, from Britain to India, from France to Mexico. Moreover, especially in western Europe, much of their social and industrial legislation became a permanent part of the legislative code of their countries. Partly this represented a full recognition of working-class parties within the political system, but it was also a rejection of the older capitalist ethos. Pragmatism with respect to the role of government in society was associated with an inner conviction that government action was almost inevitable in conditions of crisis. This was a reversal of capitalist ideology, so complete as to justify the abandonment of the word.

Finally, once again the war enormously accelerated technological and scientific development — radar, missiles, nuclear weapons, penicillin are all examples — and in the Cold War the scientific-military establishment became institutionalised. It developed a logic and a path of development of its own, dragging governments and the economy after it. Wernher von Braun, who had tried to destroy London for Hitler, sent Americans to the moon. The American economy was organised round Wernher von Braun. So was the Russian. Capitalism was over, and the age of science had arrived.

Managerial capitalism

The end of the war and the immediate period of dislocation was followed by a burst of production the like of which had never been seen. By 1950 world output levels attained unprecedented heights. International trade revived. Full employment was maintained. Productivity rose to record levels. The devastation of the war was fully repaired by 1952, although armaments expenditure was only slightly reduced from its wartime levels. Above all, political stability was established throughout the world (compared with the interwar instability) in régimes of all political types.

In this context, what did 'capitalism' mean, if anything ?

The communist dictatorships lumped together all

the American allies, and the benevolent neutrals, as capitalist régimes. What was their characteristic?

Many of them had parliamentary systems, which varied in effectiveness, but there were some dictatorships (notably Spain, Portugal and the Latin American military dictatorships). In the major countries, Germany, Italy, France, Britain, Canada, America, as well as the smaller western European states, the parliamentary régimes were associated with personal liberty, freedom of speech and freedom of movement. This was in striking contrast to communist and fascist régimes. The liberal tolerance that marked the countries of western Europe and North America, and their associated states in Australasia and Japan, was a creation of capitalism, and almost uniquely associated with it. To the extent, therefore, that political liberalism was synonymous with capitalism, the west was capitalist.

It was capitalist in another sense. Despite the extension of state ownership of industry, especially to public utilities like railways, electricity and coal, the bulk of industry and commerce was in private hands. It was from this private sector that the greater part of the rise in productivity came. The achievements were prodigious. Agricultural output, for example, rose so rapidly as a result of technical improvements in food production that the western countries achieved food surpluses by the mid-1950s, even in conditions of full employment when demand was high. Europe passed through a housing boom greater than that of the United States in the 1920s. Above all, the output of consumer durables — cars, television and radio sets, laundry equipment, kitchen equipment — increased by leaps and bounds. There was a transformation of the standard of living. Many of the products and services were new, and rested upon steady technical progress in many fields. The older industries — coal, steel, railways — were gradually either run down or their output growth slackened as new industries took their place. Chemicals, plastics, light engineering based on aluminium and new alloys, electronics, and biologically based products represented the new advances.

Industry (and the very rapidly expanding service sector) took new organisational forms, and these were

The post-war boom

Exports 1945-67 (in millions of US dollars)

	UK	FEDERAL REPUBLIC OF GERMANY
1967	17,186	17,352
1966	16,107	18,023
1965	15,619	17,472
1964	15,415	14,613
1963	13,523	13,019
1962	12,516	12,280
1961	12,286	10,941
1960	12,640	10,104
1959	10,806	8,478
1958	10,096	7,361
1957	10,960	7,499
1956	10,413	6,617
1955	10,483	5,793
1954	9,129	4,571
1953	9,025	3,771
1952	9,296	3,814
1951	10,540	3,491
1950	7,035	2,697
1949	6,831	1,123
1948	6,647	646
1947	4,862	319
1946	3,915	143
1945	1,818	20

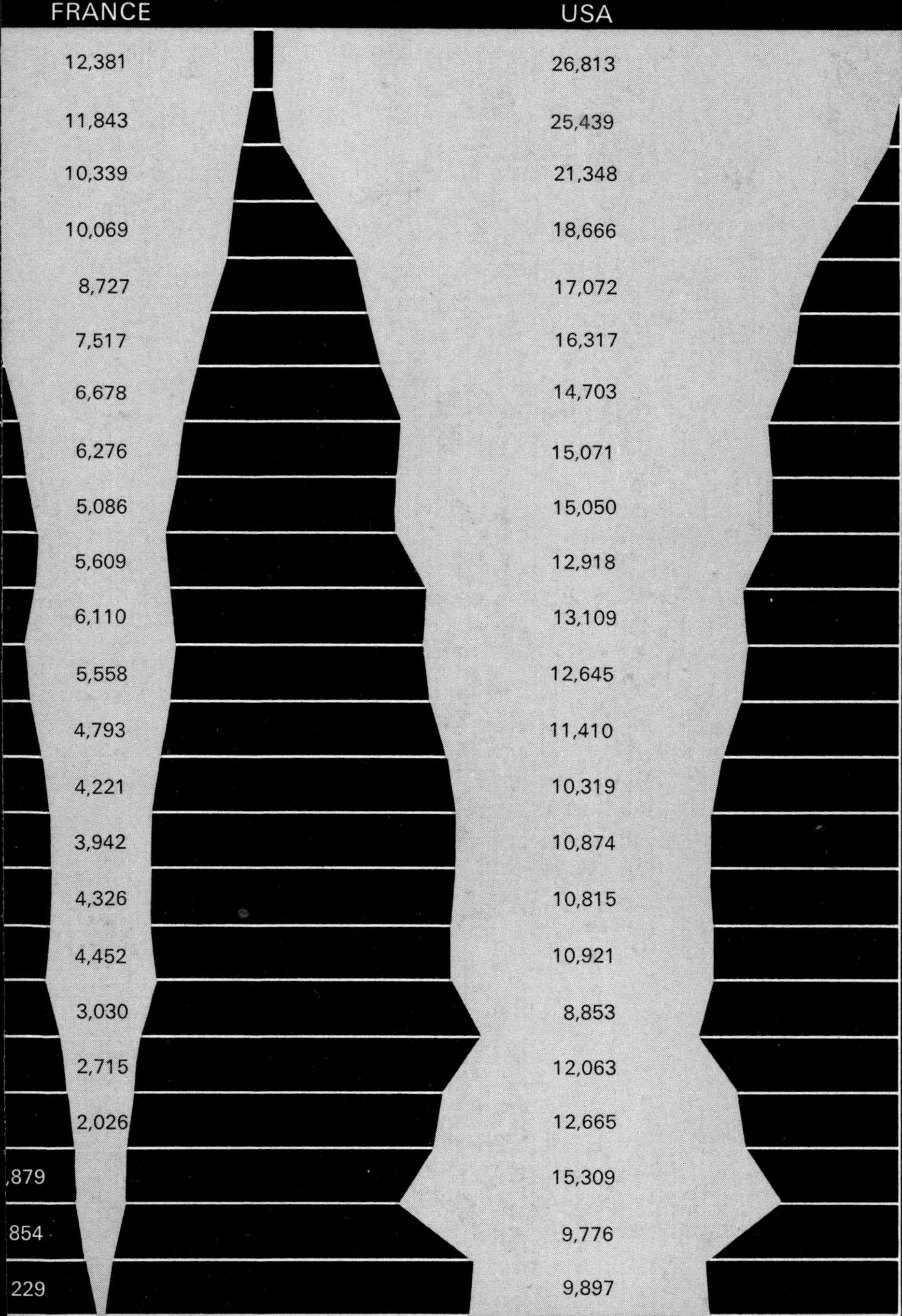
FRANCE
USA
12,381
26,813
11,843
25,439
10,339
21,348
10,069
18,666
8,727
17,072
7,517
16,317
6,678
14,703
6,276
15,071
5,086
15,050
5,609
12,918
6,110
13,109
5,558
12,645
4,793
11,410
4,221
10,319
3,942
10,874
4,326
10,815
4,452
10,921
3,030
8,853
2,715
12,063
2,026
12,665
,879
15,309
854
9,776
229
9,897

what came to be known as managerial capitalism. Industry tended to organise in federations and trade organisations, to negotiate with government and the trades unions. Competition, in significant respects, was replaced by cooperation. This was represented most dramatically, perhaps, in France in the French planning system. The industrialists, civil servants and trades unions in an industry proposed targets for their output, and negotiations took place with other industries to see that the supplies of materials, capital goods and skills, and markets for the final goods were available. While it was probably the case that what caused the effective modernisation of France was the continually rising demand for final goods, springing from the steady inflation of the currency under the Fourth Republic, the cooperation of the state and industry did not slow up technical advance and probably helped it.

Though much technical progress was due to small firms that grew rapidly as they exploited new markets available for new products (Xerox is an example), the typical postwar firm was an international giant corporation, with thousands of employees and shareholders and a professional management. It was the characteristics of these firms that caused the term 'managerial capitalism' to be invented.

The firm was an entity in itself in which it was possible to serve, as in a church or an army, for one's working life, to give absolute loyalty, and to expect in return care and concern for one and one's family for a whole lifetime — death and retirement benefits, care in sickness, housing, medical care, education, and a sense of personal worth based on an identification with the firm's ideals.

The firm ploughed back its own surplus and rarely turned to outside sources for capital. The shareholders, a transient body, consisting often of insurance companies, pension funds and other institutional investors, were treated as *rentiers*, expecting a conventional return, and in no serious sense the 'owners' of the firm. The firm had obligations, it was said, to see that its shareholders were fairly treated, but its true obligations were to its employees, its customers, and to society in general. A 'good' firm would therefore offer its employees steady employment in good conditions, for good wages, and it would expect in return considerable loyalty. It would go to great lengths to encourage democratic consultation and participation especially in industrial relations.

It would sell a product, or a series of products, that it genuinely believed to be an essential element of the good life.

In the market that came into existence, depending on advertising, and with competition between different products rather than between prices, the atmosphere of insincerity indissolubly linked with over-assertion was palpable. But, to the outsider, the 'company man's' belief in his product seemed obviously sincere and (to be fair) it was often justified.

The firm owed a duty to the community. Its executives would serve the government voluntarily (as Macnamara left Ford to become Secretary of Defense, or Catherwood left British Aluminium to serve the National Economic Development Office); they would encourage science and the arts; they would encourage youth movements and provide welfare facilities for the communities where their factories were.

Underlying this was a philosophy of responsible management. The management of the firm often had little or no financial stake in it. They served it for a salary. Their self-respect depended on recognition of their disinterested service for the company and its ideals. Management became a profession with its own codes of behaviour, its own education and training process. The emphasis was on responsibility to workers, the community and to customers (with shareholders as an afterthought).

The similarities to the great professions of medicine, law and the church, were obvious, and so, too, were

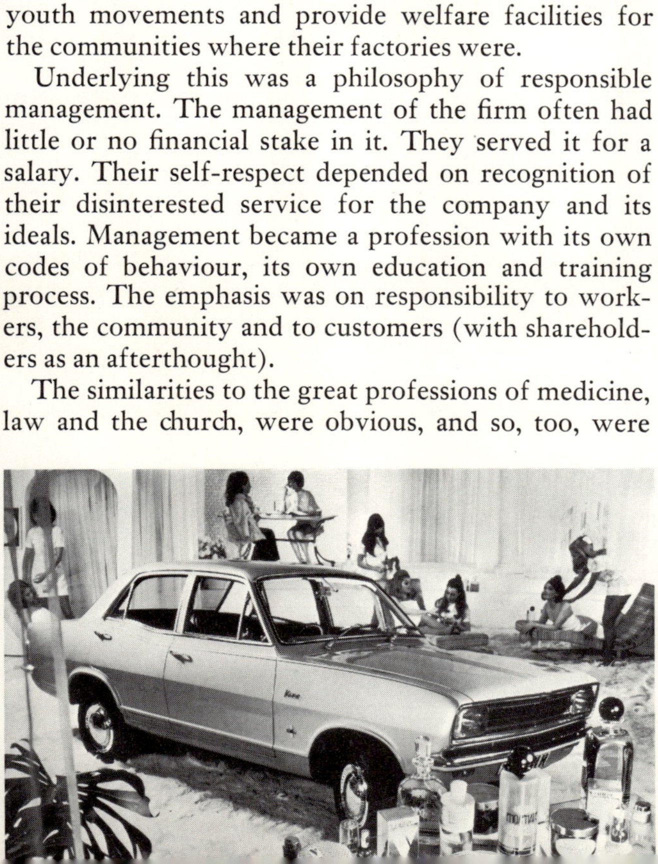

'Vauxhall use six kinds of make-up to keep the body beautiful': one of the most striking developments in post-war capitalism has been the increasing sophistication of advertising.

The growth of large towns

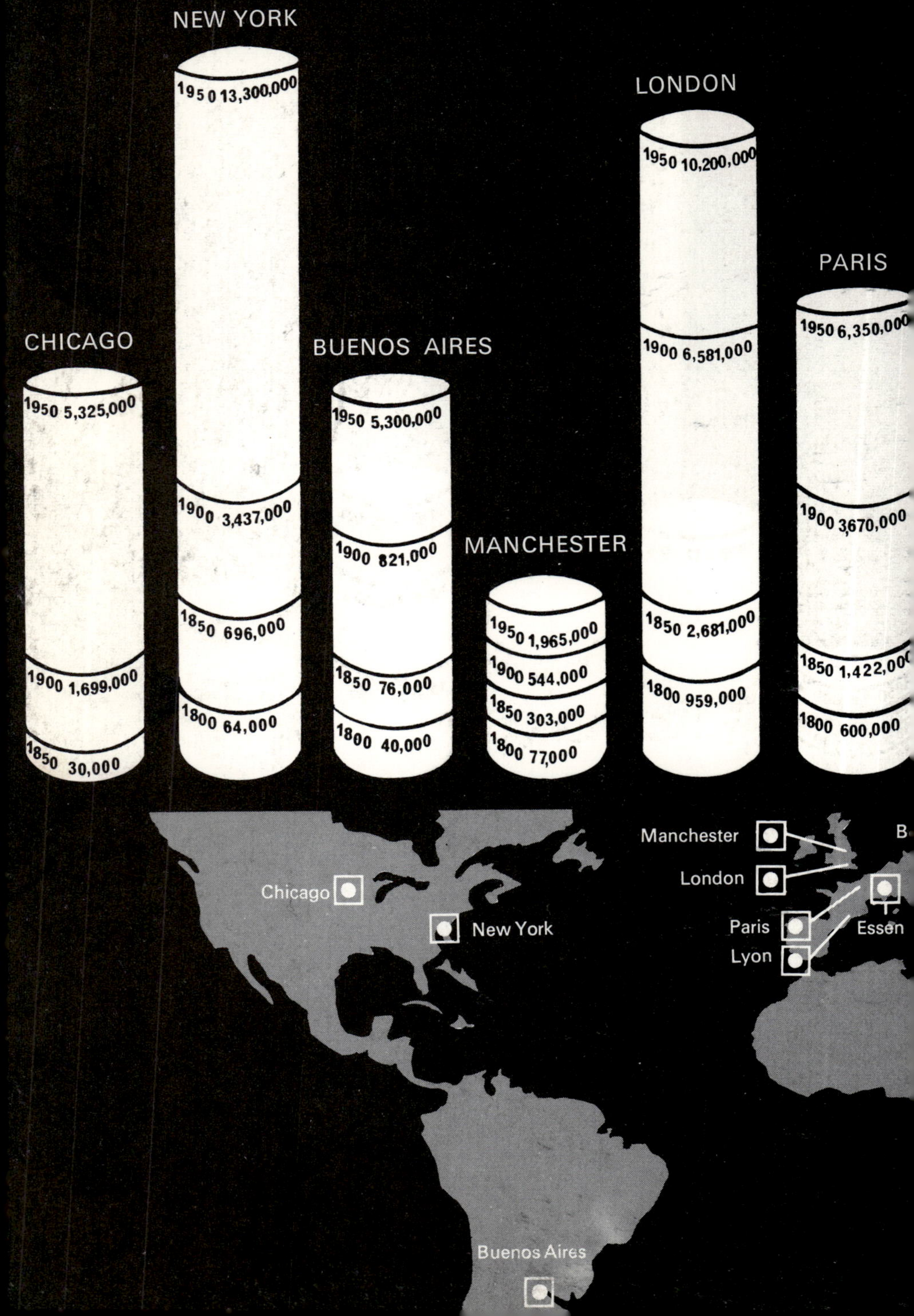

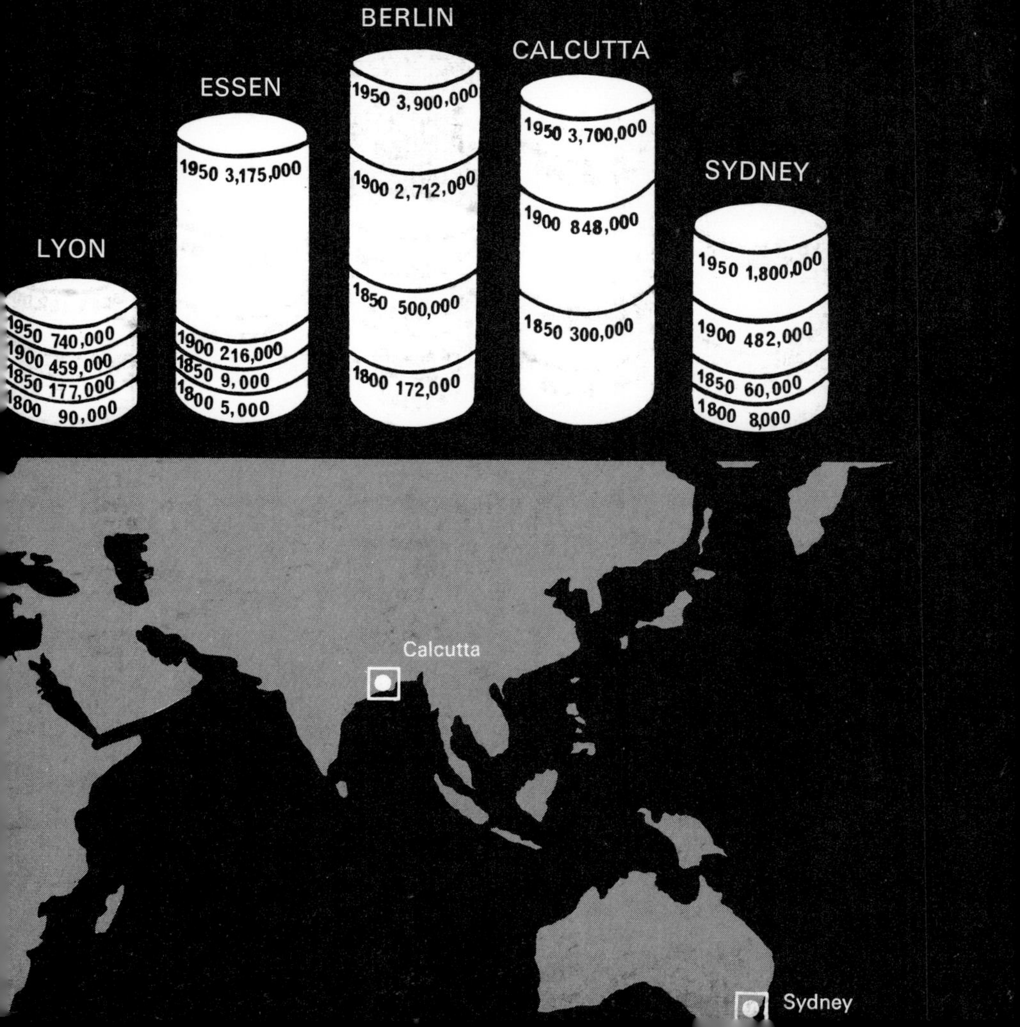
LYON
1950 740,000
1900 459,000
1850 177,000
1800 90,000
ESSEN
1950 3,175,000
1900 216,000
1850 9,000
1800 5,000
BERLIN
1950 3,900,000
1900 2,712,000
1850 500,000
1800 172,000
CALCUTTA
1950 3,700,000
1900 848,000
1850 300,000
SYDNEY
1950 1,800,000
1900 482,000
1850 60,000
1800 8,000
Calcutta
Sydney

the similarities to the civil service and the army, with their selfless anonymity, their concept of service to the community rather than self-aggrandisement, and of a balanced and objective approach to all questions.

It was this type of man, in this spirit, who dealt with the postwar problems. Their astonishing success in raising productivity, in solving social problems and in beginning to tackle international political questions, was the dominant feature of the 1950s and the early 1960s. Managerial capitalism was not capitalism. It also had its flaws. It ignored the real problems of the poor countries, nationalism, and the loss of morale among the really poor in the affluent countries.

Is it still capitalism?

Scientific advance dragged the world along after 1945. No sooner was a discovery made than attempts were made to see whether it had any conceivable technological applications. The finance for the development was always forthcoming, usually from government. Once the development had occurred, it was exploited. A new market was invented (as for television) and rapidly saturated.

Thus the original ethic of capitalism was reversed. Far from the market initiating the conditions for technical progress, the opposite occurred. Technical development led to a market.

Capital no longer sought solely profit, but rather, a variety of objectives, of which the security and responsibility of the firm were the chief. A big corporation, like US Steel, or Ford, or Imperial Chemical Industries, closely resembled a publicly owned corporation, like the National Coal Board or the *Société Nationale des Chemins de Fer*. Its capital came from internal sources, and its profits were used for further investment and research. *Rentiers* accepted a conventional return.

The market was managed by advertisers and mediated through large chains of retailers. Price competition ceased to exist as a major means of transmitting market decisions.

Above all, government took a central role in three key areas. First, in promoting scientific research and technological development, often as a byproduct of

The twentieth century has continued to build its urban night-mares: **opposite and overleaf:** Buenos Aires today.

Nineteenth-century capitalism left many countries with a legacy of industrial slums, like these in Leeds.

military endeavour. This was the engine of the economy.

Next, economic development depended on the skills and education of the labour force. This was almost wholly a governmental responsibility. The astonishing recovery of Germany after the Second World War, and the development of Japan, for example, owed everything to the skills of the labour force.

Thirdly, as social problems revealed themselves, only governmental agencies could attempt to cope with them. The western civilisation based on huge conurbations spread throughout the world. The whole east coast of North America, from Washington to Boston, the west coast from San Francisco to San Diego, Chicago, London, the Rotterdam complex, the Ruhr, Paris, Milan, Tokyo — all these great conurbations generated social problems on a terrific and terrifying scale. Crime, traffic control, ghettoes with hideous slums and acute poverty among immigrant groups, lawlessness, riots, drugs — all these represented threats to the postwar order. Private initiative could offer palliatives but it was widely agreed that a major programme of social reconstruction was both inevitable and desirable, and that only public bodies could achieve it.

Thus the role of government, in promoting science and technology, providing education and coping with social breakdown, was central to the economy. In addition, the corporate ethic and its liberal political counterpart seemed to be worthy but irrelevant.

There was, first of all, the problem of the developing

countries. Two thousand million people lived outside affluence, and they were neglected by the concept of managerial capitalism. It would require international effort to raise their living standards, and their political struggles threatened constantly to disturb the delicate balance of terror between the American and Russian alliances. This was a geo-political problem to which managerial capitalism seemed irrelevant. Its solution — not a once-for-all solution, but a working through its problems to some sort of constructive and positive action — depended on international action at a governmental, political level, on much the same lines as the scientific-military complex tackled the problems of the arms race. Indeed, all proposals for coping with 'the Third World' of underdevelopment depended on some analogy with the military-scientific approach to strategy.

'The boss needs you, you don't need him' — A French student poster of May 1968 denouncing capitalism as a system of exploitation.

Next, as the managers comforted themselves with an ideology of benevolence, students and the disenchanted denounced it as paternalistic and as a manifestation of the rationalist, technological outlook which had come to dominate the world, and which, in their view, was destroying it literally (because of the probability of nuclear and biological warfare) and metaphorically, because of the deterioration in the quality of the culture and its increasingly mechanistic nature which had destroyed the springs of originality, freshness and vitality.

The most telling point was that in many respects Russian society and western society were similar. The corporate identity, the dominance of science and technology, the culture — all had strong common features. There were grounds for calling the new society the scientific-military society.

The major difference was a significant one. Though under attack, liberal politics survived, battered but still upright. It was uniquely associated with capitalism. If capitalism meant liberalism, then there was a case for saying capitalism was still going on. But if the communist states could go liberal (as Czechoslovakia and Yugoslavia seemed at one time likely to do) the case would fall. Liberalism would be a political concept independent of the forces of industrial ownership and control, and capitalism would pass into history.

'Capitalism is going under' — another poster of May 1968. With all the modifications that capitalism has undergone since 1914, and in the face of increasing opposition, its continuing existence is called into question.

Bibliography

The classical primary and secondary works on capitalism are legion. In this selection, the most interesting and accessible for the concerned reader are cited.

CLASSICS

Adam Smith *The Wealth of Nations*
T. R. Malthus *An Essay on Population*
David Ricardo *Works* (ed. P. Sraffa)
Karl Marx *Capital*
John Stuart Mill *On Liberty*
Alfred Marshall *The Principles of Economics* London 1890
A. C. Pigou *The Economics of Welfare*
J. M. Keynes *The Economic Consequences of the Peace* London 1919
A Treatise on Money London 1930
The General Theory of Employment Interest and Money London 1936
J. A. Hobson *Imperialism*

COMMENTARIES ON CAPITALISM

The most significant are:

Joseph Schumpeter *Capitalism, Socialism and Democracy* New York 1942
J. K. Galbraith *The Affluent Society* London 1958
Andrew Shonfield *Modern Capitalism* Oxford 1964

There are some general introductions to economic history:

J. B. Clough *The Economic Development of Western Civilization* New York 1959
Barry Supple *The Experience of Economic Growth; Case Studies in Economic History* New York 1963
Max Weber *General Economic History* New York 1961

THE ANCIENT WORLD AND CHINA

Jean-Philippe Levy *The Economic Life of the Ancient World* Chicago 1967
F. M. Heichelheim *An Ancient Economic History from the Paleolithic Age to the Migrations of the Germanic, Slavic and Arabic Nations* Leyden 1958 and 1964
C. P. Fitzgerald *A Concise History of East Asia* London 1966
Edwin O. Reischauer and John K. Fairbank *A History of East Asian Civilization* Boston 1960–64
J. Needham *Science and Civilization in China* Cambridge 1954–65

EARLY CAPITALISM

Maurice Dobb *Studies in the Development of Capitalism* London 1946

EUROPE AND THE NORTH ATLANTIC

Cambridge Economic History of Europe vols. I, II, III, VI Cambridge 1942–65
John Clapham *The Economic History of Modern Britain* 3 vols. Cambridge 1930–8
Henri Sée *Histoire Economique de la France* Paris 1948–51
Werner Sombart *Der Moderne Kapitalismus*, 3 vols. Munich 1921–8
Douglas C. North *Growth and Welfare in the American Past* Englewood Cliffs, N. J. 1966
Dudley Dillard *Economic Development of the North Atlantic Community* Englewood Cliffs, N. J. 1967
J. K. Galbraith *The Great Crash* Boston 1955
Simon Kuznets *National Income and Its Composition 1919–1938* New York 1954
League of Nations *World Economic Survey* Geneva, 1932–44

Acknowledgements

The photographs in this book are reproduced by the kind permission of the following: Archiv Gerstenberg, Frankfurt am Main, 12a, 38c, 149 ; Frau Anne-Dora Arnold, 182 ; Atelier Populaire, 217a and b ; Austrian National Library, 38b ; Bank of England, 34 ; Bibliothèque Nationale, Paris, 116, 163 ; Biltmore Estate, Asheville, N. Carolina, 103 ; Frau Dagny Björnson-Gulbransson, 169b ; British Museum, 12b, 15c, 27b, 32b, 35, 45, 79, 83, 88a, 104, 105, 112, 130, 136, 144, 147 ; British Waterways Board, 61 ; California State Library, 106 ; Camera Press, 106 ; The Corcoran Gallery of Art, Washington, 129 ; Culver Pictures Inc., endpaper, 53, 152, 173-4, 178, 190, 198 ; Deutsche Fotothek, Dresden, 165 ; Dennis Dobson, 217a and b ; Esso Petroleum, Texas, 88b ; Fitzwilliam Museum, Cambridge, 14, 48, 65 ; Ford Motor Co., 141 ; John R. Freeman, 12b, 35, 45, 79, 83, 88a, 104, 105, 112, 119, 121, 136, 144, 147, 157, 162, 169b, 182, 183, 186, 192a ; Giraudon, 8, 10, 24 ; John Hillelson Agency, 137 ; Historia-Photo, 135 ; Keystone Press Agency, 204 ; Library of Congress, Washington, 70, 102 ; The London School of Economics, 158 ; Stefan Lochner, 186 ; Louvre, 8, 10 ; The Mansell Collection, title page, 11, 15a and b, 38a, 50, 58-9, 67a, 78, 94, 95, 97, 98, 99, 107, 124, 125, 140, 146a and b, 155 ; Peter Mathias, 14, 65 ; Metropolitan Museum of Art, New York, 134; Museum of the City of New York (Byron Collection), 138 ; National Aeronautics and Space Administration, Washington, 204 ; National Monuments Record, Leeds, 216 ; Public Record Office, London, 77 ; Radio Times Hulton Picture Library, 32a, 109, 172, 176, 189, 192b ; Franklin D. Roosevelt Library, New York, 197 ; Royal Institute of British Architects, 133 ; Science Museum, London, 28, 55, 56, 67b, 71, 75 ; Erich Seemann, 162, 183 ; Snark International, 116, 163, 168 ; Staatsbibliothek, Berlin, 27a ; Tasiemka, 119, 121, 157, 192a ; Ullstein Bilderdienst, Berlin, 30, 139, 167 ; UNESCO, 213-15 ; Vauxhall Motor Co., 209 ; Victoria and Albert Museum, 44, 46, 47, 73-4, 169a ; Josiah Wedgwood and Sons, 62 ; Derrick Witty, 158, 169a ; C. H. Wood Ltd., 216.

Index

absolutism, 114, 117, 139
advertising, 143, 146, 179–80, 209
Africa, 118, 120, 149, 157
agriculture, 14–16, 49, 81–7, 109, 110, 142–3, 172, 175, 205; Chinese, 19; medieval, 28; Roman, 17; Russian, 171; US, 196
agricultural workers, 94, 146, 153; *see also* farmers *and* peasants
America, 30–1, 118, 120, 121; *see also* Latin America *and* USA
American Civil War, 73, 140, 142, 146, 154
American merchant navy, 61
anarchists, 116
Ancient World, 17–19
antisemitism, 139, 150
Antwerp, 25
Arabs, 14, 21–4
aristocracy, 51, 103, 113, 115, 159
armaments, 154, 156, 196, 197, 198, 200, 204
armed forces, 154, 192
arts, 132–6, 139
Asquith, Herbert H., 163
Augsburg, 27
Australia, 13, 78–9, 118, 120, 127, 172
authoritarianism, 154, 188, 189, 191–4
automobiles, 142, 143, 179
aviation, 183
Aztecs, 26, 31

Bagehot, Walter, 106, 114
Balkans, 203
Bank of England, 105–7, 177
bankers, 34, 39, 40, 177, 182, 192
banking, 16, 27, 29, 104–8, 125, 191, 195
banks, 34, 105
Belgian Congo, 127
Belgium, 57, 64, 70, 74, 175
belle époque, la, 135–9
Bengal, 94
Bentham, Jeremy, 112, 117
Berlin, 161, 169, 186, 187
Birmingham, 57, 60, 71, 72
Bismarck, Prince Otto von, 110, 154, 158
Black Death, 25, 26
Boer War, 157
Bolsheviks, 161, 163, 168, 191
books, 80, 91, 145
booms, 96, 140–3, 206–7
boot and shoe manufacture, 79
Booth, Charles, 157
Boulton, Matthew, 54
bourgeois state, 12–13, 16, 41, 54, 60
'bourgeoisie', 41, 53, 111–14, 116, 117
brass work, 71, 72
Braun, Wernher von, 204
breeding, selective, 49, 87
Bretton Woods Conference, 201–2
brewing, 16, 40, 45, 143
Bright, John, 60
Brindley, James, 63
Britain, banking in, 105–7; and trade, 108–11, 189–90; in the 19th century, 57–60, 118–21; Edwardian, 156–60; post-war I, 160–3, 164, 165, 166, 172, 175–6, 188; and World War II, 201–2, 203
British Empire, 31–3, 110, 118, 203
British merchant marine, 72
Bruges, 25
budgets, 92–3, 175, 176, 197
building, 37, 63, 81, 103, 178
bureaucracy, 16, 113, 117, 155–6
business, 41, 193
Byzantium, 19, 21–4

Calcutta, 33
California, 118
Calvin, John, 28
Canada, 118, 121, 127, 129, 172
canals, 61–4, 73
capital, accumulation of, 10, 33–6, 53–4, 76, 183; fixed and circulating, 40, 51
capitalist class, 37–41
capitalist régimes, 205
cartels, 147–8, 187
Catherwood, H. F. R., 209
Catholicism, 28, 89, 139, 193, 194
centralisation, 199
Chamberlain, Neville, 188
Chartist movement, 115
Child, Sir Josiah, 37
China, 9, 13, 17, 19–21, 33, 118, 121
Churchill, Sir Winston, 186
Cipolla, Carlo, 45
cities, 16, 25, 37, 86, 140
civilisations, impact of trade on, 31–3
class struggles, 53–4
cloth manufacture, 27–8, 36, 39–40; *see also* textile industries
coal, 36, 40, 45, 48, 55, 56–7, 60, 66, 67, 148, 172
Cobden, Richard, 60; treaty with France, 16, 110
Cold War, 183, 203
collective bargaining, 196
colonialism, 118–24, 127, 190, 192, 203
communications, 57, 61, 131, 156
communism, 54, 96, 161, 168–71, 191–2, 193, 194, 200, 201, 203–4
companies, 63–4, 72–3, 102–3, 147; *see also* corporations, firms *and* mergers
competition, 40, 157, 208, 209, 212
Constantinople, 21, 24, 36
construction trades, 81, 178, 179; *see also* building
consumer goods, 45–8, 76–81, 91, 166, 175, 178, 179, 205

consumer society, 143–8, 178–82
consumption, 91, 145–6
contracts, 11, 113
conurbations, 216
Corn Laws, 53, 109
corporations, 149–50, 179, 184, 212
Cort, Henry, 48
cotton, 47–8, 77–9
craft unions, 150–1
credit, 34, 39, 104–8, 184–5, 187, 195
credit institutions, 182, 185
Cromwell, Oliver, 39
Crusades, 14, 24
culture, 127, 130, 132–5, 217
currency, 105–6, 164, 177, 195; reserves, 164, 191

Dalton, Hugh, 188
Dangerfield, George, 159
Darby, Abraham, 48
Darwin, Charles, 13, 131
Deere, John, 84
defence, 183, 196; *see also* armaments
deficit finance, 190, 197, 199
deflation, 164, 165, 175, 185–6
democracy, 159, 187–8, 189
Denmark, 84–6
depressions, 140, 143, 182, 184–91; *see also* slump
developing countries, 216–17
disarmament, 175
distribution, *see* service industries
domestic goods, 80–1, 136–7, 144–5; *see also* houses
domestic servants, 145, 146, 153
Dreyfus, Lt.-Col. Alfred, 139
Durham, 55, 66

East India Co., 21, 31, 118
East Indies, 33
economic theory, 50–4, 176–7, 183–4, 197, 198–200
economy, 106–7, 114, 216
education, 87, 89–90, 114, 130, 131, 154, 157, 171, 178
electricity, 88, 142, 143, 166, 171, 179

Empire State Building, 37
empires, 29–33, 118–21, 203
employment, 51; *see also* unemployment
energy, 40, 44–5, 46, 54–60, 61, 64; *see also* coal, electricity *and* steam power
Engels, Friedrich, 16, 54, 98
engineering, 13–14, 46, 48, 57, 67, 87–9
entertainment, 178, 180
Europe, 29–33, 36–7, 81, 160–8, 180, 185–90
exchange rates, 185, 191; controls, 190
exploitation, 98, 100, 115
exports, 56, 60, 77–8, 106, 108–9, 164, 175, 176; *see also* international trade

factories, 47, 77, 79, 97–101, 179–80
factory acts, 116, 155
families, 39, 138, 178–9
famine, 48, 77, 82–3, 109
farmers, 39, 40, 49, 87; *see also* agriculture
fascism, 161, 167, 191–4
feudal system, 25, 26, 53
firms, 208–9, 212; *see also* companies
Flanders, 27
Florence, 27–8
food supply, 48–9, 52, 71, 81, 82, 86–7, 96, 121–4, 205
Ford, Henry, 142
Ford Motor Co. Ltd., 209, 212
France, 16, 41, 49, 90, 108, 110, 113, 151, 159, 160, 161, 163, 208; agriculture, 82, 84; railways, 74; roads, 65; revolution, 112–13, 115; *la belle époque*, 135–9; Third Republic, 136, 138–9, 161
franchise, 156; *see also* suffrage
Franco-Prussian wars, 138, 154
free trade, 16, 51, 60, 108–11, 124–7, 157, 189–90, 198
freedom, 138, 171, 194, 199–200, 205

gas, 56, 80
Geneva, 168

Germany, 41, 60, 70, 108, 110, 130, 131, 157, 158, 159, 216; agriculture, 84; industry, 89, 110, 111, 114, 141, 142, 148, 149; social services, 154, 155–6; state, 114; trades unions, 151–2; after World War I, 160, 161, 164, 165–6, 167, 172, 177, 186, 190, 191–4, 197, 201
Gladstone, William E., 154
gold, 33, 34, 105–7, 108, 118, 188; standard, 104–5, 111, 124–7, 162–3, 164, 176, 185–6, 187, 188–9, 195
government, 50, 51, 52, 112–14, 154, 156, 199–200, 209, 212–17; intervention, 72–6, 100–1, 155–7, 164, 167, 175, 177, 180, 183, 190, 195, 202–3, 204; *see also* state
Great Depression, 140, 143, 182–91
Greece, 17–18, 24
Green, T. H., 110

hand-workers, 77, 79, 81, 94
high capitalism, 30, 118–71
Hitler, Adolf, 161, 177, 191, 193, 195, 201
Holland, 14, 19, 49
Hoover, Herbert C., 188
houses, 45–6, 81, 103, 178, 205
Hudson Bay Co., 31
Hundred Years War, 26
Hungary, 82, 169
Huntsman, Benjamin, 48
Huskisson, William, 109
Hussey, Obed, 84

immigration, 30, 90, 118, 128–30, 167; to USA, 86, 90, 98, 100, 111, 128–9, 153; laws, 167
imperialism, 29–33, 111, 118–21, 122–3, 150, 156, 157
import duties, 109–10; *see also* Corn Laws *and* tariffs
Incas, 26, 31
India, 31–3, 51, 72, 76, 118, 120, 127, 203

industrial areas, 60, 216
industrial organisation, 196, 205–8
industrial reconstruction, US, 196
industrial revolution, 13–14, 40, 45–7
industrial work, 97–101
industrialisation, 55–60, 77–81, 91–6 ; of Soviet Union, 171
industrialists, 39–40
industries, change from heavy to light, 178–82, 205 ; chemical-based, 84, 88, 110, 179, 183, 205 ; local, 118, 127
inflation, 18, 166
insurance, 124, 154, 158
interest, 34
internal combustion engine, 143, 179
international finance, 102, 192, 201–2
International Monetary Fund, 202 ; system, 102, 125–7, 201–2
international trade, 108–11, 121–8, 164–7, 175, 186, 194, 195, 199, 201–2 ; *see also* trade routes
internationalism, 127, 128–31
inventions, *see* technology
investment, 101–4, 162, 172, 184–5
investment goods trades, 172, 175, 185
Ireland, 63, 71, 96, 128, 159, 163 ; famine in, 48, 77, 82–3, 109
iron, 48, 54, 57, 67
Islam, 24, 36
Italy, 14, 24, 110, 158, 167, 201

Jacobins, the, 115
Japan, 33, 120, 197, 201, 216
Jews, 24, 130, 166, 183, 192, 201
joint stock companies, 102–3, 147 ; *see also* stock exchanges
Joyce, James, 134, 135

Kerensky, Alexander F., 168–9
Keynes, John Maynard, 176, 177, 190, 197, 198–200
Krupp, Alfred, 148, 149, 193

labour, 50–2, 71 ; force, 48–9, 85, 98–101, 216 ; skilled, 87–90 ; specialisation of, 39, 40, 50, 108 ; *see also* slavery, trades unions *and* working class
Labour Party, 159, 187–8
laissez-faire policies, 57–60, 114, 116, 155, 157, 159–60, 162, 202
Lancashire, 47, 56, 57, 60, 77–9
landowners, 34–5, 41, 49, 50–1, 52–3, 101, 103, 169
Latin America, 31, 33, 34, 200
law, systems of, 113–14, 155
Lenin, Vladimir Ilyich, 54, 111, 150, 161, 168–71, 191
Lever, William, 148, 149
liberalism, 108, 158–60, 188, 205, 216, 217
Liebig, Justus von, 131
Litvinov, Maxim, 201
Lloyd George of Dwyfor, 163, 190
London, 34, 74, 76, 124, 136, 186–7 ; City of, 39, 102, 108, 161
Luther, Martin, 28

McAdam, John, 65
McCormick, Cyrus, 84
MacDonald, Ramsay, 187
machine-tool industry, 57, 142
machinery, agricultural, 83–4, 179 ; industrial, 39–40, 46–8, 57, 76, 79–80, 97, 100
McNamara, Robert, 209
Malthus, T.R., 52
management, industrial, 98, 100, 184, 208–12, 217
Manchester, 60, 63
manufactures, 132, 144 ; *see also* mass production
market, 40, 50–3, 81, 82, 199, 212
Marshall Plan, 165, 202
Marx, Karl, 16, 52, 53–4, 91, 98, 100, 111
mass production, 80, 81, 141–3, 145–6, 166, 178
materials, raw, 33, 53, 172–5
Maudslay, Henry, 57
medicine, 89, 155, 182
Medicis, 27, 37
merchants, 11, 14, 24–5, 27, 33–4, 37–40
Merchant Venturers, 29, 31–3, 39
mergers, 147–8, 187
Metcalf, John, 65
Middle Ages, 21–9
militarism, 138
Mill, John Stuart, 117, 131
minerals, 33, 34, 88, 118 ; *see also* gold, iron *and* steel
mineral oils, 88 ; *see also* oil
monarchy, 111, 113, 159
money, 11, 17, 104–8, 166 ; *see also* currency *and* gold standard
monopolies, 54, 147–50
Mussolini, Benito, 167, 177, 191, 193

Napoleon Bonaparte, 36, 87, 90 ; Napoleonic code, 114 ; Napoleonic wars, 101
nation states, 28
National Debt, 105–6, 165
nationalisation, 74, 169, 205
nationalism, 127–8, 138, 158–60, 161, 163, 191–2
Navigation Acts, 72, 109
nazism, 166, 175, 183, 191–4
New Deal, 177, 188, 191, 195–7, 200
New England, 91
New York, 64, 74, 76, 162, 186–7
Newcomen, Thomas, 45
Nicholas II, Czar, 169
Norman, Montagu, 177
Northumberland, 55, 66

oil, 88, 127, 143, 147, 179
opium war, 21
Ottoman Empire, 120, 121
overseas businesses, 111
Owen, Robert, 150–1

Paris, 102, 103, 115, 136–8, 169
Parliament, 16, 41, 66, 113, 115, 205

Pasteur, Louis, 131
paternalism, 74, 116–17, 217
patriotism, 156; *see also* nationalism
peasants, 16, 41, 49, 169, 171
Peel, Sir Robert, 60, 109
pensions, old-age, 154–5
Peterloo, 115
philanthropy, 52, 97
Pittsburgh, 175
planning systems, 171, 208
Polo, Marco, 20, 24
poor, 35, 52, 94–7, 137, 138, 146, 176, 212
Poor Law, 53, 57–60, 96, 154
population, 26, 35, 49, 52, 77, 86, 91
Portugal, 28, 30, 31
pound sterling, revaluation of, 176
poverty, 146, 157–8, 172, 216
pragmatism, 198–9, 204
price competition, 209, 212
'price revolution', 34–5
printing, 57, 80, 91
private enterprise, 74, 76, 198, 205
productivity, 50–4, 204, 205
profits, 11, 35–6, 51, 52–3, 54, 101–4, 212
proletariat, 12, 53–4, 91–7, 171; *see also* labour force *and* working class
Protestantism, 28, 89
Prussia, 90, 114–15, 117, 138, 139, 154, 155, 156; farming, 82, 84; railway, 74
public utilities, 74, 205
public works, US, 196, 197

radicals, 156
railway stock companies, 64, 72–3, 74, 101–3, 147
railways, 61, 66–71, 72–6, 87, 149, 155; American, 70–1, 73, 147; British, 66–7; European, 70, 73–4, 155; Indian, 76; Russian, 76
refrigeration, 121, 142
religion, 28–9, 131
retail structure, 143, 145, 178, 212
revisionism, German, 152
Ricardo, David, 52–3, 195
river transport, 61–4
roads, 17, 44, 64–5
Rockefeller, John D., 147, 149
Roman Empire, 17–18, 21
Rome, 9, 11, 17–19, 24
Roosevelt, Franklin D., 175, 177, 188, 190–1, 195–8, 200, 202
Rothschilds, the, 102
Ruhr, the, 175
Ruskin, John, 116, 117
Russia, 41, 49, 74, 76, 110, 111, 113, 127, 130, 201, 202, 203, 204; farming, 82, 84; industrialisation, 171; 1917 revolution, 161, 163, 168–71; *see also* Soviet Union

sailing ships, 14, 24, 26, 44, 61, 65
Salazar, Antonio, 177, 191, 193
Salisbury, 3rd Marquess of, 115
sanitation, 81, 96
savings, 102, 104, 199, 200
science, 9, 13, 17, 87–9, 131, 132, 141, 182–4, 204, 212, 216–17
scientific-militarism, 212–16, 217
Scotland, 63
service industries 50, 145, 180, 181, 205
sewing machines, 79–80
shareholders, 208
shares, transferable, 63–4, 66, 72, 74
Sheffield, 80
Sherman Anti-Trust law, 147
ship-building, 72
shipping, 36, 72, 108, 109, 124, 175; *see also* sailing ships *and* steamships
slavery, 16, 18, 33, 45
slump, 96, 128, 184–90
Smiles, Samuel, 14
Smith, Adam, 50–1, 108
social democracy, 187–8
social problems, 212, 216; *see also* poor *and* poverty
social security, 117, 150, 154–5, 157–8, 159, 160, 175, 176, 196, 203
socialism, 54, 60, 139, 159, 160, 163, 176, 203–4; *and* trades unions, 151–3
socialists, 116, 177, 191
society, 145, 200, 217; criticism of, 134–5
South Africa, 118, 157
Soviet Union, 138, 171, 200
Spain, 24, 26, 28, 30, 31
Spanish Civil War, 194, 201
speculation, 184–5
Staffordshire potteries, 63
Stalin, Josef V., 171, 201
standard of living, 91, 205
Standard Oil, 147
standardisation of products, 143–4
starvation, 96
state, 111–15, 116–17, 183, 192; bourgeois, 12–13, 54, 116, 154–6; corporate, 193; rivalry, 121; state ownership, 205; welfare, 117, 202, 203; *see also* social security *and* government
steam power, 14, 44, 45, 46–7, 57, 60, 72, 87; engine, 45, 54, 56–7, 66; ships, 57, 61, 71–2; *see also* railways
steel, 14, 48, 141–2, 143
Stephenson, George, 66
stock exchanges, 72, 74, 76, 101–2, 147; collapse of, 184–5; *see also* joint stock companies
strikes, 158, 159, 175–6, 186
subsidies, government, 157
Suez Canal, 121
suffrage, 156, 158, 159–60
supply and demand, law of, 176
surpluses, utilisation of, 16, 50–2
Sweden, 121, 176, 177, 190
Swindon, 67

tariffs, 51, 110, 112, 127–8, 157, 190
taxes, 110, 112, 156, 159
technology, 9, 13–14, 36, 42–3, 44–8, 50–1, 52, 87–9, 141, 157, 162, 163, 166, 172, 178–9, 183–4, 204, 205, 206, 212, 216, 217
telegraph, electric, 67, 73, 90
Telford, Thomas, 65
textile industries, 40, 44, 45–8, 77–80; *see also* cloth, cotton *and* wool

timber, 48
tools, 46; machine-, 57, 142
Tories, 116, 117
totalitarianism, 191, 198, 200
towns, 41, 210–11; *see also* cities; medieval, 25–6; industrial, 60, 81–2, 96
trade, *see also* free trade *and* international trade; medieval, 22–3, 24–9; and empires, 29–33
trading posts, 30
trade routes, ancient, 14, 17, 26–8
trades unions, 150–3, 192, 193
transport, 44, 57, 61–76, 142; *see also* canals, railways, river transport, roads, *and* shipping
travel, 67, 111, 127, 145
trusts, 147–8
turnpike trusts, 44, 65, 73

Ukraine, 48, 168, 171
unemployment, 96, 146, 158, 171, 172, 176, 179, 185, 187, 188, 200
unions, 100, 150–1; *see also* trades unions
United States of America 60, 81, 112, 113, 117, 159; agriculture, 82, 83–4, 86; cartels, 147–8, 149; immigrants, 86, 90, 98, 100, 111, 128–9, 153, 167; industry, 89, 98, 100, 110, 141, 142, 157; railways, 70–1, 73; rivers, 64; shipping, 72; trade, 110; trades unions, 151, 153; post-war I, 161–3, 164–5, 166; 20s boom, 178–90; slump, 184–6, 188; New Deal, 191, 195–8, 200; and World War II, 201, 202, 203, 204
usury, 28, 34, 112

Vanderbilt, Cornelius, 147, 149
Veblen, Thorsten, 141
Venice, 14, 24, 25, 37
Vienna, 102, 186, 187
Voltaire, François, 132

wages, 12, 52, 96
Wales, 66
war, 36, 154, 157, 179, 200; *see also* armaments
watermills, 27, 44–5, 54
waterways, *see* canals *and* river transport
Watt, James, 45, 54
Webb, Sidney and Beatrice, 158
Wedgwood, Josiah, 16, 63
Weimar republic, 161
welfare state, *see* state
windmills, 44
women, 55, 98, 100, 101, 153, 158, 159, 163, 178
wool, 27–8, 78–9, 118
working class, 12, 16, 41, 53–4, 91–6, 115–17, 131, 135, 150–3, 169, 171, 191, 202, 204; *see also* labour
world trade, *see* international trade
World War I, 74, 127, 139, 146, 160–8
World War II, 139, 183, 194, 195, 196, 200, 201–4
writers, 133–5, 139

Xerox, 208

Yorkshire woollens, 78

Zola, Emile, 134